UNIVERSITY OF NOTTINGHAM
WITHDRAWN
FROM THE LIBRARY
1003104445
UNIVERSITY LIBR

KV-648-837

# THE INTERNET, DEMOCRACY AND DEMOCRATIZATION

## BOOKS OF RELATED INTEREST

*Factional Politics and Democratization*
edited by Richard Gillespie, Michael Waller and Lourdes López Nieto

*Democracy and North America*
edited by Alan Ware

*Civil Society: Democratic Perspectives*
edited by Robert Fine and Shirin Rai

*Democratization and the Media*
edited by Vicky Randall

*Social Democracy in a Post-Communist Europe*
edited by Michael Waller, Bruno Coppieters and Kris Deschouwer

*Post-Communism and the Media in Eastern Europe*
edited by Patrick H. O'Neil

*Ecology and Democracy*
edited by Freya Mathews

*The Resilience of Democracy: Persistent Practice, Durable Idea*
edited by Peter Burnell and Peter Calvert

# THE INTERNET, DEMOCRACY AND DEMOCRATIZATION

*edited by*

PETER FERDINAND

*University of Warwick*

FRANK CASS

LONDON • PORTLAND, OR

*First Published in 2000 in Great Britain by*
FRANK CASS PUBLISHERS
Newbury House, 900 Eastern Avenue
London, IG2 7HH

*and in the United States of America by*
FRANK CASS PUBLISHERS
c/o ISBS, 5804 N.E. Hassalo Street
Portland, Oregon, 97213-3644

*Website:* www.frankcass.com



British Library Cataloguing in Publication Data:

The Internet, democracy and democratization. –
(Democratization studies)
1. Internet (Computer network) – Political aspects
2. Political participation – Computer network resources
3. Communication in politics
I. Ferdinand, Peter
323′.042′02854678

ISBN 0-7146-5065 X (cloth)
ISBN 0-7146-8114 8 (paper)
[ISSN 1465-4601]

Library of Congress Cataloging-in-Publication Data:

The internet, democracy, and democratization / edited by Peter Ferdinand.
p. cm. – (Democratization studies, ISSN 1465-4601)
This group of studies first appeared in a special issue … Democratization.
Includes bibliographical references and index.
ISBN 0-7146-5065-X (cloth) – ISBN 0-7146-8114-8 (pbk.)
1. Democracy. 2. Democratization. 3. Internet (Computer network) –
Political aspects.
I. Ferdinand, Peter. II. Democratization. III. Series

JC421.I57 2000
321.8 – dc21 00-29032

This group of studies first appeared in a Special Issue on
'The Internet, Democracy and Democratization' of *Democratization*
(ISSN 1351-0347) 7/1 (Spring 2000)
published by Frank Cass.



Printed in Great Britain by Antony Rowe Ltd., Chippenham, Wiltshire

# Contents

# The Internet, Democracy and Democratization

PETER FERDINAND

The Internet has recently celebrated its thirtieth anniversary. Originally designed around 1969 to allow the exchange of packets of bits between computers, it remained for a long time restricted to the exchange of scientific data between scientists and secure information within government. Then electronic mail and bulletin boards became increasingly popular among those with access to it. It was only in the 1990s that it has become a popular means of communication. In 1993 the federal government opened up the network to commerce, and the creation of the Hypertext Mark-Up Language (HTML) laid the basis for universal accessibility.

Since then the growth has been phenomenal. A survey towards the end of 1999 suggested that 259 million people were now Internet users. Of these 111 million were in the United States, six times as many as the next largest figure which was for Japan. The survey predicted that the figures would rise to around 490 million by the end of the year 2002.[1] Another recent survey claimed that over 28 million people visited the World Wide Web every day and confirmed that it was now spreading rapidly outside the US. Foreign domains already account for nearly 50 per cent of all Internet traffic. In fact, since American Internet Service Providers (ISPs) moved into foreign markets, these figures have understated actual usage by non-Americans, since AOL and the like have a non-country specific domain name. So all AOL clients whose home is outside the US would still be counted as American.[2] Internet traffic at present is doubling every 100–120 days.[3]

As a means of communication it has the potential to revolutionize political activity far more profoundly than the telephone or television ever did, for unlike them it offers the possibility of direct two-way interaction between the citizens and politicians. This has led to predictions that it will completely revolutionize government and democracy, even that the outcome will be a new wave of democratization world-wide, as authoritarian regimes find it difficult to survive and as established democracies are transformed. Grossman, for instance, argues that technological change is about to bring a third great era of electronic democracy, following the earlier ones of classical Greek and then representative democracy.[4] The purpose of this collection of studies is to examine that process.

Nevertheless the greatest impact of the Internet so far has not been in politics. Until now it has rather been upon business and commerce. It has already transformed marketing, procurement and recruitment functions of corporations in the United States. Now the impact is spreading to other parts of the world, partly through the socializing role of multinational corporations. At the same time the Internet has created opportunities for a whole host of new companies, principally dealing with information technology. Whilst making the use of the Internet as a core business function certainly requires the acquisition of technical skills, in other respects it may reduce the costs of entry into the marketplace for new companies. For example, they may be spared many of the start-up costs of acquiring premises because they can deal directly with clients or customers.

The first benefit of the Internet to be seized was its ability to reduce the costs of internal administration. It has considerably speeded up communication with colleagues and clients. It has also reduced the costs of transmitting data. And business commentators predict that one of its chief effects will be to reduce the number of intermediaries between the original providers of goods and services, and the final consumers. This 'disintermediation' will challenge the traditional economic functions of wholesalers and retailers, agents, and so on. At least in theory it offers the prospect of more direct selling and more convenient buying. The more futuristically minded suggest a world with fewer large shops as people shop through the Internet, with fewer large offices, as individuals work from home, and fewer publishers, as writers, composers and performers distribute their creations directly through the Internet. They even suggest that the Internet will create a new paradigm of economics.[5]

But in addition, as Internet usage caught on, and as people increasingly turned to the Internet to provide information services for others, it has become an increasing source of reference too. Instead of having to go to a library, individuals could surf the web and use search engines, to acquire an enormous amount of information. Whilst not underestimating the problems of the reliability of information to be found there, and the security issue of hackers possibly altering web sites without the site-owners even being aware of the fact, it nevertheless makes available a wealth of information on up-to-the-minute developments in the world that already far exceeds anything to which an individual could have had access previously. This will transform education, but it will also transform other agencies that need to process large amounts of information.

As a result, the institutions as well as individuals will be able to achieve much more. For example, the government of Finland has taken to the Internet for internal communication, and for diplomacy too. Previously the Finnish Foreign Ministry was unable to afford a presence in a large number of countries or a large research staff. It did not have sufficient information about diplomatic issues in many parts of the world to be able to make a constructive contribution to developments. Now that it can rely much more on the Internet to keep abreast of what is happening around the world, it feels capable of a much more significant role in international diplomacy. Similarly the Peruvian and Ecuadorian governments were quick to try to take advantage of the Internet for diplomatic advantage.

## THE INTERNET AND GOVERNMENT REORGANIZATION

To some extent, the same vector of organizational transformation has penetrated government. It began with internal organization, but then gradually spread more widely to include government's relations with outsiders, whether businesses or citizens. Certainly part of the impetus for change came from businesses that had begun to adapt to the new technology and expected government to do the same. But in addition the US government recognized from early on the potential for the Internet both to increase the efficiency of its administration and also to reduce its cost. An efficiency report in 1994 pointed out that at that time the US government was afflicted by both spiralling costs and increasingly disjointed and ineffective administration:

> And yet, waste is not the only problem. The federal government is not simply broke, it is broken. Ineffective regulation of the financial industry brought us the Savings and Loan debacle. Ineffective education and training programs jeopardize our competitive edge. Ineffective welfare and housing programs undermine our families and cities.
>
> We spend $25 billion a year on welfare, $27 billion on food stamps, and $13 billion on public housing – yet more Americans fall into poverty every year. We spend $12 billion a year waging the war on drugs – yet see few signs of victory. We fund 150 different employment and training programs – yet the average American has no

> idea where to get job training, and the skills of our workforce fall further behind those of our competitors.[6]

The Chairman of the Government Information Technology Services Working Group that was responsible for this review added:

> It is an opportunity to use the power of information technology to fight the war on crime, to deliver entitlement benefits to the needy in a secure and efficient manner while eliminating fraud and cheating, to improve health care delivery, to find missing children, to improve privacy protection for all citizens – in short, to completely reshape how government delivers its services to its customers.[7]

This possibility of enhanced efficiency through increased coherence of government policies has attracted countries from around the world. The Blair government in Britain, for instance, has been much attracted by the opportunities afforded by the Internet to provide 'joined up' government. A large part of the rationale for the 'third way', for instance, rests upon the possibility of uncovering resources that can be diverted to the poorer members of society, not by increasing taxes on the rich or public ownership of industry, but because of the savings that can be achieved through increased efficiency. It was no coincidence that Demos, one of the think-tanks associated with New Labour, has devoted quite a lot of attention to new technology, government and democracy.[8]

In East Asia the Malaysian government of Prime Minister Mahathir Mohammed proclaimed the ambition of making the country as advanced as any in the West by the year 2020 on the basis of Information Technology. Singapore set out a programme for putting all the population on-line by the year 2000. And even a country such as China, whose leaders are suspicious of the impact of the Internet upon their people and who prevent completely free interaction with people abroad through it, has become converted to the ambition of putting China on-line. Beijing announced that 1999 was to be the year when Chinese government was put on-line.[9] Even more significantly, in addition to the efficiency advantages that attracted the Chinese government, and the perceived need to provide an IT environment that would invigorate Chinese businesses so that they could compete with western counterparts, the official announcement also pointed to the increasing 'transparency' that going on-line would bring to administration. The Chinese word – *toumingdu* – was the same as was used to translate *glasnost'* before the collapse of the Soviet Union. This was probably not directed so much at increasing popular control over administration, as was the case in the Former Soviet Union (FSU), as increasing the control of the centre over the periphery in China. The stubborn persistence of obscurity and deceit practised by lower-level officials in their dealings with Beijing in the post-Mao era no doubt explains the enthusiasm of the leadership there for the new technology. Nevertheless, greater transparency was also explicitly linked with democratization and would certainly be a precondition for it.

## THE INTERNET AND DEMOCRACY

Thus one kind of innovation that the Internet might bring to politics has been managerial. It has been linked with the assumption that current government, even in established democracies, is too dominated by outdated and out-of-touch bureaucracies. This viewpoint is expressed both by individuals and by companies that have a great deal of contact with government agencies. Whether it is welfare claims, or taxation, or planning applications, the experience of those outside the government was that traditionally the bureaucracy seemed to run their affairs primarily for their own benefit, and to avoid embarrassment to the party in power, rather than for the good of the public.[10]

Those who argue along these lines believe that the new technology will also open up the processes of administration to outside observers much more effectively than before. In so doing administration will become more transparent, and more amenable to democratic pressures. This will lead to a virtuous circle of increasing transparency leading to greater efficiency and then to greater democracy. This impetus has lain behind many of the proposals for reform at both the national and local levels, namely simply bringing administration closer to the people.

Others wishing to apply benefits to government through applications of the Internet have focused upon local rather than central government. In many western countries, local government has suffered from popular apathy and/or official neglect. The Internet offered an opportunity for improving local government services, and also possibly a new way for ordinary citizens to participate more directly in the decisions that will affect their immediate living conditions.[11]

Within Europe too there has been an increasing interest in using the Internet to (re)create a new sense of community, especially at the local level.[12] The European Commission has actively encouraged the formation of new networks of local authorities in various countries, for example the Civic Community network, which have achieved a pioneering success. And even though English is, at least for the moment, still the predominant language of the net, some ethnic communities have taken it up enthusiastically as a way of establishing an international presence for themselves, their region and their language. The government of Catalonia, for example, has made a great effort to establish an Internet presence, so as to increase their freedom of manoeuvre *vis-à-vis* Madrid.[13] Irrespective of whether these opportunities are also used to increase democracy within localities, they do represent an increase in the democratic expectation within one region that it should be treated as the equal of another, where previously it felt inferior.

There is, though, a second approach linking the Internet and democratization that is more radical. This is the school of thought that believes in direct democracy as an ideal, or at the very least in 'strong democracy'. This term, created by Benjamin Barber in the early 1980s, symbolizes many of the more radical aspirations.[14] In many ways the ideal was Athenian democracy. There all the citizens were able regularly to gather together so as to debate and decide public policy. This ideal of direct contact between all those eligible to vote has long seemed outdated, if only because of the much greater size of the modern state. But if new technology could enable citizens to come together in some 'virtual' forum, then it might be possible to restore a more genuine, and more profound form of deliberative democracy.

For example, it might be possible to organize regular plebiscites on important issues. Already this happens with increasing frequency in states in the United States. Switzerland, too, is an example of a state that has practised fairly regular plebiscites with apparent success. So, Budge argues, after a thorough review of the evidence on the way that plebiscites have worked there: 'Direct democracy can therefore be seen as the logical way to modernize our existing regimes.'[15] For him a crucial factor that supports this conclusion is the changes that have taken place in western European society this century. In particular he points to the extended education and increasing political sophistication which citizens can now bring to deliberation over issues of public policy. So the need of citizens for representatives to make decisions in their name is no longer so great.

But to make that work, there will also have to be a change in the ways in which citizens approach democratic debate, especially if at least part of it is going to be mediated through the Internet. However better educated these people may be, this type of behaviour will not come naturally. This has led Barber and others to set up a web site called Civic Exchange, that should help citizens to play this role more effectively. The other chief organizer of this project is Noveck and her article in this collection typifies this plea for a new type of democratic debate and the need for the creation of the conditions to realize it.

Others have tended to argue the same case, though from a slightly different starting-point. For them what is striking is the growing popular disenchantment with existing forms of democracy in both the United States and Western Europe. In almost all countries public opinion polls suggest that dissatisfaction with parliaments is reaching worrying levels. Membership of political parties is declining. Indeed political activism is declining in general. So is voter turn-out in countries where voting is not compulsory. The only exception to this apparent decline in popular interest in politics would seem to be support for single-issue causes – and that can be spasmodic. For some commentators this points to a serious potential problem for the future: will the 'democracies' finally be outgrown by alienation or a sense of irrelevance?

Whether or not the solution to this problem lies in direct democracy, there is no doubt that the new technologies are a challenge to established democratic, political institutions. In this collection, Bieber reminds us of the problems that face German political parties today – 'drying and ageing', as he and others put it. In other words the political enthusiasm of party members dries out as they, and the parties, age. Whether or not the Internet will replace or supplement parties' activities, he shows how the main German parties have tried to take advantage of the new technology to modernize their workings, rejuvenate their appeal, and stimulate policy debate both within the party and also with outsiders.

In this collection Stromer-Galley looks at a parallel issue: the impact of the Internet upon American political parties. She shows how professional party organizers have rapidly embraced the new technologies for campaign organization. And because these techniques are relatively cheap, they have  also enabled individuals and groups who would otherwise have been unable to compete for lack of funds to make a more dramatic impact. The Internet has enabled at least some individual candidates to escape from the tyranny of fund-raising for television advertisements. Nor is the superiority of the Internet limited to its greater cheapness. It also has been used by political campaign-managers to identify potential supporters and target more personalized appeals to them, rather than relying upon general advertisements on television.

It may also be the case that those who are more enthusiastic users of the Internet are also more optimistic about the possibilities of reviving democracy using the new technology, at least in the US. A survey appeared in *Wired* magazine in 1997 of what it described as 'digital citizens'. This suggested that a higher proportion of those who most actively used the new interactive technologies had 'a lot of confidence' in the American political system compared to those who used them less (the proportions were 59 per cent versus 42 per cent in a total sample of 1440). The general ethos of this group was optimism about the future, the political system included. It was true, though, that actual support for the current two-party system in the US was less strong.[16]

Of course the challenge is not only to political parties. Parliaments too have suffered from eroding public confidence. For them the problem of contemporary relevance is becoming equally intense. A special issue of *Parliamentary Affairs* in 1999 was devoted to the issue of 'Parliament in the Age of the Internet' and it included articles on developments in a number of countries: the United Kingdom, Australia, Germany, the US, South Africa, Denmark, Slovenia. A common conclusion was that almost all of these parliaments had seriously embraced new technology to bring greater efficiency to parliamentarians' office work, as well as in terms of presenting their activities to the electors. All of them had their own web sites to enable citizens to get a much clearer picture of their activities and of their legislative procedures. At least to that extent, the advent of the Internet had broken down barriers between parliament and the citizen.[17]

Conceivably, however, the impact of the Internet upon this relationship could go much further. Since the Internet facilitates both wider access to information on-line, and also direct communication between representatives and their electors, one possible effect could be to change the relationship between the individual parliamentary representative and his/her political party. One of the contributors predicted:

> It will become easier for individual Members of Parliament to have his or her own network of people and groups and to maintain it, coordinating research, focus groups, poll people throughout society, and coordinate activities in large groups than is possible today. This makes Members of Parliament more independent from central infrastructure, be that from the Parliament or the Party.[18]

And the greater availability of parliamentary documents, including documents on decision-making obtained from the government, may also mean that individuals and groups will be able to mount much more professional campaigns to win support inside parliament.[19] Thus the triangular relationship between citizens, parties and parliament could also change.

One way in which that could change can be seen in an initiative of the German parliament, the Bundestag. This has begun using its Internet site to begin regular discussions of issues of current national concern, with leading figures from the major parties represented there helping to lead the discussion. Each issue is discussed for around six weeks and then a new one is launched.[20] As a way of attempting to bring closer citizens and the parliament, and also encourage a more informed debate of issues, it represents a step in the direction of the 'strong democracy' that Barber and others have called for. There are of course a lot of other alternative sites for encouraging political debate in various countries, but it is unusual in that attempts directly to involve the national parliament. The Danish parliament attempted something along these lines with on-line public debates in 1999 on the Danish constitution and possible changes to it, but so far these have only been a one-off event.[21]

Existing parliaments in democracies, however, have tended to be more interested in applying the new technologies to help them become more effective, rather than adopting innovations that might undermine their traditional status and authority. In the United Kingdom this has certainly been true of Westminster. But in Scotland and Wales the creation of new devolved Assemblies has been viewed as an opportunity to think of new ways of encouraging participation so as to establish their popular legitimacy, especially as these new Assemblies were deprived of major tax-raising powers. In Scotland in particular the new Assembly was the first to establish an interactive web-site, although sites for Wales, Northern Ireland and Westminster itself are now apparently under construction. But in Scotland, too, the Assembly web-site set aside space for two debating areas under the headings 'opinion' and 'think-tank', both intended to provide opportunities for citizens to debate political and policy issues.[22]

One other benefit that the Internet could bring to the workings of parliament has been the subject of an experiment in the European Parliament. Its Science and Technology Committee has sought to take advantage of the increased speed of communication brought by the Internet. Previously the Committee had relatively formal, but limited panels of scientific experts who would regularly discuss the policy implications of scientific discoveries. The disadvantage of this approach, however, was that the real experts on a particular breakthrough might not be members of the appropriate committee, since the numbers on any committee are necessarily limited. So assessments of the policy implications of particular discoveries and inventions might be made by scientists who were not really expert in that field. The European Parliament introduced the innovation that it would post details of new discoveries and procedures on the web and it would invite responses from any scientist who wished to comment within a certain time-frame.[23] In this way the Committee could tap a much wider spectrum of opinion than previously. Here the fact that Internet usage is currently still largely limited to elites was turned to advantage for policy assessment.

Equally importantly, though, the Internet offers the possibility for full reintegration into political life of minorities that have been marginalized in the increasingly money-dominated world of democratic elections. At least for the moment, the Internet offers the possibility for individuals or organizations to make much more of an impact on voters and at much lower cost. Especially in the United States, where free local telephones make Internet access very cheap and where the Internet is already well established, it is quite possible for individuals to make a play for votes without having to become the candidate of one of the main parties. Will this then mean that the poor will acquire new opportunities for political participation and leadership? Lekhi's article in this collection addresses this issue as far as African Americans are concerned.

On the other hand, the poor and disadvantaged are not the only groups in society whose participation in democracies is disproportionately low. There are other groups too on the margin of society who want to transform it so as to put themselves at the core of the new society. They could also take advantage of the opportunities that the Internet offers for increased participation and leadership. One such category of users is the far-right militias in the US, that have taken advantage of the web to counter the, as they see it, conspiracy of the Federal government and the commercial media to mislead the American people about the general direction of public policy.[24] In this collection Chroust has written a study that focuses upon two communities like this: the neo-Nazis in Germany, and the Taliban in Afghanistan. What is their strategy for social transformation and how do they attempt to put the technology to use for them? Are they a threat to 'democracy' in the more conventional sense? And if so, what would be the best way to counter them?

Another way of trying to increase public integration in democracy is at the local level rather than the national one. Here, too, some suggestions have been radical. They envisioned the use of the Internet to bring direct democracy to citizens at the local level. Some, such as Christa Slaton and Ted Becker have been advocating 'electronic town meetings' to allow citizens a direct say so as to determine local issues and they have organized experiments to see how this would work.[25]

It was at the state level in Minnesota that the first election victory was recorded that could be attributed to a superior campaign based on the

Internet. There in 1998 Jesse Ventura was elected Governor, despite the fact that he was not the candidate of either of the two main parties. Actually, he was the candidate of Perot's Reform Party, but the crucial difference, according to Stromer-Galley in this collection, was his use of the Internet. Since he had very limited financial resources, the Internet provided an excellent alternative way of appealing to voters at very low cost. He spent perhaps one tenth of the money used by his other major rivals and yet he still won. In particular he was able to use the Internet to target those voters identified as potential supporters, and also to create political events that provoked a lot of public reaction. Possibly one factor in his success was the fact that one of the largest Internet organizations committed to e-democracy, especially at the local level, was also based in Minnesota. In between elections it hosts a state-wide discussion forum to develop the practice of using the web for political debate.[26] So the habit of looking to the Internet for political information and participation was already quite well-established there. And now the habit is spreading - well over 200 American towns and cities have established their own community networks of one kind or another.

Lastly we should mention two organizations that have come to play an important role in stimulating public debate and reflection on politics and public policy in the US at all levels, especially around the time of presidential elections. They are the Democracy Network (DNet) which is run from California and the Web White and Blue, which originated in Minnesota. Both of these are funded by non-profit organizations and they aim to strengthen the debates between civil society and candidates for public office.[27] They would see their mission as helping to create the kind of 'strong democracy' that Barber and others advocate.

## THE INTERNET AND THE INTERNATIONALIZATION OF DEMOCRACY

So far this discussion has focused upon the impact of the Internet upon politics within individual states. One of the most striking effects of the Internet, however, has been its ability to spread ideas and products across national boundaries. It is one of the most effective forces of globalization. In addition, however, its own architecture, which was designed to enable the US to withstand nuclear strikes where any particular transmission station could have been knocked out, can be very effective in preventing censorship. The fact that messages on the Internet will be broken up into separate 'packets' of information as they leave the sender, directed across various telecommunications routes, and only reassembled at the computer of the receiver, means that it is impossible for outsiders like governments to intercept them en route without destroying most of the efficiency gains that such a technology can bring. The only options available to anyone who would wish to attempt this would either be to restrict very considerably the possible routes through which traffic could travel, or to monitor continuously and intensively the receivers. Either way this would seriously slow down the general speed of communication. And even if governments attempt to close down the senders of messages within a particular country that are deemed harmful, it is quite easy to set up 'mirror sites' abroad that can continue to receive and rebroadcast trafffic.[28] Already Stonier predicted in 1985 that this change would pose an increasingly serious challenge to Soviet power as the USSR became increasingly reliant upon micro-electronics to bring economic growth.[29] And a leading official in the Pentagon cited a comment by *Rolling Stone* about authoritarian regimes in 1995:

> The Internet is the censor's biggest challenge and the tyrant's worst nightmare … Unbeknown to their governments, people in China, Iraq and Iran, among other countries, are freely communicating with people all over the world.

As he put it:

> The Internet is clearly a significant long term strategic threat to authoritarian regimes, one that they will be unable to counter effectively. News from the outside world brought by the Internet into nations subjugated by such regimes will clash with the distorted versions provided by their governments, eroding the credibility of their positions and encouraging unrest. 'Personal' contact between people living under such governments and people living in the free world, conducted by e-mail, will also help to achieve a more accurate understanding on both ends and further undermine authoritarian controls. Information about violations of human rights and other forms of oppression will be increasingly conveyed to the outside world by the Internet, helping mobilize external political forces on behalf of the oppressed.[30]

This feature will become even more important in the future as the Internet's penetration spreads to more and more countries. Looking to the not so distant future, the same official envisaged the emergence of new political parties operating chiefly through the Internet. These could be local, national or even international. As he says, these parties would make the political scene much more complex, for they would be able to respond much more rapidly to political changes, though party discipline would be a serious problem.[31] Bieber gives an example of an attempt to create a 'virtual' party branch in the Social Democratic Party, but he also shows the difficulties that even this modest initiative has faced.[32]

How has all this affected the political systems of states so far? The best known example of the Internet being used from outside to bring about political change inside particular countries came in Mexico with the Chiapas uprising in 1994. At the beginning of that year a group of guerrillas led by Subcomandante Marcos seized control of the main urban areas bordering the Lacandon forest in the province of Chiapas. They were protesting about the lack of respect for the rights of the indigenous people there. This was not the first such protest there. Very quickly, however, news of the events spread abroad and support began to mobilize on the Internet. As Moreno Toscano mentions when analysing the Chiapas events in Mexico:

> The newness in Chiapas' political war was the emergence of various senders of information that interpreted events in very different ways … The flow of public information reaching society, through the media, and through the new technological means, was much greater than what conventional communication strategies could control … These alternative opinions, made possible by open media, or by closed media that felt the pinch from the open media, called into question forms of construction of 'the truth', and induced, within the political regime as well, a variety of opinions. The view from power became fragmented.[33]

Castells himself adds that:

> Extensive use of the Internet allowed the *Zapatistas* to diffuse information and their call throughout the world instantly, and to create a network of support groups which helped to produce an international public opinion movement that made it literally impossible for the Mexican government to use repression on a large scale.[34]

Without this use of the Internet, it seems highly likely that this uprising would have suffered the fate of all its predecessors. But now that the actions of the Mexican government were being scrutinized much more closely abroad, simple repression became much more difficult. Without the Internet connections, there seems little doubt that the Chiapas guerrillas would have been destroyed by the Mexican army far from any prying eyes. Now, however, a group of analysts at the Rand Corporation remarked that 'Mexico, the nation that gave the world a prototype of social revolution early in the 20th century, has generated an information-age prototype of militant social netwar on the eve of the 21st century'.[35]

Two other more recent examples can be mentioned here. The first is from Serbia, the second from Malaysia.

The collapse of the former Yugoslavia and the civil war that followed led President Milosevic to crack down on political opposition inside Serbia. Nevertheless a radio station inside Serbia became one of the chief opponents of the regime, despite official attempts to silence it, and it relied heavily on the Internet. It was called B92. As it tried to present alternative views of Serbia's domestic policies, including towards Kosovo, it was put under serious official pressure. In the end its transmitters were cut off. The station, however, had established itself as the first ISP inside the country and it responded by sending its broadcasts abroad over the Internet and then having them rebroadcast back into Serbia from sympathetic stations in Montenegro, and later by CNN, the BBC and others. However much pressure the regime continued to put on the station, it could not stop the flow of news. Then the station evolved into an alternative news agency, as other elements of the media turned to it for help in getting their material published too, because of its communications links with the outside world. So it helped to arrange for newspapers to be printed abroad and then their material redistributed inside the country after they had been officially closed. It also became involved in training journalists in the use of the Internet. And in time it also became linked with a network of foreign news stations and newspapers so that they distributed news from abroad inside Serbia, and news from Serbia abroad.

Similarly the Democratic Party of Serbia, one of the parties opposing President Milosevic, faced a ban by the authorities in the run up to elections. It responded by sending the text of its platform abroad so that it could be rebroadcast back to the country from a mirror site on the Internet. In this way it managed to avoid being silenced and it ran a credible election campaign. Then it formed an alliance for a while with an independent news agency in Belgrade that spread alternative information about official policies both inside and outside the country. In particular it concentrated upon official treatment of Kosovo as tensions mounted. This was an interesting example of a party, with its own political platform, being forced into providing 'objective' information about politics to counter official propaganda because of repression by the regime. In the end, as the fighting in Kosovo intensified, it became impossible for this alliance to survive, and the party went back to using its web site to broadcast its own commentaries on recent events. However critical the Democratic Party may have been of the regime, the latter could not prevent it from doing so because of its Internet presence.[36]

The second example comes from Malaysia. In 1998 Prime Minister Mahathir Mohammed suddenly had his deputy, Anwar Ibrahim dismissed and arrested on sex charges. Previously Anwar had been acting prime minister and it had been assumed that he was the heir apparent. His dismissal provoked a storm of protest inside and outside the country, but the media inside Malaysia presented the official account of the reasons for this. Anwar's supporters, however, set up Internet sites to mobilize support and explicitly to challenge the official account of events. For Malaysia this was completely new, and an unexpected consequence of the government's determined push to put the country on-line as part of its 2020 Vision. For months these web sites kept support alive during the court case that followed and they provided an opportunity for political critics to get together and protest without having to fear what the authorities would do. They also publicized the support that they were winning from abroad, such as from Presidents Habibie of Indonesia and Estrada of the Philippines – things that the Malaysian authorities would have kept quiet if they had been able. They spread to Malaysia the word *Reformasi* – reform – which had just become extremely popular in neighbouring Indonesia and through this they kept up the pressure on the Malaysian government. For the first time since independence it seemed as though Malay support for the ruling Barisan coalition government, led by the United Malay National Organization (UMNO), was divided. This then both kept open and widened the possibilities for political reform.[37]

A third case where the Internet played a big part in upsetting an authoritarian regime was the Suharto regime in Indonesia, where the Internet provided a virtual forum for disaffected Indonesians inside and outside the country to collect and protest. Surprisingly quickly, these protests gathered momentum and culminated in the collapse of the regime. These events are studied by Hill and Sen in this collection.

Beyond the impact on individual states, their political systems and civil societies, which is caused by activists within them trying to make the most of the technologies that are on offer, there is also the possibility of outsiders using the Internet to try to encourage change within societies. Insofar as this happens, it could be part of a possible emerging international civil society, or it could represent an attempt by one government or group of governments to induce change in a certain direction within another state. Two papers in this collection are devoted to this theme. One, by Bray, looks at efforts by non-governmental organizations in the west to put pressure on the Chinese authorities to change their policies in Tibet. The other, by Ott and Rosser, looks at possibilities for developed countries to use the Internet to bring about democratic change in Africa. In general terms they address the role of the Internet in supporting the emergence of civil society at both the national and the international levels.

## NOTES

1. Cyberatlas at http://cyberatlas.internet.com/big_picture/demographics/article/0,1323,5911-1511 51,00.html
2. StatMarket at www.statmarket.com/SM?c=stat061599
3. Peter Schwartz, Eamonn Kelly and Nicole Boyer, 'The Emerging Global Knowledge Economy', in *The Future of the Global Economy: Towards a Long Boom?* (Paris: Organisation for Economic Co-operation and Development, 1999), p.91.
4. Lawrence K. Grossman, *The Electronic Republic: Reshaping Democracy in America* (New York: Viking, 1995).
5. See, for example, Don Tapscott, *The Digital Economy: Promise and Peril in the Age of Networked Intelligence* (New York: McGraw-Hill, 1995); Schwartz, Kelly and Boyer make a related point, that the knowledge revolution will transform the basis of market economics and make market estimates of the 'real' value of ideas extremely problematic, in 'The Emerging Global Knowledge Economy', pp.81-90.
6. Cited in Tapscott, *The Digital Economy*, p.160.
7. Report of the National Performance Review, *Creating a Government that Works Better and Costs Less* (Washington, DC: Silicon Pr., 1994), p.32.
8. See, for example, Roger Freeman, *Democracy in the Digital Age* (London: Demos, 1997); and George Lawson, *NetState: Creating Electronic Government* (London: Demos, 1998).
9. www.gov.cn/news/xinw2.htm and and www.gmd.com.cn/gm/19990127/gb/17950^GM9-27 16.htm
10. Tapscott, *Digital Economy*, pp.160–62.
11. For a review of experiences, see *Modernising Local Government: Moving Towards E-Democracy* (Northampton: Society of Information Technology Management Services Ltd., 1999).
12. For examples, see Roza Tsagarousiannou, Damian Tambini and Cathy Brian (eds.), *Cyberdemocracy: Technology, Cities and Civic Networks* (London: Routledge, 1998).
13. See the basic web site www.catalonia.net as well as the sites linked to it.
14. Benjamin Barber, *Strong Democracy: Participatory Politics for a New Age* (San Francisco, CA: California University Press, 1984); an update can be found in Benjamin Barber, 'Three Scenarios for the Future of Technology and Strong Democracy', *Political Science Quarterly*, Vol.113, No.4 (1998–9), pp.573–89.
15. Ian Budge, *The New Challenge of Direct Democracy* (Cambridge: Polity, 1996), p.193.
16. Jon Katz, 'The Digital Citizen', *Wired* (December 1997), pp.68–82, 274–5.
18. Bert Mulder, 'Parliamentary Futures: Re-Presenting the Issue', *Parliamentary Affairs*, Vol.52, No.3 (1999), p.561.
17. Parliament in the Age of the Internet, *Parliamentary Affairs*, Vol.52, No.3 (1999).
19. Ibid., p.560.
20. See www.bundestag.de especially the 'Diskussionsforum'.
21. Karl Lofgren, Kim V. Anderson and Mette Frithiof Sorensen, 'The Danish Parliament Going Virtual', *Parliamentary Affairs*, Vol.52, No.3 (1999), pp.493–502.
22. www.Scottish-parliament.com/thinktank/index.shtml and www.Scottish–parliament.com/opinion/index.shtml For a discussion of the existing use of the Internet at Westminster, see

Stephen Coleman, 'Westminster in the Information Age', *Parliamentary Affairs*, Vol.52, No.3 (1999), pp.371–87.

23. For the report that surveyed American experience and laid the foundation for the change, see *Transparency and Openness in Scientific Advisory Committees: The American Experience* (Luxembourg: Scientific and Technological Options Assessment (STOA), European Parliament, PE 167 327/Fin.St., 1998).
24. For a discussion of their significance in this context, see Manuel Castells, *The Power of Identity. The Information Age: Economy, Society and Culture*, Vol.2 (Oxford and Malden, MA: Blackwell, 1997), pp.84–97.
25. www.auburn.edu/tann
26. See www.e-democracy.org/
27. See www.dnet.org/ and www.webwhiteblue.org/ An account of the Democracy Network can be found in Sharon Docter, William Dutton and Anita Elberse, 'An American Democracy Network: Factors Shaping the Future of On-Line Political Campaigns', *Parliamentary Affairs*, Vol.52, No.3 (1999), pp.535–52.
28. For a full discussion of the issues involved, see Robin Whittle, '"Refused Access Lists"? Why Internet communications cannot be reliably blocked', at http://www.ozemail.com.au/~firstpr/contreg/refused.htm
29. Tom Stonier, 'The Microelectronic Revolution, Soviet Political Structure and the Future of East/West Relations', *Political Quarterly*, Vol.54 (1983), pp.137–51.
30. Charles Swett, *Strategic Assessment:The Internet* (Washington, DC: Office of the Assistant Secretary of Defense for Special Operations and Low-Intensity Conflict (Policy Planning), the Pentagon, 17 July 1995, as posted on the Internet by the Project on Government Secrecy of the Federation of American Scientists, at www.fas.org/cp/swett.html
31. Ibid.
32. See below p.71–2.
33. Alejandra Moreno Toscano, *Turbulencia politica: causas y razones del 94* (Mexico City: Moreno, 1996), p.82, cited in Manuel Castells, *The Power of Identity*, p.73.
34. Castells, ibid., p.80.
35. David Ronfeldt, John Arquilla, Graham Fuller and Melissa Fuller, *The Zapatista 'Social Netwar' in Mexico* (Santa Monica, CA: Rand, 1998), p.1.
36. For the Serbian Democratic Party web site, see www.dssrbije.org.yu/index.html. For B92, see www.b92.com. For a long and very detailed account of B92's problems and the ways in which it attempted to cope with them, as well as recommendations for western countries in dealing with similar situations in the future, see www.nyu.edu/globalbeat/balkan/Matic0299.html
37. For examples of web-sites devoted to Anwar Ibrahim and *Reformasi*, see (i) http://members.tripod.com/Anwar-Online/main.htm (ii) www.geocities.com/Tokyo/Flats/3797/berita.htm (iii) http://members.xoom.com/Gerakan A fairly full index of such sites can be found at http://members.tripod.com/~REFORMASI_MALAYSIA/resources.htm

# Paradoxical Partners: Electronic Communication and Electronic Democracy

BETH SIMONE NOVECK

A cultural fascination with the accelerated immediacy of interactive Internet technologies – be it euphoric or cataclysmic – predictably accompanies the transition to a mysterious new millennium. Rapid-fire chat and conversation outlets are prevalent in quantity (albeit not in quality) with new interactive applications, such as ICQ, Third Wave, Gooey, Yahoo! Chat and new forms of collaborative groupware, competing for a share of the seemingly insatiable market for interaction. E-mail is, without a doubt, *the* 'killer app'.[1] The potential for an increase in interpersonal interaction, what has been called 'the ecstasy of communication', is responsible for the Internet's exponential growth and attractiveness as an entertainment medium.

The logical but false conclusion is that this communications revolution will profoundly strengthen the fabric of political culture in wired societies. Despite the explosion of outlets for communication, there is in fact no noticeable improvement of the democratic quality of political institutions. Traditionally, free communication is integral to the flourishing of a robust civil society, where conflict is managed through conversation, rather than violence, and free communication enables responsible citizens to participate vocally in their own governance. In the nineteenth century Alexis de Tocqueville marvelled at the din of democracy he encountered on his travels in America. He wrote:

> No sooner do you set foot on America soil than you find yourself in a sort of tumult; a confused clamor rises on every side, and a thousand voices are heard at once, each expressing some social requirements. All around you everything is on the move: here the people of a district are assembled to discuss the possibility of building a church; there they are busy choosing a representative; further on, the delegates of a district are hurrying to town to consult about some local improvements … One group of citizens assembled for the sole object of announcing that they disapprove of the government's course … .[2]

In the midst of this technological revolution in human communication, a paradox is emerging that blurs the vision of civil society for the next century. The essence of the paradox is this: even as we enjoy limitless information, we are at risk of obtaining less knowledge. Though protected by powerful tools to control how we present ourselves to the world, these technologies concomitantly destroy our privacy. The Internet offers decreasing marginal costs of communication access and yet the web is becoming thoroughly commercialized and devoid of interactive 'public' spaces. Finally, these technologies make community possible and yet encourage atomization.[3]

Counter-intuitively, the marriage of communication and democracy is being undermined by the very technologies which offer the promise of unlimited communications, cheap and easy access to mass media, the broadcast of independent and original content and the linkage of individuals across vast distances into communities of interest. Hyper-connectivity brings more and more people in touch with each other faster yet it does not bring them closer together. Instead of democracy's din, the Internet seems to be creating a hyper-speed cacophony of dissonant shouting voices. Instead of widespread virtual democracy, founded on interpersonal electronic interaction, it is more common to find intrusive personal messaging, cantakerous e-mails, cross-posted to dozens of listservs and inundating millions of in-boxes. Those visitors who do not merely lurk exchange lengthy diatribes or random utterances, without any incentive to engage others or even commit to take part in an electronic conversation, aptly known as 'chat rooms'. In any given on-line discussion, the development of community is easily derailed by individuals pulling the conversation off its fulcrum, typing, 'MARIA CALLAS IS CRAP!' in the midst of a focused, even fun, debate about the significance of opera as a musical form. There is a marked absence of spaces for deliberative, independent, thoughtful dialogue among 'wired' citizens, confronting new ideas and people in the course of civil conversation. We are 'hugging the shore' of these technologies, to paraphrase John Updike, rather than sailing into the alluring waters of their political possibilities for the creation of new institutions of civil society.[4]

Every revolution throughout history has given birth to a counter-revolution that stands in dialectical and sometimes bloody juxtaposition to the movement from which it emerged. The transformation of public life by network technologies creates the conditions for revolutionizing and reinvigorating civil society and, at the same time, for a world of ultimate totalitarian control by government, by unaccountable commercial interests and by virtue of our own enslavement to the alienating quality of the technology. On the one hand, our computer is a window on to new communities of association and communication. But it is also a mirror reflecting narcissistic isolation, behind an opaque screen that withers genuine civil society and public consciousness. The umbilical cord of swirling cables connects us and yet also ensnares participants in a strangling embrace, shackling man to machine. Networks can connect or they can create a misperception of community where segregation predominates. We have the impression that we are linked to remote people and places. In fact, we are enamoured of the *process* of getting linked, rather than mindful of the ensuing character of the interaction.[5] That is to say, if getting 'wired' becomes more important than the question of what content comes across those wires into homes, schools and public places, then it is the ends of the technology – more, faster, more connected – that are served, rather than the goals of the participants.

Despite the flourishing of electronic commerce and the doubling of the web's size every few weeks,[6] there is no concomitant growth in electronic democracy. There is much information, but no guarantee of knowledge; a lot of chat but little debate. Seeming transparency and openness lead to but a loss of privacy, rather than the emergence of a virtual public sphere. Where are the clearly demarcated, easily accessible, welcoming and independent sites – sites not restricted only to election-time, candidate-centred campaign discussions – for community conversation and deliberation, expressly designed for interactive usage, not passive browsing? Where are the 'public technologies' designed to breed citizens, not consumers? These information-getting web-sites intended to inform the electorate in preparation for elections reinforce the representative system of democracy that has flourished in the television era, but do little to push the envelope into new democratic uses that take advantage of the particular advantages of unmediated conversation empowered by computer networks.

It is not technology per se which either fosters or denigrates the connection between communications media and participatory democratic culture. Technology exists within a framework of values and ideals both inherent to it and imposed by the external legal and institutional structures. Avoiding the negative potential requires solutions that engage law and public policy. But, because network communications are global, decentralized and uncontrollable, we must also utilize the *technology itself* in maximizing the civic and democratic potential. Without 'programming democracy' into the code – building it into the architecture – of virtual spaces, the way we design public spaces for maximum advantage in real space, little can be made of the promise of digital network communications media. In the same way that we consciously construct buildings with space for public displays of art or with handicapped access or that we design rooms with acoustic panels to facilitate conversation and musical performance, we must also purpose-build public chat-rooms and cyber-fora.

The absence of politically relevant discussion spaces on the net is not surprising given that we are trying to force our public debates into spaces designed for private and commercial interaction. Just as we have parks and meeting halls in real life, we need to devise a 'public architecture' in cyberspace to take advantage of the communications potential. By building the ground rules into the architecture, people can access information and discussion and govern their own conversations. The technology can be enlisted to create conversation that is on-point, stays on-point and models the flexibility and dynamics of real-time conversation.

## SELF-GOVERNANCE THROUGH PUBLIC CONVERSATION: WHICH DEMOCRACY FOR THIS TECHNOLOGY?[7]

In an era of increasingly centralized, professionalized and mediated politics, where Washington and Brussels appear, not only geographically distant, but on another planet, and our political experience comes to us spun through the lens of commercial media conglomerates, the Internet promises to reinvigorate an improved kind of localism based on reasoned public discourse. The focus is not the specific political flavor or form but on the inculcation of deliberative forms of self-governance into public life and into the discussion of themes of public import. Put another way, 'our continual observations upon the conduct of others', facilitated by the interactivity of networks, 'lead us to form to ourselves certain general rules concerning what is fit and proper either to be done or to be avoided.'[8] Through communication and confrontation with others and their ideas, we learn and grow as citizens and take part in governing our own communities.

Individuals could have a new-found influence on political and other decision making processes on all levels. Discussion of issues of central importance to geographical communities and dispersed interest communities can form a basis for consensus-building and political organizing. The ready availability of information to inform the conversation disperses power from an educated elite to all participants. Imagine a New England-style town meeting where disenfranchized minorities and physically challenged users can participate equally, using those technologies that facilitate conversation across distances. Any Internet user knows its potential for political debate and organizing. For those with access to the tools, and to the education necessary to use them (already major hurdles), the Internet could be a revolutionary boon to the quality of public life, tying reasoned public debate of issues of common interest to the mechanisms of governance and decision-making.

Deliberative political culture depends upon reasoned language and debate to tie individuals together into a web of discourse and self-governance. 'There is an intimate connection between informal conversations, the kind that take place in communities and virtual communities, in the coffee shops and computer conferences, and the ability of large social groups to govern themselves without monarchs or dictators.'[9] No communications medium could be better suited to participatory activity than the Internet, which offers the means for collective discussion and choice among equals. Therefore rather than inquiring here as to the Internet's viability as a faster polling system or a more accurate vote aggregator, the central emphasis is on how the new capacity for interpersonal dialogue can and will serve the creation of public institutions based on public discourse. Government by-the-people-for-the-people makes sense where people have the means for the airing of views and expression of public consensus. The New England town meeting, the citizen council, neighbourhood associations and other citizen-based forms of communal association are integral institutions to enfranchising and empowering individuals. From community conversation arises community action. Cultivating the means for community dialogue across geographical boundaries is possible with computer networks and a *sine qua non* for establishing genuine democratic governance, that is, by the *demos* itself.

It is difficult to infuse any discussion new technologies with terms like democracy or civil society without sounding like preachers, raining on the entertainment parade of the Internet, or like elitists, failing to appreciate the essential populism of these communications technologies. Public discourse can be lively and entertaining on the net and offers a broad appeal for a large new audience interested in participating in public dialogue and improving the quality of political culture. The tendency to speak of e-commerce needs no additional promotion because it takes care of itself. A *public* Internet, however, needs the support and attention the market cannot provide and can be most readily accomplished by letting democratic goals drive the design of the technical architecture, seizing the advantages of technology to enhance our democracy.

## PARADOX 1: INFORMATION WITHOUT KNOWLEDGE

Information is a cornerstone of political education and socialization. The ability to find out about issues of public importance, to inform oneself about the workings of government and its policies, the availability of information on candidates prior to an election, the contents of governmental files and reports, scientific and historical data, are but a few examples of the information essential to the education of the informed and responsible citizen. Germany's Basic Law, like many European constitutions (and unlike the First Amendment in the United States), does not enshrine the freedom of expression but the right to inform oneself freely and to disseminate opinions. This rhetoric squarely places the emphasis on the necessity for independent and trustworthy information to facilitate meaningful communication. Yet in this era of information overload, the subtle but vital difference between information and knowledge needs to be drawn in order to create virtual places that promote political education in the broadest sense. It is not, in fact, information per se which is useful to the democrat but knowledge, information which has been distilled and contextualized so that it can impart meaning.

Neil Postman wrote in his classic work, *Amusing Ourselves to Death* (1985):

> What Orwell feared were those who would ban books. What [Aldous] Huxley feared was that there would be no reason to ban a book, for there would be no one who wanted to read one. Orwell feared those who would deprive us of information. Huxley feared those who would give us so much that we would be reduced to passivity and egoism. Orwell feared that the truth would be concealed from us. Huxley feared that the truth would be drowned in a sea of irrelevance.[10]

The Internet is the ultimate reference library, chock-full of obscure data supplied by individuals and institutions from around the world, usually for the free use of all comers. The web's growth inheres to the breadth of information being made available by over 200 million individual users and hobbyists worldwide, maintaining private and institutional sites through volunteer labour, such as collecting recipes, political observations, and statistics.

The danger of the Internet is that it threatens to overwhelm us with so much information – too much information – so as to give the appearance of democratizing and enriching our political lives while actually drowning us in irrelevancies. The mere existence of a web page with a candidate's voting record does nothing to educate us as to the political context, what it means, how we should understand or process this data, how reliable it is and how we should find it in the first place. Internet users know all too well that the abundance of informational riches can have a paralytic effect, rendering the viewer helpless to find anything. The sheer quantity of information available creates an inverse relationship between speaking and listening, between information and understanding, between broadcasting and reception. The more people speak, the fewer people will actually be heard. In fact, the deluge of data ensures that we cannot find anything and that we become even more dependent than in the days before the flood on information arbitrageurs who push, trade and sell us access to sources of information. We depend on familiar and accepted media brands but also on unaccountable, commercialized search tools and information filters to sort information and make it meaningful. Although these editors are machines, they are not neutral. The values and choices are embedded deep within the code and often not obvious to the user.

The major search engines sell priority retrieval to those willing to pay to be listed first. Currently, the leading supplier of networking equipment, Cisco Systems, is advertising a product which would allow a cable company to block or restrict consumers from reaching pre-set web-sites in Internet-over-cable service. This technology also includes the function to slow down access to unaffiliated sites at the cable company's choosing in order to frustrate users and turn them away from that content.[11] In a world of 75 million, instead of 75 channels, companies will pay premiums to ensure the greatest number of eyeballs. Though, in theory, every individual with access to the right technology and education can be his or her own broadcaster on the web, this does not imply that each of us has equal power to be heard in an information society dominated by a handful of players who occupy the prime real-estate on-line and obscure the way to alternative content because of their ability to enter into strategic, cross-media, eyeball-capturing alliances.

The profusion of information, only some of which is reliable, prevents the creation of a true knowledge economy on-line. In real space, where we are familiar with various brand names, such as CBS or the *New York Times*, we might be willing to experiment with an obscure alternative that comes along such as *Brill's Content*. In the on-line arena, where there are so many available channels in the form of millions of web-sites, we are *more*, not less, dependent on those familiar and trusted media brand names. Moreoever, on the web, where commercial actors who formerly sold tangibles, now offer information services, well-known brand names will also be relied upon as media sources. Information is melding into and becoming indistinguishable from advertising. Companies use content to attract consumers on-line and, as a result, the quality and independence of content is compromised. This is not to say that AT&T, Big Blue, DaimlerChrysler and other giants of industry should not provide informational content but that there should also be clear access to sources of public, non-commercial, independent information and conversation.

The answer to the problem of 500 informational channels and no knowledge lies in new media law and policy as well as in the architecture of the technology itself. Both government, by mandating open access rules, and industry, by market mechanisms, can promote content in the public interest, independent search and filtering tools, which strive for value neutrality and an independent assessment of the relevance and priority of web pages. However, the solution must also come from within the technology itself. There need to be spaces on-line where the information can be trusted and labelled as such. There need to be places for conversation and debate on-line that are closely linked to sources of information so that participants segue seamlessly between learning and speaking, reading and participation. Imagine an on-line town-meeting where, instead of shouting at one another, participants could marshal competing data to present countervailing arguments and bring relevant knowledge to bear on the discussion. There are news sites which currently offer chat rooms and discussion fora to accompany timely content offerings. Yet these sites do not link between the information offerings and the debate at hand, though the technology would permit it. Instead, web-sites compete to put on the most dazzling display of information overabundance, further reinforcing users' reliance on commercialized and non-transparent tools for sorting, filtering and editing information. What calculators have done for arithmetic literacy, these technologies risk doing to critical faculties of discernment and the ability to translate information into knowledge.

## PARADOX 2: PRIVACY OR SURVEILLANCE?

At the dawn of the communications revolution the second democratic paradox is between two competing trends: one toward electronically enhanced privacy and, the other, toward, digital monitoring. The same technologies that facilitate anonymity and arm's length interactions with the world also provide the ultimate means of surveillance. Through recent media reports following the adoption of the European Data Protection Directive and stories of various abuses of consumer data privacy by unscrupulous data processors,[12] the problem of on-line data privacy has become well known. The technologies which enable us to surf and sort the web also make possible the web's monitoring of how and what we surf and sort – not unlike the panopticon or prison devised (but never tried out) by the utilitarian philosopher Jeremy Bentham. Content appears on a web page customized to our interests, sometimes as we have chosen, or often enough as the web-site chooses for us. The problem of technology and privacy is not new. Credit card companies track every transaction and use this data to create and market customer profiles. Telephones, credit cards, check cashing cards, club cards, computers, cell phones, television, even cars are equipped to gather information which can be gold to data brokers and telemarketers. From Martha Stewart to Walmart, vendors regularly mine private information to sell more product. Governments have been in the business of snooping since the beginning of time.

Cyberspace has exacerbated the problem and our sensitivity to it. On-line every click on a web-site or completion of an on-line registration form could reveal personal information which, when combined with readily available public records about who we are and where we live, destroys our privacy. A recent poll by Louis Harris and Associates revealed that 86 per cent of net users who have bought products via the net are 'concerned' about privacy and 55 per cent are 'very concerned'. Though GeoCities, a web site company, had been telling its customers that it protected their privacy, it actually sold its databases of customer information to direct marketers. A recent survey conducted by Forrester Research (Cambridge, MA) called on-line privacy 'a joke'.[13]

The Internet has so far failed to spawn public spaces, and it is also in danger of destroying privacy and intimacy. Sun Systems' Chief Executive, Scott McNeely, declared, 'privacy is dead, get over it'. It may well be that privacy exists only as an illusion. Corporate data mining techniques are a threat because they are insidious, pervasive and difficult to rout given the underlying profit-motive. But the culture of on-line life – its developing mores – is another danger: instant messaging, rapid fire e-mails at every and all hours, PC cameras, and cookies erode intimacy in the name of getting 'wired'. Though normally secluded alone with our machines, our solitude is a chimera. We cannot perceive the intrusion into our private lives the way we would an invasion of our homes. But the silent surveillance of on-line habits, the popping up of 'buddies' with 'instant message' demands or chat-seeking ICQ (I-Seek-You) requests stealthily siphon off our privacy.

The conveniences of the Information Society need not come at the cost of disclosing intimate personal data. We do not need targeted marketing 'pushing' the goods which data miners claim we want. When there are technologies, such as electronic search engines, that enable us to 'pull' the information or product we choose, and when we freely give up our personal information to receive targeted marketing, we are actually allowing companies to sell us back our own personal preferences at a profit. We suffer not only the financial loss to us as consumers of the worth of our personal data, but the immeasurable moral loss as citizens of the value of privacy.

The danger is not necessarily the diminishing of any absolute measure of privacy but the deception that we enjoy privacy when, in effect, we can become subject to the tyranny of our tools. The erosion of data protection and privacy is not the inevitable result of the new information-harvesting or personal messaging technologies, but of our failure to demand social change, namely privacy legislation from government, ethical privacy principles from business and a culture of respect for personal privacy from ourselves in on-line (and off-line) activities. Beyond the legal question of how to regulate or promote individual and industry self-regulation with regard to privacy, technological controls can be built into the architecture of the software to allow users to protect their privacy preferences. Encryption can be used to secure commercial transactions (digicash and digital signature) but also to protect user personal privacy and the privacy of communications.[14] Technology, such as encoding and scrambling software, can do end-runs around governmental and corporate censorship by increasing the transaction costs associated with blocking or censoring content or invading the privacy of electronic communications. Encryption is the mortar to forge structures where users choose how their personal information is used and revealed.[15] Encryption technologies can help to patrol the tenuous border between openness and a dangerous destruction of civil liberties on-line. In addition to encryption, the inter-activity of the Internet as a communications platform can and should be used to promote a conversation around the issue of privacy and its importance which, in turn, generates norms for the appropriate use of personal information.

## PARADOX 3: FREE NOT PUBLIC

The third paradox of democracy's future in the information age, already obliquely alluded to, is the disjunction between the sudden availability of relatively cheap and easily accessible means of communication without the concomitant emergence of public spaces on the net. The greater the number of outlets for communication, the more the Internet reinforces privatization and the expression of private desires, rather than expressions of public interest. There are no parks, band assembly or meeting halls yet in this media space. To an extent, this is also one of the strengths of these technologies; the facilitation of individuated choice can be empowering. But the absence of mechanisms to transform individual preferences into an expression of collective intent is a failing which threatens the development of deliberative processes on the Internet. The technologies of freedom which enable us to customize and personalize everything about the net, creating My-Browser and My NewsSite, encourage thinking only about what is good for *me*, rather than what is good for the world in which I live. The worldwide web is dominated by personal consumption outlets for the individual purchase of information, goods and services. Personal agents help trawl the net extracting select information and eliminating serendipitous browsing. Many of these items are 'free' in that they exact no monetary remuneration, though they extract payment in the form of attention to advertising or personal data, yet they are not public because they do not catalyze congregation and consensus. Missing are the on-line institutions about 'us', that actually foster decision-making and action.

The Internet offers the possibility for every individual to be his own broadcaster at almost no marginal cost. Networks empower users to communicate their ideas to one recipient or to a general public. But with so many voices speaking, who has time to listen? It is similar to the dilemma of excessive information. Too much direct participation, where everyone is inputting and no one heeding, transforms even political speech into random chatter. Network technology implies flexibility and user empowerment. But the hypertext links and multimedia options which allow each person to 'do his own thing', taken to the extreme, can emasculate community. If everyone is the king, who obeys? Diversity enriches the fabric of social life and the quality of dialogue in the public sphere, but excessive diversity leads to strife and the breakdown of dialogue. For the public sphere to function, citizens have to be able to hear themselves think and hear each other speaking.

In the on-line world a user can download exactly what she wants, when she wants it. But, in the same way that pay-per-view destroys television as a common platform, hyper-segmentation of information and communications channels on the Internet can eviscerate the 'public' in participatory and deliberative democratic life. Where is the public interest component of media when media exist just for me? When it becomes possible – and even necessary given the high noise to signal ratio on-line – to create the 'me-channel'. When I only see what I want to, and become an information consumer, rather than a participant, then I have isolated myself. There is no integrator of common views and interests if I design my own filter to suit my tastes alone. Max Frankel, media commentator for the *New York Times Magazine* writes:

> The romantic experience of a nation united by a live comedy, a political convention or a Presidential funeral has been shattered by electronic inventions. First, tape, then the remote control, followed by cable TV, the launching of satellites, the creation of new networks and, increasingly, one-subject channels. The more we have been wired together, the faster we have been spun apart … And now comes the web, the ultimate slicing machine, to divide and deliver us to market, by group for sure, and even one by one, where possible. Some hail the web as a liberation, rendering all voices equal. I suspect we will be equal only in our digital loneliness.[16]

Deliberative, participatory democracy requires careful editors and good filters to engage in a mediated, educated debate. But too much filtering isolates users who share no common platform and cannot, therefore, meaningfully discuss issues of self-governance. The lack of common moral basis – the destabilization of any meaningful conception of 'public' – makes resistance to tyranny increasingly difficult.

So-called collaborative browsing and collaborative rating technologies, though interesting and exciting software advances for the Internet, are also not about collectivity or deliberation. These technologies aggregate individual preferences and prejudices. They do not demand of users to think socially. Rather, in the collaborative browsing model, where the server suggests a site to visit based on the aggregated preferences of previous users, or a collaborative shopping tool, where product recommendations are made based on what a defined category of other shoppers bought, the machine creates the relevant society. The user has no interest or incentive to consider anyone beyond himself. The deployment of the latest generation of Internet toys expose two apparently contradictory trends, one toward an extreme individualization (me-business, my-browser, me-commerce) and the other toward interactive groupware and 'chat' applications. The former capitalizes on the unique flexibility of network technologies and the sale-ability of user-empowerment tools. In addition, personalisable technologies also facilitate increasingly targeted monitoring and marketing of individual habits and preferences. The latter exploits the two-way marvels of the Internet as distinct from the uni-dimensionality of television and permits a certain kind of non-committal, unengaged sociability.[17]

The addictive ease of our connectivity has us frenetically clicking and jumping around the web, yet at times our attention spans are reduced to that of immature children. Even when we all herd to the same web-sites to follow slavishly the latest breaking news story, we are not using the web as a public medium, but as a private viewing box, no different than television except for its extreme speed and that there is even less time for evaluation and critical reflection of the content on the screen. Falsification is cheap, easy and instantaneously replicated like a virus across the Internet. With the demand for constantly changing, always up-to-date content, we have few guideposts to identify truth and reliability. We are overwhelmed by new data – or newly repackaged data – accompanied by graphs, charts, photographs, movie clips, 'factoids', and links, and are so concerned with absorbing the volume of information that we have no time to assess why we need it or to what end. Without reflection and deliberation, there can be no conversation and therefore no public self-governance – no town meetings or community councils.

The building of genuinely public places necessitates the creation of architectures conducive to the values of public conversation. A public place on the web needs, first and foremost, to be easily and freely accessible. In the same way that municipalities do not charge admission fees to public parks, there be no costly barriers to entry or discrimination among those wishing to join in the debate. Those costs are measured not only in dollars charged but personal data taken, time and attention abused, and independence compromised by commercialization. Discrimination can also take many forms, including the exclusion of those without the 'right technology or technological sophistication'. They have to be identifiable as public spaces and easy to find. A well-equipped and comfortable meeting hall is of no use if no one in town knows where it is, no one can get there or park, or dedicated participants must watch commercials and traverse a shopping mall before being allowed to join in the town meeting. It is not a public park if sunbathers are bombarded by advertising billboards and hawkers, selling, not only cold drinks, but products unrelated to the enjoyment of the public park and its public aims.

Yet this is precisely the situation we have in cyberspace and it is getting worse. Some good political sites exist but there is no simple way to find them or to happen upon them, especially when richer commercial sites can afford to buy priority on the major search engines and to purchase eyeball-catching advertising time on other media, including television and newspaper, to attract people to their sites. In real space, we make room –

albeit ever dwindling – to public media and public gathering places. These independent entities are neither state-controlled, nor commercial, but institutions of the 'third way', of civil society, between the state and the market. Even if there is a paucity of such spaces in real life, there is still the hope of building them in cyberspace. We have to strategise to set aside public space in cyberspace by legal and policy means, mandating, if necessary, the protection of the independence and carriage of public sites, but also by technological and market mechanisms which enhance the profile and accessibility of such sites. We have to take responsibility for building attractive, vital, fun and enticing public sites without advertising, banner ads, endorsements, and paid-for linking arrangements. If they are to take hold, we also have to frequent such sites and demonstrate a demand for them. Developing this demand is perhaps the most difficult prescription, given our non-participatory and commercialized political and media culture.

Once we get to the park or the meeting hall, if the atmosphere is not conducive to conversation, because there is no place to sit and hang out, the acoustics are terrible, one person is able to monopolize the conversation, and certain individuals are excluded, they cannot fulfil their function as public spaces. We need 'public architectures' on the Net which facilitate conversation, interaction, deliberation, education and engagement. In the same way as we build e-commerce solutions honed to shopping atmospherics, we can also built sites tailor-made for political, social and cultural uses. Instead of facilitating the instantaneous availability of information, more web-sites need to build in 'speed bumps' that allow users to slow down, ponder, deliberate and reflect before speaking. By limiting the word length of postings or disabling the 'speaking' powers of an abuser, technology can be employed to prevent one user from monopolizing the conversation. With the necessary support, special groupware, designed explicitly to serve as public architectures, could be the wave of the future. Unfortunately, because such projects cannot, by definition, be commercialized or state-run, their development will depend partly upon the generosity of those both in the private and state-sectors willing to contribute to such projects they will not control. Yet from them we will all benefit.

## PARADOX 4: COMMUNITY OR ANOMIE?

Information Society pundits have written extensively extolling the virtues of virtual communities, which have and can coalesce around the interests of their members, in addition to adhering to geographical boundaries. In the early days of BBSs, such as The Well, participants wrote of the companionship, conversation and genuine community dialogue they experienced. The interactive potential of networks enhances the possibilities for communicative discourse which binds people with the ties of common dialogue around subjects of shared interest. Yet out of this promising beginning, the illusory nature of on-line community has also manifested itself. There are exceptions, but the wider-spread truth is that the superficial quality of conversation on the net makes lasting and politically relevant community thus far impossible. The appearance of community masks the reality of isolation and atomization fed by life behind the screen.

The desktop box leads us to exist in a disconnect from reality. The dangerous disjunction between chat on the net and action in the real world risks emasculating the politically interesting relationship between discussion and democracy. That is not to say that debate and discourse in any medium must be linked directly to political action. To the contrary, deliberative democracy depends upon thoughtful, reasoned even languorous conversation about issues of common public import and interest for its own sake. This process of self-education and socialization creates more mature citizens and community members. However, where a medium like the net is so pervasive and all-encompassing to the exclusion of other outlets, the smothering dominance of irrelevant 'chat' jeopardizes opportunities for deliberative conversation and debate. The speed, accessibility, affordability and multilateral anonymity of the net encourage the chatter by making it so easy to speak without thinking. The prevalence of irrelevant dialogue, in turn, prevents the development of a concomitant responsiveness by decision-makers in real space. To be sure, there are many exceptions and examples of how the Internet has influenced the policy making process by disseminating news and public opinion at lightening speed[18] with the help of television's coverage of Internet activity.

Debate in the public sphere presumes not only an educated public but an honest debate. Not only in cyberspace, but also in traditional media, the blurring between truth and fiction raises grave political questions. The more isolated the consumer, the more he must rely exclusively on his own judgement. Given the power of the media to influence, to create stars and to destroy lives and the speed of new media to disseminate falsehoods, the frequent confusion of authentic information with the make-believe renders any optimistic prediction of an electronic public sphere naive. The marketplace of ideas presumes perfect information, not imperfect falsehoods. Legitimate political processes are made possible by the erection of institutions which instill a sense of trust in participants because of their integrity and professionalism. Although television is inherently about illusions, it is able to instill a sense of trust by making the images on the screen more immediate and real. But if there are no guarantees in cyberspace of the authenticity of experience and information, cyber-institutions cannot function as trust-building public bodies. Instead of serving as a locus for political action, there will be so many people speaking – with no guarantee of who is speaking the truth – that no single voice will command any respect or lasting legitimacy.

Again, the technology can aid in overcoming the problem, if it is used to demand accountability of participants in the disembodied debate and to inculcate a culture of truth and responsibility. If certain chat rooms, instead of permitting users to post anything and everything and disappear, required participants to commit to a minimum level of participation in a discussion with a limited number of participants, familiarity and trust might begin to develop. In meta-moderation systems, for example, participants rate each other for the quality of their postings and, in one model, are given either more or less time to speak, based on these ratings as a technological mechanism to encourage polite and reflective behavior. The meta-moderation idea has deep flaws, including that it would allow a disgruntled participant to rate someone for the content of their remarks, rather than rating for quality and politeness. In an alternate system, a web site might demand of participants, wishing to join in the debate, to read something on point before jumping in to speak or the design of the site might physically limit the length of a posting or permit the users in the group to silence someone who persistently and in bad faith strays from the topic. There are limitless 'architectural' possibilities to design for public and community use as an alternative model to the mushrooming me-sites that abound in the e-commerce web space.[19]

## PUBLIC TECHNOLOGIES: IF WE BUILD IT WILL THEY COME?

If we recognize the potential of the technology and its pitfalls for conversational democracy and public discussion and build sites that take advantage of the deliberative and interactive promise of the Internet, the empirical question remains: will anyone use these sites? Can the architecture of the net be reconstructed in such a way as to encourage actual political participation and to catalyze a reinvigoration of off-line political culture through vital on-line institutions? The proof will only manifest itself in time, if we experiment with and experience genuine democratic life on-line. All forms of democratic life depend to greater and less extent on a conversation between the citizenry and government and among citizens.

Though wonderfully different from sitting in a cafe or in a meeting hall, conversations in cyberspace offer the necessary modicum of true human interaction for shopping, but not for conversation. It is still very difficult to express urgency, importance, sympathy and attention. These emotional and visual clues that undergird basic human interaction are among the most fundamental and taken-for-granted building blocks of democratic institutions that we have to consider in designing institutions. Yet for all the sophistication of network technologies and the boon to democracy that they offer from being text-based, they lack these basic indices of interaction. Only by building public sites on-line, 'architected' to serve the goals and meet the needs of deliberation and self-governance, can we know how the paradoxes will resolve themselves; if electronic communications will continue the tradition of communications media in the service of democracy or if we are entering a new era of information without knowledge, privacy without intimacy and networks without community.

## NOTES

1. PriceWaterhouseCoopers' 1999 Consumer Technology survey found that 48 per cent of United States users polled said they went on-line for e-mail, whereas 28 per cent said they went on-line to do research. The previous year those figures were exactly in reverse, making e-mail the primary reason people now go on-line. Reuters On-Line Report of 1 October 1999, available at http://www.reuters.com.
2. Alexis de Tocqueville, *Democracy in America* (New York: Doubleday, 1969) p.242.
3. It is also the case that the dyads of the paradox enumerated above suggest different outcomes resulting from the spread of the on-line-life, not all of which are antithetical to democracy *per se*. To an extent, they describe a natural rift within modern democratic culture where private and public, individual and community are in dynamic tension. For example, the pull between virtual community with collaborative decision-making and enhanced individual choice empowered by personalizable technologies reflects choices we must make as to the flavour of our future political culture in an on-line world. The threat to privacy from surveillance technologies, on the other hand, presents a danger to the future of our civil liberties.
4. John Updike, *Hugging the Shore: Essays and Criticism* (New York: Knopf, 1983).
5. Notes to speech of Rabbi Lee Paskind, delivered on 19 September, in Lakewood, New Jersey. Notes on file with author.
6. For helpful information regarding size and growth rate of the Web, see http://www.nua.ie/surveys
7. For more on this, see, Beth S. Noveck, 'Transparent Space: Law, Technology and Deliberative Democracy in the Information Society', *Cultural Values*, Vol.3, No.4 (Oct. 1999), pp.472–91.
8. Adam Smith, *The Theory of Moral Sentiments* (Indianapolis: Liberty Classics, 1982, first published 1759), p.159.
9. Howard Rheingold, *Virtual Community: Homesteading on the Electronic Frontier* (New York: HarperCollins, 1994), p.281.
10. Neil Postman, *Amusing Ourselves to Death: Public Discourse in the Age of Show Business* (New York: Viking Penguin, 1985).
11. http://www.glinks.Net/items/glitem.4904.htm, visited 25 Sept. 1999.

12. 95/46/EC of the European Parliament and of the Council 24 October 1995 available at http://www2.echo.lu/legal/en/dataprot/directiv/directiv.html. See also European Directive 97/66/EC of the European Parliament and of the Council of 15 December 1997 concerning the processing of personal data and the protection of privacy in the telecommunications sector at http://www2.echo.lu/legal/en/dataprot/protection.html.
13. See the Forrester Research website at http://www.forrester.com.
14. For a list of privacy tools and resources, see http://www.epic.org/privacy/tools.html.
15. For example, Novell's digitalme™ is software designed to give consumers the ability to control their personal information and manage their online relationships. New users fill in a profile form containing a wide range of information which is encrypted and stored in a secure, private directory. When a digitalme user elects to register with a new web site, a personal proxy system intercepts the necessary registration forms, automatically fills them in, and provides a completed form for review. The next time the user accesses the Web site, digitalme automatically handles the sign-on process.
16. Max Frankel, 'One TV Nation, Divisible: The Union of Media Giants Carves the Audience into Ever Smaller Units', *New York Times Magazine*, 3 Oct. 1999, p.30–31.
17. There are exceptions, of course, including the close-knit communities described so elegantly by Howard Rheingold in *Virtual Community*. However, the norm is increasingly toward dysfunctional on-line communities where there is no sense of responsibility, engagement or lasting commitment.
18. An excellent example of this was the web-based campaign in the United States to derail the Communications Decency Act (CDA) (also known as the Exon Amendment) in 1995.
19. Designing such prototypical sites is the goal of the Civic Exchange: Strong Democracy in Cyberspace Project, a collaboration of the Yale Law School Information Society Project and the Walt Whitman Center for the Culture and Politics of Democracy. The aim of Civic Exchange is actively to encourage uses of the Internet that exploit its vital conversational inter-activity and potential for direct communication among citizens. The Project's goal is to design spaces for deliberative, trusted, independent, thoughtful dialogue where 'wired' citizens can think and rethink issues, confront new ideas and people and change their minds in the course of civil conversation. The focus is on strengthening 'strong democracy', where knowledgeable, engaged and accountable citizens can face each other in ongoing civic discussion about issues of public interest and importance. For more information, visit http://www.law.yale.edu/infosociety.

# Democratizing Democracy: Strong Democracy, US Political Campaigns and the Internet

JENNIFER STROMER-GALLEY

## STRONG DEMOCRACY

In 1984, Benjamin Barber wrote a book offering a new conception of direct democratic rule. He faulted liberalism, the current form of government in the United States, and claimed that this 'thin democracy' is based on premises not genuinely democratic. The liberal paradigm constructs people as autonomous from all other individuals, acting only when necessary to preserve one's own private self-interest: 'We are born into the world solitary strangers, live our lives as wary aliens, and die in fearful isolation.'[1] We solitary strangers appeal to knowable, independent grounds 'from which the concepts, values, standards, and ends of political life can be derived by simple deduction'.[2] Politics, then, is a tool for preserving individual self-interest. The average person does not behave politically in daily life, but rather only when moved to do so for self-interest. Those who act politically are specialists, 'elites' whose only special qualification is that they engage in politics.

Barber believed that direct democracy is true democracy when properly conceived and executed. Called 'strong democracy', his design provides balance lacking in other forms of direct democracy, such as majority rule and communitarianism. Strong democracy is 'politics in the participatory mode where conflict is resolved in the absence of an independent ground through a participatory process of ongoing, proximate self-legislation and the creation of a political community capable of transforming dependent, private individuals into free citizens and partial and private interests into public goods'.[3] Strong democracy necessitates that government is comprised of citizens active in a process to resolve conflict, not through

The author thanks W. Russell Neuman, Richard Davis and the participants of the Caught in the Web Conference at the Annenberg School for Communications at the University of Pennsylvania, in April 1999.

appeals to natural rights or market forces, but as part of the communication process in which there is no appeal to independent grounds. He emphasized the notion that citizens are active and are able to govern themselves in a strong democratic system. Individuals act politically *in their daily lives* rather than only acting politically when called to out of a necessity to preserve self-interest. Citizenship is viewed as a condition of human nature, and individuals are social beings who exist in a community of other social beings. He explained:

> Community grows out of participation and at the same time makes participation possible; civic activity educates individuals how to think publicly as citizens even as citizenship informs civic activity with the required sense of publicness and justice. Politics becomes its own university, citizenship its own training ground, and participation its own tutor.[4]

One of the key activities in this process of individuals becoming citizens is talk, which serves several functions including community building, persuasion, and agenda-setting. These talking citizens are amateurs not elites. They have no speciality and engage each other as such without the 'intermediary of expertise'.[5]

Barber outlined a program for enacting his vision of strong democracy. It relied heavily on communication technology to provide for easy information access, for efficient electronic balloting, and for increased communication in local and national political spheres. Throughout the 1980s, civic activists and democratic theorists in the United States and elsewhere put their hopes into interactive television. Although it never caught on in the national marketplace, it was used in a select set of programmes around the United States for town hall meetings in which people could phone in questions or comments on local talk shows with government officials or political activists and elites.[6] Interactive television spawned a research and activist agenda centred around the political possibilities created through 'teledemocracy'.

Because it was never actualised in the United States, researchers and activists now look to the Internet to supply the kind of communication channel for information gathering, deliberation, and voting that are essential for direct democracy. The question is, can the Internet offer the features necessary for direct democracy of the strong sort that Barber envisions? In this essay, I define and explain six characteristics of the Internet and their functions within the context of the political campaign. Increasingly, in the United States, they use the Internet as an additional channel through which to convey their message. I argue that the characteristics of the media that comprise the Internet suggest, if applied properly, a more democratic turn in the political sphere of daily life – a move towards Benjamin Barber's strong democracy. The complicating factor in predicting a more democratic turn lies in the candidates, the staff and the purposes to which they put this new communication technology.

## THE RISE OF THE INTERNET

At least part of the impetus for direct democracy focuses on citizens' general malaise towards elected government. Hacker argued, citing focus groups conducted by the Kettering Foundation, which is a US public interest organisation, that citizens are disenchanted because they feel they have no meaningful way to participate in the process of government – in setting the political agenda on issues of which they are concerned and in participating in the approval or rejection of proposed policy. Hacker set his sights on the Internet as offering the possibility to reverse this trend.[7]

In this modern era of the television, most citizens experience their government second-hand, through the lens of the camera or through the pen of a journalist. The media act as a filter for information. Journalists and editors determine what stories will have the most drama and interest for readers. Economics is a factor in the news industry. Newspapers must be sold and eyeballs must be brought to the screen to bring in advertising dollars. To do so, political news often has the narrative structure of a story, complete with characters, conflict, a climax, and resolution.[8] Orren wrote: 'the media like to report news events as mini-melodramas, with heroes, villains, and underlying plots; political leaders are rarely cast as the heroes'.[9] In this context, political actors and the government they represent are cast in an unflattering light. Experimental research points to the conclusion that the way in which the press covers politics, with their focus on comparisons with horse-races and on scandal, increases readers' cynicism towards politics.[10] There is hope that the Internet may offer an alternative space for people to gain their information about government and the people who comprise it.[11]

There also is hope that the Internet, in either its global capacity or in civic networks established for local communities, will create a 'space' for citizens to participate in setting the political agenda and assist in decision-making.[12] Speaking as the US Vice President, Al Gore in his address before the International Telecommunications Union (ITU) in Buenos Aires heralded the Internet as 'promote[ing] the functioning of democracy by greatly enhancing the participation of citizens in decision-making'.[13] Hacker offered the thought that the Internet, though its technical feature of interactivity, will make it possible for citizens more easily to provide feedback to government officials, thereby placing them within the process of governance.

In testing these claims, researchers have not found such promising results in the United States. Davis conducted a detailed study of the content of political web-sites and the participants on-line and found that the players in the traditional media are becoming and will continue to be key players on the Internet. He found that the major political parties and their political candidates had sophisticated web-sites that were distinguishable in content and quality from the lesser-known party and candidate sites. Furthermore, he found that of the 100 political campaign sites he studied in the 1996 election cycle 75 per cent of the candidates used interactive features, such as e-mail addresses, on their sites. None of the candidates, however, used the Internet for public discussions with citizens and they could choose what e-mail messages needed a response.[14] The hope that Gore held of citizens participating more directly in the process of governance via the Internet does not seem to hold true from Davis's analysis of political campaigns.

An analysis conducted of candidate web-sites during the mid-term elections of 1998 offered no more promising results, even though the technology had had two more years of tinkering. Kamarck conducted a content analysis of candidate web-sites. Of the 1,296 candidates running for Congress or Governor, 43 per cent or 554 had a campaign web-site. Most contained both issue positions and biographical information of the candidate (81 per cent). It appears that people can learn important information about the candidate, information that is relevant to determining how the candidate will conduct him or herself in office. On the more interactive features of the medium, however, the candidates left much to be desired. In Kamarck's coding scheme only two candidates were 'fully interactive', that is, users visiting the site had some ability to engage in a dialogue with the candidate or campaign staff.[15]

On a more positive note, a recent study conducted by the Pew Research Center for the People and the Press, an independent, non-profit, public opinion research organization in the US, indicated that a small but growing group of people are using the Internet to learn about politics and political candidates. Of people who use the Internet, 16 per cent visited the Internet at least once in 1998 to get election news or information. Mid-term elections typically do not garner the same amount of press and public attention as presidential election years. Indeed, the same question asked in 1996 of

Internet users reveals that 22 per cent reported going on at least once during the election for news and information. Of those who went on-line for news and information about the elections in 1996, 25 per cent reported visiting a candidate web-site. In 1998, the number dropped to seven per cent. This drop speaks more to the lack of interest in mid-term elections than to a general drop in interest in political news and information.[16]

An assumption in research on the Internet and politics is that the Internet has features, qualities, or characteristics that will provide citizens with an increased role in the political process. This assumes that (a) citizens want more of a role in the process; (b) the current channels available to them are inadequate; and (c) the Internet offers those channels. It is that third assumption that I wish to address. Researchers, such as Browning[17] and Hacker,[18] often point to the interactive character of the Internet as being the primary channel through which the Internet may provide a gateway through which citizens can find greater participation in politics. The question is: what is this character and how do candidates use it?

In order to begin testing whether the Internet genuinely offers democratization, or a threat of anarchy, or perhaps worse, the status quo, we must understand the characteristics of the Internet to begin gauging the opportunities it may offer. The focus of this analysis is political campaigns. Political campaigning is an important area of study because campaigns place policy issues and general politics, through television advertisements, direct mail, fund-raising, and grass-roots efforts, into the laps of the average person. The political campaign and election is an important ritual in which it seems possible for a new political agenda to be set or to affirm a current or older agenda. Often when scholars discuss direct democracy and a changing political context, they do not look to political campaigns, they look to non-profit and activist organizations. Barber cited examples of strong democracy as those kinds of organizations as well as governmental initiatives that encourage citizens to engage in community building. Scholars tend to look at progressive organizations for that is where change can be seen. For Barber's plan to work, however, the existing institutions must change, too. Eisenstein and Marvin both show how technological advancements such as the printing press[19] and electricity[20] historically have altered institutions. Political campaigns, in my estimation, are indicative of the state of the institution. The degree to which democratic language and practice suffuses campaign communication indicates the degree to which genuine democracy exists. If a given technology makes an invitation possible to participate in the process of setting the agenda with the candidates and the candidates do so, then there exists a spirit (if not a practice) of democratic participation by the populace.

Some commentators might argue that the purpose of political campaigns, however, is for the candidate to win the election.[21] Others might challenge that political candidates should not allow the citizenry to set the agenda, because political candidates must demonstrate their ability to lead on the issues. Both of these stances, however, favour a liberal democratic agenda over one that favours strong democracy. Political candidates can energise the democratic environment by inviting deliberation and offering information not only on the issues they favour but also on providing factual evidence to back their policy positions. The question is: do the characteristics of the Internet offer a turn towards direct democracy?

## CHARACTERISTICS OF THE INTERNET

There are six characteristics of the Internet that theoretically contribute to a democratizing effect: cost, volume, directionality, speed, targeting, and convergence. Illustrations from the 1996 and 2000 presidential elections and the 1998 gubernatorial elections in the United States will supply evidence for the existence and use of these characteristics. The 1998 illustrations are of ten states' gubernatorial campaign. The table indicates which states, the names of the candidates, and their incumbency status.

TABLE 1

TEN STATES, THE CANDIDATES, PARTY AND INCUMBENCY STATUS

| State | Candidate | Party | Status |
|---|---|---|---|
| Arizona | Jane Hull* | Republican | Incumbent |
| | Paul Johnson | Democrat | Challenger |
| California | Dan Lungren | Republican | No incumbent |
| | Gray Davis | Democrat | |
| Colorado | Bill Owens* | Republican | No incumbent |
| | Gail Schoettler | Democrat | |
| Florida | Jeb Bush | Republican | No incumbent |
| | Buddy Mackay | Democrat | |
| Illinois | George Ryan | Republican | No incumbent |
| | Glenn Poshard | Democrat | |
| Iowa | Jim Ross Lighfoot | Republican | No incumbent |
| | Tom Vilsack | Democrat | |
| Maryland | Ellen Sauerbrey | Republican | Challenger |
| | Parris Glendening | Democrat | Incumbent |
| Minnesota | Norm Coleman | Republican | No incumbent |
| | Hubert Humphrey III | Democrat | |
| | Jesse Ventura | Reform | |
| Oregon | Bill Sizemore | Republican | Challenger |
| | John Kitzhaber | Democrat | Incumbent |
| Texas | George Bush Jr. | Republican | Incumbent |
| | Garry Mauro | Democrat | Challenger |

*Note*: *Candidate did not have a campaign web-site.

*Cost*

Thc Intcrnet is a cost-effective way to communicate. The hardware is plentiful and reduces cost caused by high demand and short supply. The hardware is increasingly inexpensive to produce through mass production and through inexpensive synthetic materials. Finally, the system of passing information is more efficient, allowing more information to flow. As a result the cost per message decreases.[22]

For the political campaign, after the initial cost of purchasing hardware and software (between $1,000 and $2,500 for a standard desk-top machine in the United States), and a connection to the Internet, a political campaign's other fees can include paying for staff to build and maintain the site, a domain name for the web-site, and a host to provide server space for it. All of these costs can be kept minor, especially if volunteers can be found to build and maintain the site and businesses can be found that will provide server space and web hosting free or at a reduction.

Creating and maintaining a web-site is significantly cheaper than creating a television advertisement – the primary way in which candidates communicate to the public. Producing a television advertisement requires access to expensive cameras, a studio for filming, editing equipment, actors, and so on. Most politicians hire a consulting company to produce their advertisements for them. Their costs, however, are steep. It is not uncommon for a candidate to spend $2 million on purchasing a small, national advertisement for just one month. In the United States the high cost of running a campaign can be attributed to the current perception that a strong television advertising presence is a key component of success. Even at the local level of politics, such as a mayor's race, candidates spend millions of dollars on advertising. In Philadelphia, 1999 was a mayoral election year. Total funds raised were in the $25 million range – the most ever spent in the city. Most of that money was spent on television advertising.

web-sites also are inexpensive 'storage spaces' for a campaign. Creating an advertisement or a flyer to be sent to voters' homes requires planning. The message must be crafted and the medium designed for the message. At present, most campaign web-sites are used not as a host for original content but for warehousing content produced from advertisements, flyer, and press releases. As such, message content has already been produced and then placed on the Internet. Once the initial purchase of the computer and software is made, and the connection to the Internet established, storing content is virtually free.

Money spent on a web presence differs from campaign to campaign. Most use volunteers to build and maintain the site, whilst supporters host it. For these campaigns, utilizing the Internet for communication is practically free. For example, in Minnesota the gubernatorial campaign of Hubert 'Chip' Humphrey III, grandson of Vice-President Hubert H. Humphrey, had volunteers create and co-ordinate the web-site. Other campaigns hire people to build the site and host it, such as Jeb Bush, son of former President George Bush, creating a communication context in which the Internet added cost to the campaign. Presidential candidate Dole's campaign paid staff to build the web-site and hired an outside company to host it. Rob Arena, who worked on Dole's campaign on the web-site, explained that the site cost one-tenth of one per cent of the overall campaign budget. Even hiring professionals is still a small fraction of the expenditures of the entire campaign.

Volokh argued that new communication technology will have an equalising effect as candidates and parties with less money will be able to have an equal footing on the campaign trail with the better funded because the message would be cheaper to produce.[23] Because the cost of producing a web-site is minimal, a cash-poor candidate could create the same quality web-site as a cash-rich candidate. Moreover, once a candidate was on-line, access was equal with any other candidate, rich or poor. The candidate's web presence was there for anyone to find, regardless of ones' purchasing power in other media. Davis found in his content analysis of campaign and party web-sites in 1996 that incumbents and those with major-party backing had more access in that they were linked to official government sites or major-party sites, thus giving their name and the web-site more visibility than those of less-known candidates. One could argue, however, that although not every candidate can buy television air-time, once a candidate has a web-site, journalists, when writing stories about on-line campaigns, will often provide the web address of all candidates running for the election, including minor party candidates, thus bolstering name-recognition in ways not possible before.

Davis's research also found that a distinction could be made between rich and poor candidates in the quality of a web-site. Although Davis is correct in that often a valid distinction can be made, but even so the amount of money spent on a web-site does not necessarily guarantee a web-site that appears higher in quality. Humphrey's web-site appeared as professional as Bush's web-site. The Humphrey site had high-quality layout, similar to that of an on-line newspaper, and used technical devices such as electronic newsletters and a web-based bulletin board. It is less the amount of money spent on an on-line presence and more the people who create the web-sites and their relationship to the campaign that make the difference. The volunteers who designed the web-site for Humphrey were highly trained computer experts. Moreover, the volunteers were dedicated and trusted members of the campaign. Ted Johnson, campaign manager, reported that by the end of the campaign, the volunteers were an integral part of the development team, brainstorming content and design. The critical factor is not necessarily money but planning by the campaign staff, and dedication of the campaign volunteers or hired help. It is not always the case that 'you get what you pay for'.

For some campaigns the reduced cost of using the Internet for communicating allowed them to use it as their central communications medium. The state of Minnesota in 1998 featured prominently in the news because one of the candidates who threw his hat in the ring was a former professional wrestler. Running on the third party ticket of the Reform Party, Jesse 'The Body' Ventura, ran a campaign on a shoestring budget. Although he qualified for state funds for campaigning, the funds are not released until after the election, creating a situation where Ventura had to borrow money to finance his campaign. He did not purchase television advertising until the last weeks of the campaign. The primary mode of communication for the campaign was the Internet – a web presence, 'JesseNet', and a web based bulletin board. Phil Madsen, Jesse Ventura's web creator, explained that the web-site's total cost was roughly the start-up cost of $200.00 and a monthly fee thereafter of $30.00. Overall, Ventura spent $650,000 on his campaign, while his opponents spent a combined $15 million. Most of their money went to television advertising. But Ventura won the race.

*Distance*

Physical distance has little direct bearing on on-line communication. On the Internet, a woman from Germany can visit a web-site in Australia about backpacking, then visit a chat area about travelling and have a discussion with a Japanese couple who recently travelled to Australia. Distance no longer poses an obstacle to communicating with people or reading information housed in far-away places.

Some criticise the death of distance brought about by the Internet. Doheny-Farina would question whether the ability to hold conversations with someone in Australia about the Barrier Reef has much value in the context of generating community. He argued that genuine community can only be forged through the bonds of physical location.[24] The kind of community one finds on-line is based around hobbies, interests, or activities. There is often little enforcement of social norms or agreed-upon rules; disagreement can lead a person easily to abandon one 'community' for another where they have more in common. In physical communities, people have to learn to get along in a context in which they may not agree with or like those in that physical space. When social norms or rules are broken, punishment exists to enforce those norms and rules.

Doheny-Farina's argument raises an important question about the role of distance in politics. The eighteenth-century Genevan philosopher Jean-Jacques Rousseau theorised that a democratic form of government necessitated physically small communities in which people interact with and know one another.[25] Democratic governance can only be successful in that context. Rousseau probably would doubt that true democracy could exist in a physically vast country such as the United States. Indeed, the representative form of democracy was designed, in part, for a physically dispersed electorate. Barber offered communication technology as a solution to distance. It can close the distance and bring people into a sphere of communication necessary for direct democracy.

A problem for politics in general is the tension between local and national governments. Should local administration inform national politics or should national administration dictate local politics? Communications technology may aggravate this tension. The movement towards direct democracy in states such as California, which has a strong tradition of state legislation by direct referendum, will be empowered by the Internet. Barber's vision of democracy rests on a strong local political structure in which neighbourhoods, regions, and cities move to advance issues and suggest policies affecting those in the neighbourhood. Neighbourhoods would hold town hall forums that also would communicate frequently with those in other areas and with the national administration – developing a network of political information exchange and deliberation in which neither local nor national has primacy in developing and passing legislation.[26] The actual outcome of such exchange may prove to be less balanced than Barber's vision and more a pendulum in which power swings from local to national and back again. None the less, the Internet makes such a vision possible.

In the domain of the political campaign, the death of distance, coupled with minimal cost and increased speed, is a boon for campaign organising. In national campaigns, such as the presidential race, the campaign offices can stay co-ordinated through the use of e-mail, real-time chat, and the web. When press releases are generated at headquarters, all auxiliary offices can know the latest message.

Jesse Ventura's campaign staff organised a 72-hour drive around the state solely through the Internet. The campaign used a voluntary e-mail list called 'JesseNet' to send messages to 3,000 subscribers. The content of these messages typically included criticism of debate organizers for excluding Ventura in televised debates, appeals to send money, and reminders to vote and turn out friends to vote on election day. During the 72-hour drive, messages were sent notifying people of Ventura's itinerary so that people could meet him at these scheduled stops. The campaign also used a web-based bulletin board to post notices of Ventura's schedule. The campaign did not use advance teams to organise the stops ahead of time. People who supported Ventura or who were just curious showed up when their e-mail or the web board said when he would arrive. This organizational feat may be a first for political campaigns.

*Volume*

What makes computers both intriguing and terrifying is their capacity for storage. Boyle explored in depth the fear that the rise of computers will mean the death of privacy.[27] Corporations and enterprising entrepreneurs can traffic in the demographics of individuals and groups, purchasing data on habits, hobbies, or biological and genetic traits. Computers greatly reduce the cost of storing information and of sifting that information for patterns. The digital nature of computer-stored information makes it easy to index, categorize, sort, and transmit. Indeed, one of the current economic tensions between the United States and European countries is the United States' lax data privacy policy. The Council of Ministers of the European Union in 1995 adopted a directive on the processing and transfer of personal data. The purpose of the directive was to establish a common high level of privacy protection in the flow of personal data between European countries and elsewhere. The United States government has paid lip-service to data privacy protection and to upholding the standards adopted in Europe to protect Europeans' private information generated through business transactions. However, it has done little but threaten United States corporations if they do not abide by the directive.[28]

Gathering data on people raises important questions about privacy. The negative side to data storage and analysis is the possibility that individuals will lose their privacy – having their names and personal data sold again and again to the highest-paying advertiser, political organization, or business. One organisation, the Center for Democracy and Technology (CDT) evaluated all the web-sites of the presidential candidates running for election in 2000. Specifically, the CDT noted which candidates explicitly stated how personal information supplied by visitors would be used, whether privacy was guaranteed, and how prominently that guarantee was on the web-site. Six of the major-party candidates did not pass the CDT's evaluations; however, a staff member on George Bush, Jr.'s campaign, one of the candidates who failed, announced that a privacy statement was an oversight that they were going to correct in the near future and did.

On a more optimistic note, volume on the Internet allows campaigns to provide a depth of information to voters. Television advertisements, direct mail, and radio spots are bounded by space, time, and cost limitations; the volume of content is restricted. Successful television and radio advertisements stick to one message or one main idea as a result. In comparison, a web-site is not bounded by those constraints. The volume of information on a web-site is as much as the campaign wishes to provide the Internet user and as much as the visitor is willing to tolerate. Multiple messages, ideas, and purposes are possible on a site.

Of the gubernatorial campaigns studied in 1996, the candidate who offered the greatest volume of information was George Ryan, Republican candidate in Illinois. He offered issue positions on taxes, education, job growth, crime, and transportation. For each of these issue positions, he offered several detailed explanations of what he would do for each area. For example, on taxes, eight different 'pages' outlined his stance. Moreover, his policy positions were clearly detailed and evidenced. He placed his 'no taxes' pledge within a context – offering detailed information on Illinois's rank nationally in state income and property taxes. In arguing for increased federal funding of Illinois roads, he provided actual figures of the projected need from a credible source, the Illinois Department of Transportation. His web-site detailed his plan to get increased federal assistance through preserving the federal gas tax, working with the Illinois congressional delegation, and pushing to change the funding formula. Voters would have great difficulty finding that much information on Ryan's issue positions from any other information source.

One problem for campaigns posed by the increased volume of information exchange is the magnitude of e-mail messages received from potential voters, journalists, and others. The release of the Starr report on the worldwide web provided an important moment to gauge people's use of the Internet to provide feedback to the government. It also served as an omen of things to come for political officials or hopefuls. The Starr report – the report by the independent prosecutor alleging legal wrongdoing by President Bill Clinton during an affair with a White House intern – was released at the same time via the Internet as it was to the United States legislature, which would conduct hearings into the allegations. As legislators read the report, so, too, did the people who had access to the Internet. Where once elites would have had the first sight of such an important document, both elites and the citizenry now had an equal opportunity to peruse this document.

Reports following the release of the Starr report indicated that many citizens contacted their Senators and Representatives in unprecedented levels. Although legislators received much of their correspondence via telephone and postal mail, electronic mail was also a major conduit for citizens' opinions. Senator Mike DeWine's (R, OH), press secretary reported that the Senator had received approximately 6,700 e-mail messages over a four-day period after the release of the report. The volume of e-mail traffic was heavy enough that the managers of the Senate Internet server sent a message to each office stating, 'We are currently experiencing Internet E-mail delays due to extremely high volumes of mail.'[29]

Political candidates have to tackle the same kind of problem. Ellen Sauerbrey's campaign manager reported that her campaign for governor in Maryland received approximately 700 e-mail messages in the last week of the campaign. That magnitude makes it almost impossible to provide any response to the messages. Because of that fear of being swamped with e-mail messages, staff members of both Republican Bob Dole and Clinton's presidential campaigns in 1996 reported that their campaign managers decided not to provide an e-mail address on the web-site to contact the campaign. Rob Arena, Dole's web creator, and Laura Segal, assistant to Clinton's communication director, explained that the presidential candidates had neither the staff nor the time to handle the potential bombardment of e-mail messages. Arena explained that his campaign feared people might be annoyed when they visited Dole's web-site and found no way to e-mail him, but the campaign was more willing to risk that than to offer an e-mail address to which people could send messages. In that scenario there was a high likelihood that Dole and his staff would not respond. In Arena's estimation, a lack of response to an e-mail message could be more damaging and alienating than not providing an e-mail address at all. The volume of e-mail that campaigns receive and the perplexing question of how and if to respond to messages will continue to daunt the on-line campaign.

### *Targeting*

Because data are easily stored and sifted for characteristics, targeted messaging becomes even easier. Specialized magazines are on the rise because advertisers have determined that effective advertising is targeted advertising. If a company sells kayaks, advertising on prime time television or *Time* magazine may be too expensive and the audience not likely to be kayakers. The *Great Outdoors* magazine, however, offers the right audience at the right cost.

Targeting can be a function of the rhetoric on a web-site, or it can be through e-mail messages sent to those who have requested such e-mail or have indicated themselves as being affiliated with a political party. In the political context, the ability to target potential issue publics, donors, or general voters is invaluable. Surveys, data storing, and web-tracking devices give candidates the ability to determine what web-sites or areas of a web-site a person sees, what political affiliation they hold, what issues they identify are important. When a candidate invites citizens to receive weekly e-mail updates about campaign activities, they have the opportunity to gather important information, such as affiliation, issues that they deem important, or whether they would consider giving money to the candidate.

Targeting is one of the tricky elements of on-line campaigning. In the United States there is little toleration for 'spam', that is unsolicited e-mail messages. As a result, although political campaigns may have lists of e-mail addresses that they have gathered from the party or purchased through some other means, they take great risks if they send out a mass e-mail message. A state Senator running for Governor in the state of Georgia sent out a mass e-mail using 500 unsolicited e-mail addresses. The campaign manager reported that he was 'horrified' at some of the angry responses the campaign received.[30] The candidate sent out a personal apology the next day to pacify the angry citizens.[31]

Campaigns have had to become creative in their targeting practices. One method for soliciting e-mail addresses from people is through the e-mail 'newsletter'. Eight of the gubernatorial candidates studied invited visitors to 'sign-up' or 'subscribe' to receive a newsletter on-line. Ventura's campaign featured a sign-up sheet in which people had to supply their first and last names, street address, home phone, and e-mail to become a 'Jesse Net' member. Most candidates, however, simply asked for people's e-mail address, bypassing the possibility to gather more data about the people who visit their site. Once a person has willingly given an e-mail address, however, the campaign can use that e-mail message to send a barrage of messages if they so choose.

As mentioned above, the gathering of data makes citizens wary and political watchdog groups vociferously attend to privacy issues even if the United States has weak privacy protection laws. Just as six of the presidential contenders ran afoul of privacy protection practices, so too will future campaigns in their quest to gather information on citizens for more effective targeting for money and vote appeals. It appears that message targeting and privacy concerns are going to be difficult issues for Internet-based campaigns.

### *Convergence of Forms of Media*

The Internet can be modelled similar to broadcast, to print, to common carrier and to an amalgam of all three. Web-sites, themselves, can be modelled similar to print. The communication is one-to-one with the web-site serving as the central message source. E-mails can serve as broadcast and point-to-point communications. A message can be sent to one individual or to a mass of individuals. The e-mail newsletter is distributed as a broadcast. A response to a citizen's e-mail question is point-to-point communication.

The content of electoral sites suggests that it, too, is converging on to one space. A campaign web-site often has a 'press page' for journalists to access campaign press releases. A voter as well as staff at an auxiliary office can also read that information. Thus, the press release serves a multiple audience. Indeed, Bill Bradley, Democratic contender for the 2000 presidency, has a press section in which members of the press can sign up to access a special area of the web-site designed for them. The description of the contents states that press releases and digital images are readily available for journalists to download and use for publication. The text also assures readers that the content is the same on the press area as elsewhere: 'We *do not* intend, in any way, to exclude any information from Bradley web-site visitors who are not members of the press. Throughout the Bradley web-site, much of the same material is available, in other formats.' Bradley's assurance speaks to fears that candidates say to one group what they want to hear and then say the opposite to another group. It remains to be seen if candidates will create messages on their web-site intended for one constituency and not another.

The web-site serves another set of tasks in one space. In addition to telling potential voters about the candidate and keeping supporters and staff informed, the web-site signs up volunteers, provides a conduit for campaign contributions, and acts as an outlet for purchasing campaign paraphernalia. The Federal Election Commission, the governing body for national elections, ruled in 1999 that presidential candidates can receive matching campaign money from the federal government when they receive credit card donations supplied through the Internet. Prior to this ruling, candidates could only qualify for matching funds on contributions sent through the postal service. As money drives campaigns, the importance of the Internet to fund-raising cannot be underestimated – nor can the ability to sign up volunteers to staff phone lines, put up lawn signs, or host tea parties on the candidate's behalf. Presuming that the people who visit candidate web-sites are more likely to be supporters, the site can capitalize on that interest to conduct grass-roots campaigns. The purchasing of campaign paraphernalia, from buttons, to T-shirts, to underwear, also capitalises on the interest of those motivated enough to visit the campaign site.

Finally, there is a convergence of kinds of media on the Internet. web-sites can provide textual, audio, video, and still images. Most political candidates utilize this convergence. Jeb Bush's Florida gubernatorial campaign web-site featured still images of Bush on the campaign trail. These were taken almost daily and updated as often. Elizabeth Dole in her presidential bid for the Republican nomination for 2000 featured prominently on her web-site in its first days her 'announcement' video. In it, the viewer could watch on their computer a poised Dole sitting in a cosy living room extolling the virtues of public office and her desire to be the next president. Bill Bradley, Democratic Party hopeful for the 2000 presidency, featured on his web-site photos of his return to his hometown to deliver the speech announcing his run for the Democratic ticket. After looking at the photos, a visitor could read the text of his announcement, then take a 'virtual tour' through his hometown.

### *Directionality*

Perhaps the most important component the Internet offers in relationship to democracy is directionality or the possibility for increased interaction. Using the Internet business executives can communicate the latest memoranda electronically, and the labour force, in turn, can discuss amongst each other the appropriateness of the new policies. Parents can keep in touch with their children who have gone away to college. Marketers can put up web-sites, list the URL on their television advertisement, and ask people who visit the site for feedback on the latest colour of their new tennis shoe. A citizen angry at increased urban sprawl and poor zoning practices can do research on the laws regarding zoning in the region, create a web-site urging people to get involved in fighting the latest plan for a new strip mall, and e-mail friends to contact city council. Activism, information exchange, familial communication, business transactions can now all occur through the Internet.

In the political arena, the Internet provides mechanisms for town hall forums, political information gathering, alerting citizens to new issues and electronic balloting that proponents of teledemocracy advocated. Government agencies and officials can make current and proposed policies easy for people to access. Legislators can get feedback from citizens on agenda setting and on voting decisions. Political candidates, too, can use this channel to supply information to potential voters and gather feedback on the issues and policies voters think important.

In electoral campaigns, two-way communication between campaign staff and Internet users is rare. The kinds of invitations for two-way communication include e-mail, surveys and polls, feedback forms, and bulletin or web boards. Although most campaigns provide an e-mail address, the response is unsystematic. In a test the writer conducted early in the campaign season of the 1999 gubernatorial election, an e-mail message with a request for clarification of three issues, crime, school vouchers, and taxes, was sent to all candidates with an e-mail address posted at that time. The message was sent on 14 September, the day before a primary election in Minnesota and Maryland. Sending the message the day before the election would, I hoped, test the importance that campaigns placed on their Internet communications. Of the 20 candidates who had an e-mail address (the Minnesota campaign had four candidates running for the Democratic nomination), only eight (44 per cent) ever got round to responding. Of those, three were received within four days; the rest came up to two weeks later. Of the Minnesota and Maryland candidates, only one responded by the day of the election, indicating that their e-mail communications were indeed a priority.

Although e-mail addresses are common on candidate sites, other forms of interaction, such as web-based bulletin boards or live 'chat' forums, are rare for most campaigns. In 1996, only one presidential hopeful, Patrick Buchanan, hosted a web-based bulletin board. Messages were supportive of Buchanan and critical of his opponents. Voices critical of Buchanan were not visible on the board. In 1998, two of the candidates studied used web boards, Ventura and Humphrey, both candidates for Governor in Minnesota. Phil Madsen, Ventura's web-site director, stated that the board provided the opportunity for campaign staff and citizens to talk about the Ventura campaign and his issue positions. He also said that the campaign staff had to filter out some messages because of their inappropriate character: messages about Ventura's former wrestling career or invitations to view or swap pornography. In the 2000 presidential campaign, Bradley used a clever ploy that Clinton pioneered in 1996 – inviting people to tell stories of why they support the candidate. A select few appear on the web-site. These testimonials by average citizens, however, do not function as genuine deliberative forums, but as endorsements for the candidate. Elizabeth Dole's campaign featured a chat forum, and Gore hosted town hall forums in which for a period of an hour citizens could post messages to the campaign and a selected number would be answered live online. A trend appears to be developing in which candidates, particularly high profile candidates, are moving towards more interaction on their web-sites.

Candidates have to negotiate interaction carefully, however. The more opportunities to speak directly with the citizen, the less likely candidates can hide behind ambiguous statements. In genuine deliberation citizens and candidate would discuss the issues. The flow of such deliberation presumes that candidates would be asked about their issue positions and to elaborate if they were vague or unclear. The more elaborate an answer, the more unlikely the answer will appeal to a majority of the population. For example, the question of legal abortion is one that divides the United States. Political candidates who attempt to appeal to a majority of the population will need to remain vague on the issue. A candidate who states that she or he is 'Pro-Choice' taps into the heuristics of citizens allowing them to decide for themselves what the term connotes. 'Pro-Choice' is a large umbrella that includes the range of opinions from full and unregulated access to regulations of parental and spousal consent, and waiting periods. If candidates are pressed on the issue and state that they favour unregulated access to abortions, they potentially lose the support of those who believe abortion should be carefully regulated. In the dynamic exchange possible in chat forums, candidates put themselves into a situation in which they cannot use ambiguity to appeal to the highest number of voters.

The other risk for candidates in public communication is the potential loss of control of the communication environment. On a web board, for example, if a candidate does not filter the messages to appear on their board, they may have messages that fairly or unfairly criticize the candidate, that post inappropriate messages (such as pornography), or that use the space for unrelated messages. If the candidate's web-site is viewed as an extended advertisement for the candidate, then it is imperative that the message on the web-site 'sell' the candidate. Glenn McCalley, web developer for Ellen Sauerbrey's gubernatorial campaign in Maryland, explained to the writer that they debated whether to have a bulletin board but

> The feeling there was that we weren't sure that we wanted things going on the web site over which we had no control. We were concerned that somebody would make some wild off-the-wall comment, and then we'd be reading in the *Baltimore Sun*, 'the Sauerbrey web site said this or that', when it really wasn't us that said it. We just decided not to do that.[32]

From the campaign perspective, candidates run a tremendous risk by hosting interactive forums on their web-site. From the perspective of strong democratic theory and practice, however, interactive forums are necessary for citizens to participate in the process of setting the agenda of issues important to them and to the long-term health of the nation.

*Velocity*

The Internet reduces the time it takes to transmit and receive information. A postal letter can take days to reach a recipient. E-mail takes seconds. Finding information about government or industry used to require a trip to the library or a set of phone calls or letters to begin finding the information. Now, a person can type in a set of search terms in one of the web-based search engines to find web-sites that supply that information (assuming the search engine has the sites indexed).

Because of the reduced time in sending and receiving information, the expectancy of immediate response is high. When people send off an e-mail message to a legislator, for example, the expectation is that they will receive some kind of response – and quickly. Newhagen, Cordes and Levy conducted a content analysis of 650 e-mail messages sent to television's *NBC Nightly News*, after the programme requested feedback on a series they aired on the impact of new technologies. Specifically, Newhagen *et al.* were concerned with 'perceived interactivity'. That is, that the invitation by NBC created a perception in the minds of viewers that NBC was encouraging interactivity with the viewers. In their factor analysis of the content of the e-mail messages, they found that for those who were comfortable with e-mail and the Internet, the topics and focus of the e-mail suggested that they did perceive a higher degree of feedback. Those who were less comfortable wrote their messages more like letters to the editor, and were thus expecting less feedback from NBC.[33] In other words, they found that people who were regular users of the Internet wrote e-mail messages that suggested that they expected some kind of feedback from the television show producers.

Decreased distance and reduced cost of communication leads to increased speed of diffusion of messages. Candidates no longer have to rely on journalists or editors to run a story about the candidate's announcement of, for example, an economic agenda the candidate hopes to promote if elected. The message is up on the web-site and can be diffused over e-mail when the candidate wants without the filters placed on the message in the retelling by journalists.

## CONCLUSION

Martin Heidegger's insight on technology is relevant to political campaigning and the question of democracy. According to him, technology is both a human activity and an end in itself. Technology is instrumental and instrumentality has causes.[34] Heidegger looks back to ancient Greece and Greek philosophy on causality. There are four causes: (a) The *causa materialis*, the material out of which an object is made; (b) The *causa formalis*, the form and shape the material will take to become an object; (c) The *causa finalis*, the purpose of the object; (d) The *causa efficiens*, what brings about the effect that is the finished product.[35]

The *causa materialis* of the Internet, the network of networks and its associated characteristics of lowered cost, increased volume, directionality, targeting, velocity, and convergence when formed into a communication environment between political candidates and citizens suggests that the final product can be an environment in which strong democracy is supported. Decreased costs can level the playing field between heavily and poorly funded, the institutional and the fringe. The volume of information and the convergence of media creates an environment in which information in multiple forms is available at one's desire. If citizens have not seen campaign advertisements, they can visit a candidate's web-site, read up on the candidate's issue positions and watch a political advertisement as streaming video over the Internet. Targeting, too, when used effectively provides information to those who want it, when they want it. All of those characteristics offer an environment in which citizens have a wealth of information at their disposal, and can control and decipher that information for their own purposes. They can still turn to journalists to filter and frame information; however, they can also investigate and learn 'from the source' and frame for themselves the message and its consequences.

Perhaps the most important attraction for strong democracy is the increased speed of communication coupled with the two-way nature of the network promoting the possibility for deliberation horizontally amongst citizens and vertically between citizens and political elites. Directionality also means that feedback mechanisms can be established such as opinion polls that allow citizens to weigh in on policy positions and general issues for debate; e-mail provides a channel for citizens to provide positive or critical feedback to the candidate; town hall style electronic forms make it possible for candidates and citizens to engage in policy debate in real-time. These mechanisms lead to the possibility of a breakdown of hierarchical communication, with citizens driving the political process. On the Internet, an invitation to participate *is* possible.

The fourth cause, *causa efficiens*, makes the question of whether the Internet can promote strong democracy less easily answerable. The people who bring about the web-site can use the material offered by the Internet in a form that does not serve democratic ends, but rather more self-interested, instrumental ends, such as getting elected. The absence of a message is still communication. Absent from the 19 gubernatorial web-sites, for example, was the invitation for a real-time, town hall-type forum or an explicit request that people give them feedback about the campaign. All the candidates but one provided an e-mail address. However, the rhetoric leading to the e-mail address was typically a simple: 'e-mail us'. Dan Lungren, running for Governor in California directed people to 'Please send your questions about the Lungren for Governor campaign to info@lungren98.org.' His opponent, Gray Davis, simply directed people to 'E-mail Gray Davis'.

The most unusual rhetoric pertaining to sending messages to the campaign came from Jesse Ventura. Clicking on a hyperlink 'contact' brought people to this message: 'As a busy candidate and celebrity, Jesse receives more mail than he is able to personally handle. His campaign staff assists with the mail. To help Jesse hear from as many citizens as possible, and to help you get your message into Jesse's hands, please use the form below.' What followed included a detailed description of the process by which the candidate handled e-mail, including an explanation that although Jesse was made aware of issues brought up in e-mail, people should not expect a response back. Moreover, on no other campaign web-site was so detailed a description provided of the e-mail handling process.

As mentioned above, candidates do receive mass volumes of e-mail – more than they can possibly handle. If we are to move towards a more direct democracy, however, candidates and their staff will have to find a way to handle those messages satisfactorily – either through the strategy that the Ventura campaign utilized, or through some other means. By not providing responses, citizens will feel discouraged and their concerns unacknowledged. The democratic process ceases to be democratic. Solutions of auto-replies, a generic response thanking people for their message, are unfit for the rigours of democracy, as well.

It remains to be seen whether the presidential and congressional candidates for the 2000 election cycle will promote discussion with themselves and with other citizens on their web-sites. Early indications during the primary season suggest that candidates are moving in that direction; however, the primary season is designed for those who are already engaged in politics. The average US voter does not begin to attend to the election typically until the last month of the general election. A different audience then will be browsing the web-sites and campaign staff may find it prudent to close off communication channels for the sake of controlling the message and promoting the candidate.

Gathering information about the candidate also is not always easy on the candidate site. Absent from some candidates' web-site were issue positions, which should be a staple of any well-organized campaign. One candidate in the state of Minnesota provided only information on how to e-mail the campaign, a brief biographical summary of the candidate, and directions on sending a campaign contribution. Most candidates, however, provided statements on a set of issues they staked their campaign on. An unanswered question is whether there is depth to those issue positions and how grounded in evidence are they.

Does the technology offer the characteristics for promoting the form of direct democracy to which Barber and others aspire? The simple answer is, yes. The characteristics of the media that comprise the Internet suggest, if applied properly, a more democratic turn in the political sphere of daily life. The complexity arises in the actual uses to which the technology is put. If political candidates do not open themselves up for deliberation using the Internet or offer detailed information, then an obstacle is reached. If pressure is put on candidates by citizens to use this technology for increased input in the political process, then possibly, over time candidates will comply. That is the essence of strong democracy.

## NOTES

1. Benjamin Barber, *Strong Democracy* (Berkeley, CA and London: University of California Press, 1984), p.68.
2. Ibid., p.46.
3. Ibid., p.132.
4. Ibid., p.152.
5. Ibid., p.152.
6. See, for example, F. Christopher Arterton, *Teledemocracy: Can Technology Protect Democracy?* (Newbury Park, CA: Sage Publications, 1987).
7. Kenneth L. Hacker, 'Missing Links in the Evolution of Electronic Democratization', *Media, Culture and Society*, Vol.18 (1996), pp.213–32.
8. Kathleen Hall Jamieson and Karlyn Kohrs Campbell, *The Interplay of Influence*, 4th Ed. (Belmont, CA: Wadsworth, 1997).
9. Gary Orren, 'Fall from Grace: The Public's Loss of Faith in Government', in Joseph S. Nye, Jr., Philip D. Zelikow and David C. King (eds.), *Why People Don't Trust Government* (Cambridge, MA and London: Harvard University Press, 1997), p.99.
10. Joseph N. Cappella and Kathleen Hall Jamieson, *Spiral of Cynicism* (New York and London: Oxford University Press, 1997).

11. Bruce Murray, 'Promoting Deliberative Public Discourse on the Web', in Roger G. Noll and Monroe E. Price (eds.), *A Communications Cornucopia* (Washington, DC: Brookings Institute, 1998).
12. See, for example, Kees Brants, Martine Huizenga and Reineke Van Meerten, 'The New Canals of Amsterdam', *Media, Culture and Society*, Vol.18 (1996), pp.233–47; Kenneth L. Hacker & Michael Todino, 'Virtual Democracy at the Clinton White House', *Electronic Journal of Communication*, Vol.6, No.2 (1996); Cathy Bryan, Roza Tsagarousianou and Damian Tambini, 'Electronic Democracy and the Civic Networking Movement in Context', in Roza Tsagarousianou, Damian Tambini, and Cathy Bryant (eds.), *Cyberdemocracy: Technology, Cities and Civic Networks* (New York and London: Routledge, 1998), pp.1–17.
13. Albert Gore, 'Toward a Global Information Infrastructure' (Speech delivered at the International Telecommunications Union Development Conference, Buenos Aires, Argentina, 1994).
14. Richard Davis, *The Web of Politics* (New York and London: Oxford University Press, 1999), pp.85–120.
15. Elaine Ciulla Kamarck, 'Campaigning on the Internet in the Off-Year Elections of 1998', in Elaine Ciulla Kamarck and Joseph S. Nye, Jr. (eds.), *Democracy.com: Governance in a Networked World* (Hollis, NH: Hollis Publishing Co., 1999), pp.99–123.
16. The Pew Research Center for the People and the Press, *The Internet News Audience Goes Ordinary* (Philadelphia, PA: The Pew Center, 1998).
17. Graeme Browning, *Electronic Democracy* (Wilton, CT: Pemberton Press, 1996).
18. Hacker, op. cit., pp.227–29.
19. Elizabeth L. Eisenstein, *The Printing Press as an Agent of Change* (Cambridge: Cambridge University Press, 1979).
20. Carolyn Marvin, *When Old Technologies Were New* (New York and Oxford: Oxford University Press, 1988).
21. See for example Anthony Downs, *An Economic Theory of Democracy* (New York: HarperCollins, 1957).
22. W. Russell Neuman, *The Future of the Mass Audience* (Cambridge: Cambridge University Press, 1991), pp.53–6.
23. Eugene Volokh, 'Cheap Speech and What It Will Do', *The Communication Review*, Vol.1, No.3 (1996), pp.261–90.
24. Stephen Doheny-Farina, *The Wired Neighborhood* (New Haven, CT: Yale University Press, 1996).
25. Jean-Jacques Rousseau, *Rousseau's Political Writings* (New York and London: W.W. Norton & Co., 1988), p.124.
26. Barber, pp. 267-273.
27. James Boyle, *Shamans, Software and Spleens* (Cambridge, MA and London: Harvard University Press, 1996).
28. Robert Gellman, 'Conflict and Overlap in Privacy Regulation', in Brian Kahin and Charles Nesson (eds.), *Borders in Cyberspace* (Cambridge, MA and London: The MIT Press, 1998), pp.255–82.
29. Linda Wertheimer and Larry Abramson, 'Congress E-mail' *All Things Considered* (Washington, DC: National Public Radio, Inc, 16 Sept. 1998).
30. Peter Lewis, 'Web campaigning gains ground', *The Seattle Times* (17 Oct. 1998), p.1A.
31. William Booth, 'Politicians set their sites on the Web', *Washington Post* (17 Oct. 1998), p.1A.
32. Personal communication.
33. John E. Newhagen, John W. Cordes and Mark R. Levy, 'Nightly@nbc.com', *Journal of Communication*, Vol.45 (1995), pp.164–75.
34. Martin Heidegger, *The Question Concerning Technology* (New York: Harper & Row 1977), p.4.
35. Ibid., p.6.

# Revitalizing the Party System or *Zeitgeist*-on-line? Virtual Party Headquarters and Virtual Party Branches in Germany

CHRISTOPH BIEBER

All political parties in Germany have now established 'Virtual Party Headquarters' all of which have become the most popular on-line-presentations within the wired political system in Germany. Given the dominant position of political parties inside the German political system, this is not a big surprise. Party web-sites have already attracted the attention of a few, mostly young, German political scientists. The following account will not present another detailed – and soon outdated – analysis of a small sample of Virtual Party Headquarters. Instead it offers a short outline of the development of these on-line-services since their 'digital birth' in 1995.[1] It also attempts to describe the origins and formation of important elements of party web-sites, as well as some of the many digital dead-ends, that have in a few cases misled political parties on their way to the information society. During the short but lively history of Virtual Party Headquarters, there has been a generational evolution. The opening up of web-site structures is augmenting the growing boom in political communication on the Internet. Complementing this examination of Virtual Party Headquarters will be an analysis of a phenomenon within the German Internet landscape that is both similar and different – the rise of the Virtual Party Branch. This gives rise to even more innovative structures. Furthermore, these political on-line projects may provide some indications about the future impact of computer-mediated political communication on the German party system as a whole.

## NOTES ON THE ANALYSIS OF POLITICAL PROJECTS ON THE INTERNET

In spite of massive methodological problems well known in communications or media studies, there are some analytical steps which help identify the main characteristics of political projects on the Internet.

As a first step, the on-line appearance or layout of Virtual Party Headquarters provides some clues about their technical facilities. The web-sites of the major parties use the most up-to-date techniques of web design (that is frames, audio-/videofiles, java-applets, plug-ins, active server pages).[2] They use graphic elements to foster a consistent 'style' and they pay attention to innovative forms of presentation. Usually external multimedia agencies take care of site-design and -administration, thus the appearance of party web-sites on average is as sophisticated as that of commercial corporations. Site statistics such as 'hits', 'page views' or 'page impressions' may also be included in this category. Often underestimated is the role of the registered domain name, belonging to each Virtual Party Headquarters. In Germany, party sites usually staked their claim with the formula 'www.(party name).de'. Slight exceptions either show a more sophisticated use of this important means of positioning oneself in on-line name space, or they demonstrate radical mistakes on the way towards the information superhighway.[3] As they develop, Virtual Party Headquarters are more likely to expand their on-line presence by registering additional domains or sub-domains, for example in the case of elections, party conventions, specialized on-line services and so on. Finally, the number of external links with Virtual Party Headquarters may be regarded as a further indicator of the penetration of web-sites.

Range, accuracy and depth of site content can be seen as the second category of examination. Standard offerings of German Virtual Party Headquarters are political programmes, personal pages for high-ranking officials, organizational structure and current party activities. Inside the spacious on-line archives and libraries Internet tourists may find a selection of programmatic papers, basic issues, discussion papers, speeches, addresses, press releases or newspaper articles.[4] This collection forms a complex mosaic of texts, graphics, and sometimes moving images and sounds.[5] The longer the party sites are on-line, the broader and deeper the site content. Accompanied by the acceleration of site-updates, special coverage of party-events and the production of 'on-line only' content reveals the development of a genuine media format that easily surpasses the older modes of intra-party communication such as magazines or newsletters for party members.

The 'interactive elements' mark the third level of site analysis. Like many other on-line services, Virtual Party Headquarters try to make great use of the possibilities of the new communication environment. These include collections of e-mail addresses for direct feedback, guestbooks (all too often outdated) or the standard on-line forms for immediate membership as well as areas for downloading, games, or shops offering merchandising material to supporters. Beside these examples of simple, more complex forms of interactivity have to be mentioned. These can be found inside discussion areas or arise during on-line chats. According to the 'dimensions of on-line-interactivity' the distinctions between marketing-communication, content-provider, virtual marketplaces, and virtual communities may be transferred to the analysis of Virtual Party Headquarters.

TABLE 1

VIRTUAL PARTY HEADQUARTERS: LEVELS, ELEMENTS, INTERACTIVITY

| **1. Layout** | |
|---|---|
| • technical/design elements<br>(i.e. plain HTML, frames, graphics, video-/sound-files, Java-applets, plug-ins)<br>• domain-name<br>• site-statistics (hits, page views, page impressions)<br>• external links on the web-site | |
| **2. Content** | **3. Dimension of Interactivity** |
| • programmatic papers<br>• biographies of important party members<br>• organizational structure | marketing-communication |
| • press releases<br>• archive<br>• newsletter<br>• speeches, addresses<br>• current news and reports<br>• 'on-line only' material (e.g. on-line magazine)<br>• lists of hyperlinks, web directories<br>• guestbooks<br>• games | content provider |
| • download area (texts, graphics, tools)<br>• on-line forms (i.e. membership form)<br>• on-line shop | virtual marketplace |
| • on-line chat rooms<br>• discussion areas | virtual community |
| **4. Organization** | |
| • technical administration<br>• graphic design<br>• on-line editors | |

Finally, an accurate analysis of Virtual Party Headquarters should not exclude their off-line organizational structure. Complementing the three categories of on-line characteristics, the integration of a new means of internal and external communication of political parties into real-world processes has to be considered. First, the rise of new job profiles for public relations professionals in the field of political communication is evident. Besides the technical administration and daily maintenance provided by 'webmasters' and 'webqueens', there has emerged the job profile of on-line editors. Their prime task is to formulate and control most parts of the site content. The relative status and the still narrowly limited level of authority of webmasters and webqueens reveal their reputation in the hierarchy of intra-party organizational structures, as well of course as that of the party web-sites.

This short sketch of different analytical levels may be used as a blueprint for describing and evaluating Virtual Party Headquarters. They may equally well be transferred on to other political projects on the Internet, such as personal pages, web-sites of parliaments or legislative bodies. The basic distinction between levels of complexity, that is 'layout' (1), 'content' (2), 'dimensions of interactivity' (3) and 'organizational structures' (4) might be used as a general pattern for the analysis of political web-sites. However, it has to be complemented by consideration of their position and function inside the respective political system, since this always determines the character of political on-line projects.[6]

## DIGITAL BROCHURES

Until autumn 1998 the German Virtual Party Headquarters went through a three-year-long 'product cycle'. The first experimental phase began during 1995. In the wake of a general Internet-breakthrough in Germany the parties elected into the Bundestag were first to present digital information on-line but they displayed rather conventional HTML-pages.[7]

Already the first steps of political parties into Cyberspace were closely tied to off-line symbols of corporate identity. Of course, data tourists would expect to find a familiar environment when going on-line and checking the pages of 'their' political party. Those impressions were fostered by museum-like portraits of party heroes, welcoming surfers with friendly messages.

Pictures and symbols dominated the design of early Virtual Party Headquarters. The different parties used quite similar patterns setting up their digital architecture. The colouring of the Virtual Party Headquarters

TABLE 2

VIRTUAL PARTY HEADQUARTERS: 'OPENING DATES'

| Party | Domain-Name | On-line since |
|---|---|---|
| SPD | www.spd.de | 19 August 1995 |
| CDU | www.cdu.de | 17 October 1995 |
| Bündnis 90/Die Grünen | www.grüne.de | 29 November 1996 |
| FDP | www.liberale.de/www.fdp.de | 4 December 1995 |
| PDS[8] | www.pds-online.de | During April 1998 |

*Note*: SPD=Social Democratic Party; CDU=Christian Democratic Union; FDP=Free Democratic Party; PDS=Party of Democratic Socialism.

corresponded to the usual party colours.[9] Party labels and mainly typed slogans were the most visible graphic devices. In this styled, but not stylish environment, portraits of the party leaders resembling religious (not desktop) icons tried to captivate browsing citizens. Scans of Helmut Kohl (in 1995 still Chancellor), Oskar Lafontaine (then leader of the Social Democratic Party) and Wolfgang Gerhard (Free Democratic Party) were the first politicians to be seen by politically interested surfers. The party heroes took on the role of 'anchormen' and tried to emphasize their own parties' commitment to innovation and the development of the information society. But such symbolic enrichment was accompanied mostly by static content and poor performance: parties rarely produced information exclusively for Internet use. Only special events like national party conventions, clearly separated from day-to-day-politics, boosted innovation in the political datasphere. The new political players on the Net permanently highlighted their strong need for digital, interactive media in all-day-business, but in the early days of political on-line communication 'talking digital' was nothing but symbolic politics. Such assessments can be justified by a closer look at the design and organization of Virtual Party Headquarters, focusing on the attempt to instrumentalize the Internet as a pure tool for marketing. This experimental phase can be characterized as the big time of 'digital brochures', resembling their old-fashioned brothers and sisters, printed on glossy paper and being distributed via snail mail, in shopping malls or on city squares.

These on-line brochures were dominated by top-to-bottom structures of communication with clearly split modes of sending and receiving information, that is classical forms of marketing communication.[10] Browsing through political datasets suggested one´s importance, but the still prevalent hierarchical relationship of sender (political parties) and receiver (citizens) cemented the incongruence of participation in the political process: on the one hand political information-providers determined the content and layout of the service, while on the other hand the surfers appeared more in the role of customers than as fully accepted, participating citizens. Despite their chance to choose between a lot more digital info-options than in analogue media-environments, data tourists had no input into the construction and development of political on-line services. Setting the rules for political uses of the Internet by relying on top-to-bottom models did not correspond to the often claimed 'democracy-friendly', decentralized communication infrastructure. The pronouncement of the German Technology Council when they characterized computer networks as a 'technology of direct democracy' was massively contradicted by the rather boring and producer-centered Internet-reality of the German Virtual Party Headquarters during their early days in 1995/1996.[11]

## ON-LINE-MAGAZINES

In spite of their structural deficits the first releases of Virtual Party Headquarters started into cyberspace with good user-statistics, lots of 'hits' and a quickly increasing interest from surfers and the increasingly 'wired' journalists.

TABLE 3

VIRTUAL PARTY HEADQUARTERS: SITE STATISTICS

| | 1996 | 3/1997 | 7/1997 | 11/1997 | 4/1998 |
|---|---|---|---|---|---|
| CDU | 234,000 (9/1996) | 348,000 | 350,000 | 773,585 | 1,500,000 |
| CSU | | | 60,000 | d.n.a | d.n.a |
| SPD | 97,000 (4/1996) | 180,000 | 190,000 | 900,000 | 1,200,000 |
| FDP | 105,524 (11/1996) | 154,476 | 200,000 | 180,000 (9/1997) | 200,000 |
| The Greens/Bündnis90 | | | 31,000 | d.n.a | 150,000 |
| PDS | | | d.n.a | d.n.a | d.n.a |

*Notes:* CDU=Christian Democratic Union; CSU=Christian Socialist Union; FDP=Free Democratic Party; SPD=Social Democratic Party; PDS=Party of Democratic Socialism; d.n.a. = did not answer.

*Sources*: Heike Hillenbrand, 'Möglichkeiten der Darstellung politischer Parteien im Internet: Zustandsbeschreibung und Zukunftsvisionen' (unpublished MA thesis, Konstanz University, 1997); Marco Althaus, 'Nur einen Mausklick entfernt – Wählerstimmen sammeln auf der Datenautobahn', *Frankfurter Allgemeine Zeitung*, 19 July 1997; Hans-Martin Tillack, 'Der Wahlkampf mit der Maus', *Konrad*, No.1 (1998), pp.35–40; Angelika Eckert, 'Schlammschacht im Virtuellen Bonn', *Global Online*, Nos.4–5 (1998), pp.56–9.

The main supply of accurate and 'breaking' political news quickly was established as an important element of Virtual Party Headquarters and still is one of the cornerstones of their activity. Interactive elements such as guestbooks, down-loadable files, on-line games, web competitions or on-line polls marked the next stage of digital development.

Guestbooks may be seen as one of the ancestors of user-feedback stimulated by Virtual Party Headquarters. This area was usually well-accepted by users. Lacking sophisticated on-line statistics (the counting of hits, page views, page impressions was not yet reliable nor sufficiently comparable), the number more than the content of guestbook entries provided evidence of user acceptance of the Virtual Party Headquarters. This rather incomplete feedback channel was the foundation, on which its more complex successors were built.[12]

Moving beyond the guestbooks' conventional one-way direction of communication, on-line chats and discussion areas stimulated higher quality user feedback. Discussion areas as a permanent and extremely popular element can be used in particular to characterize the second generation of Virtual Party Headquarters. The best examples of successful discussion areas are found on the web-sites of the Free Democratic Party (FDP) and the Christian Democratic Union (CDU). Both offerings require no registration and were first to catch the interest of a large number of politically interested surfers, who are enabled to send messages or even encouraged to suggest topics for discussion.[13] Their concept as permanent, free-to-use, broad-content environment of communication much resembled the model of the classical Greek 'agora'.

While the Green Party/Bündnis 90, the Party of Democratic Socialism (PDS), CDU and FDP favoured an open model of discuission area, the Social Democratic Party (SPD) maintains with their 'Klartext'-Forum a restricted area for political discourse. Before taking part in a set of discussions about which topics are accepted by site officials, participants have to register. As a consequence, this discussion area is much less frequented than the open areas of the CDU or FDP web-sites. There might be a pre-selection of especially motivated users, which could increase the quality of ongoing discussion. No discussion area is censored by site officials, but every party claims to permanently monitor and – if necessary – control discussion activities.

Because of the intensity and the large number of messages recently, politicians are forced to take part in current on-line-discussions on their party web-site. Such messages are marked as 'official' (usually by colour). They enable direct communication between citizens and otherwise hard-to-contact high-level politicians. Also they slowly help to integrate the Virtual Party Headquarters into the internal communication structures of political parties. This may be regarded as the beginning of the development of responsive structures, stimulating political communication between elected officials, party members and interested citizens.[14]

As a new means of communication, on-line chats start to accompany and support discussion areas as another place to bring together both ends of the political process. Usually, the participation of political celebrities ennobles these events which may be considered as 'organized public places', clearly limited in time (usually about sixty minutes) and topic (such as current affairs, elections, new legislation). Scheduled either as special events or regularly planned (once per week or month), on-line chats gather large numbers of participants at a certain 'place' in cyberspace – usually the party homepage. The restriction on time, topic as well as the presence of a professional politician to be targeted by a large number of questions regarding his or her own work or his or her own party separates on-line chats from discussion areas but may empower the same 'responsive structures'.

The combination of these currently dominant modes of communication finally helps to condense the overall content of Virtual Party Headquarters. In particular, popular threads of discussion areas may well lead into 'official messages' to that forum or even an on-line chat with the party's political expert on that topic. Various communication elements of the Virtual Party Headquarters thus form a central public space, which on the content level is supplemented by three further types of information: news, service and interactive elements.

Anna Siebenborn, editor at www.spd.de, concludes: 'Our work is based on three main tasks: current news – that's the first task. The second is the field of interaction and communication, like in our discussion area. The third task is service, it's especially important for on-line-campaigning.'[15] Her colleague Susanne Land, former webqueen at www.cdu.de characterizes the advantages of the Internet thus: 'On the one hand we've got the chance to be very fast, that's much better than with other media. On the other hand, the worldwide web is an active medium for communication.'[16]

With these main emphasises the range of information offered by Virtual Party Headquarters systematically seems to resemble the style of news presentation established by the printed press. Current news and reports from daily party business become an informational basis. Speeches and addresses of politicians are archived. Special coverage of party events such as conventions, elections and polls enlarges the data body. In addition to the increasing content, the rhythm of site-updates is accelerating. Virtual Party Headquarters change their faces almost daily; consequently, for example, the CDU home page is designed in the style of a newspaper or television station web-site. In combination with the expansion of net-specific formats (link pages, annotated web directories), the 'grabbing' of user interest (guestbooks, discussion areas, chats) or interactive features (games, e-mail greetings, day-to-day polling), this process leads straight toward the rise of on-line nodes of discussion, that are closely tied to genuine party interests. Having accomplished that, Virtual Party Headquarters can be regarded as 'on-line-magazines', leaving behind the era of pure marketing communication. The second generation of party web-sites has changed their front doors from digital business cards to a frequently up-dated, information-loaded front page with quickly changing content, much more aware of the need to respond quickly in a new media environment.

New media experts still are far from happy when evaluating Virtual Party Headquarters. 'German political parties are miles away from an adequate on-line-presentation. Obviously, they consider pouring out information on party activities into the data ocean to be enough. May anyone start fishing for what he or she is interested in?'[17] But such critiques do not target the soul of Virtual Party Headquarters and ignore the various facets of successful political on-line communication. Professional web-designers usually do not judge all levels of analysis, and despite their similar look and concept. Virtual Party Headquarters must not be compared in a too simple way with 'normal' journalism-related web-sites. Because of the embedding into organizational structures that usually have grown off-line for decades, political projects are not able to do much more than copy those structures into the digital datasphere. Once landed in cyberspace, these structures have to undergo a massive change, boosted by the new rules of the digital media-environment. This difficult process is permanently monitored and partly managed by the editors of the Virtual Party Headquarters with considerable success. Now those webmasters and webqueens lead their projects slowly but surely into their next phase of life.

## POLITICAL PORTAL SITES

The transition into the next generation of Virtual Party Headquarters seems to have proceeded rather smoothly. Despite only slight movement towards new modes of digital party presentation, it is possible to make some comments on likely changes and the next developments.

Continuously growing site acceptance and, especially, the successful use of party web sites during the on-line campaigning for the Bundestag elections of September 1998 have strengthened the position of the Virtual Party Headquarters in intra-party-relationships and helped to recruit new human resources to maintain the on-line services. Taking this as a starting point for new ventures in political on-line communication, a further broadening of exclusive on-line content can be expected. A striking example of increasing usage of the party web-sites as publication channels in their own right is 'politik on-line', a weekly on-line magazine containing articles, features or reports. It is released 'onsite' at www.cdv.de. This could be seen as the latest version of the conventional press conference.

This trend points towards new forms of self-sufficient media presence, because parties try simultaneously to undermine and adopt the classical functions of typical old media gatekeepers like the printed press, radio or television. By extending their on-line efforts, political parties incorporate the means of production and distribution of editorial content. The still scattered media ammunition which includes press releases, speeches, addresses, interviews and announcements is concentrated into a 'digital periodical'. Slowly the transformation of the news-related area of the Virtual Party Headquarters leads to the rise of on-line magazines, explicitly coloured by each party's set of political ideas and programmes.

During this phase of development, discussion areas and on-line chat rooms mark the next step towards an internet presence that approximates to on-line-publishing. 'Interactive' services combined with regularly published information are indeed a characteristic of advanced web-sites.

Whereas the Virtual Party Headquarters of the first and second generation favoured modes of presentation and distribution resembling conventional 'top-down' communication, the empowering of individual or group communication induced by interactive elements emphasizes the turn towards modes of communication that make the most of the Internet's potential.

Besides the fostering of publication activities, the Virtual Party Headquarters also influence intra-party communication and information, a development proved by the establishment of high-performance Intranets.[18] In the shadow of their well-known on-line outposts, the CDU and SPD launched nationwide computer networks, intensively used for quick distribution of data, articles and speeches during the 1998 on-line campaign. It is noteworthy that intranets were introduced into party communication *after* the successful integration of the Virtual Party Headquarters in day-to-day business. Likewise the rise of on-line editors led to an internal restructuring of the communication units of at least the big players in German political party business.

The development and maintenance of the Virtual Party Headquarters thus has to be considered as a model and catalyst for future use of information and communication technologies on various organizational levels of political parties. The increasing convergence of internet- and intranet-use is possibly leading to a massive acceleration of intra-party communication. As a consequence, the points of technical and informational coordination inside the party bureaucracy gained a lot of importance – probably a general revision of intra-party work-flows would be the prime outcome of increasing internal computerization and networking. From this point of view, describing and reflecting some typical trends emerging from the on-line activity of political parties, the Virtual Party Headquarters seems to be only the tip of an iceberg of media-related reforms yet to come.

The process of digitalization and computerization became irreversible a long time ago and it may well be a logical continuation for new media services to be supplied by political parties, as they seek to put their own spin on the news. For several months the CDU and SPD have been offering HTML construction kits, helping to update and to streamline the web-sites of regional and local party structures. The formation of comfortable and easy-to-use lists of hyperlinks into the respective political spectrum is another service illustrating the new possibilites of an active, member-orientated service policy that simultaneously functions as subtle political education along ideological trenches. Future party activities may include web directories or large datasets of on-line material focusing on single issues as well as the basic functions of Internet-Service-Providers, such as free e-mail addresses for party members or a certain amount of web space for hosting private home pages.

A summary of current developments and future perspectives clearly shows that the next transformation of Virtual Party Headquarters is just taking place. The political portal sites are on the verge of coming to life, resembling pocket-sized copies of their role models Yahoo!, Excite, Geocities, Netscape or Microsoft.[19]

Although this is still a scenario for the future, individual elements of political portal sites are already to be found at various German party web-sites. Combined with overall development and the growth of the Internet, the Virtual Party Headquarters will play a significant role in the future of political parties as a whole.[20]

## VIRTUAL PARTY HEADQUARTERS – REVITALIZING THE PARTY DINOSAURS?

Recent findings of German political science focusing on the life and times of political parties are almost unanimous in highlighting 'gridlocked reforms and blocked chances for participation', or they complain about shortages in recruitment, called 'processes of ageing and drying'. Also they identify structural weakness of membership organizations and question the future of parties during the process of modernization in general.[21]

Even if this account cannot deliver hard empirical facts on either the performance or the intra-party acceptance of Virtual Party Headquarters,[22] their organizational structure and future perspective reveal a broad affinity with the various discussions on revitalizing efforts and party reform. The intensive and increasing use of the Virtual Party Headquarters significantly contrasts with the precarious situation of membership development. During recent decades political parties have been struck by a continuous decline in members, directly leading to stagnation, paralysis and an erosion of party roots. The main cause for this development is the 'lack of new membership', which in turn is responsible for an accelerated ageing process of party demographics: 'Inner-party life is dominated by senior party-members, who have joined the organization years and decades ago.'[23] As a consequence of this internal structure, the processes of inner-party decision-making are almost brought to a standstill, and the internal gap between influential and powerless members is widening – the result of this chain reaction is characterized as the paralysis of organizational life.

Various strategies intending to reform German political parties identify the deficient membership structure as an important starting point for institutional change. The discussion on party reform is mainly divided into two perspectives: on one hand the radical rejection of the paradigm of party membership, on the other hand smooth changes of the existing situation.[24] The latter concepts of smooth change dominate the discussion. Often cited suggestions for reforms are 'the revitalization of local party branches or the supplementing of local party branches by Virtual Party Branches or more flexible teams; enhanced integration of non-party-members into party or other political decisions ("plebiscitarian elements"); the opening of party structures for non-members and improving the chances for inner-party participation, namely in the form of trial memberships'.[25] A closer look on this multifaceted catalogue of the advantages for and options of Virtual Party Headquarters emphasizes their affinity to the various modes of political communication through party structures. This affinity may be described more precisely, by comparing a conventional suggestion for reforms currently under discussion as 'Liberal Clubs'.[26] 'Liberal Clubs offer an area of discussion, participation, educational services, social contacts, also on an international level, as well as a wide range of services provided by other liberal organizations. Liberal Clubs discuss problems affecting society on various levels and develop and formulate solutions.'[27]

Almost every single point of these requirements is fulfilled at least by the Virtual Party Headquarters of the CDU, SPD and FDP. Open discussion areas, fora for social contacts, educational and political service provider, contact with politicians, international flair, chances for participation – all can be found at the on-line-outpost of political parties. In addition to that, Virtual Party Headquarters are open for interested citizens and do not require party membership. Visiting party web-sites, browsing digital archives, participating in on-line discussions or single-issue debates much resembles the '*Zeitgeist*'-idea of trial membership. Still missing are authentic chances for participating in intra-party decision-making, and Virtual Party Headquarters of course are deficient in several ways. Some examples are the mistaken use of party web-sites purely as platforms for marketing and publishing, and the often poor integration of on-line services into off-line organizational structures.

## THE VIRTUAL PARTY BRANCH – MODEL FOR THE FUTURE OR JUST A '*ZEITGEIST*'-EXPERIENCE?

A quite helpful illustration of cutting-edge use of Internet-communication is provided by the 'Virtual Local Branch' (*Virtueller Ortsverein*), an organization of net people within the SPD' (www.vov.de/allgemeines/vov_faq_englisch.shtml).[28] This group has – in spite of being officially considered a working team ('*Arbeitskreis*') by the head of the party – massive problems about entering traditional party structures and is still waiting for official recognition as a modern equivalent to the conventional local party branches. This is despite the fact that this unique concentration of party-affiliated, intensely committed and politically active group of 'netizens' contrasts dramatically with the membership malaise of the SPD:

> The members of the VOV are people from all over the world. In addition to that, many members are also members of the SPD and work in some of the regional and national bodies of the SPD. Currently we have more than 820 members; unfortunately less than 10% of them are female (but on average more are active). Most of the

VOV-members claim to be members of the SPD' (www.vov.de/allgemeines/vov_faq_englisch.shtml).

The Virtual Party Branch is proud of having a rich club life, which is documented by high user acceptance and a large number of postings to the discussion area, and which is organized in several newsgroups. Party membership is not necessary for participation in on-line-activities of the Virtual Party Branch. Thus it may regarded as a 'model for a more open mode of party discussion and recruitment. … The notion of "party basis" thus is changing, it expands into the field of the politically indecisive electorate which is used as a source of external expertise – of course, the "party line" is fading'.[29]

Within the context that has been outlined, the Virtual Party Branch has to be considered as a special form of intra-party communication with tight links to the Virtual Party Headquarters. Whereas the Virtual Party Branch has functioned as a 'nucleus' for a group of politically active people held together by the use of new media within the political process, a much bigger number of users taking part in the official on-line activities of political parties are interested in a broader spectrum of topics. Yet the technological infrastructure – as well as the human resources – provided by Virtual Party Headquarters still fails to be integrated explicitly into organizational processes of German political parties. This is the most striking difference between the Virtual Party Branch – as seen in its SPD-affiliated embodiment – and the Virtual Party Headquarters.

As they observe the further development of world-wide visible party web-sites, the inclusion into traditional structures of party organizations is the most prominent task for the future of Virtual Party Headquarters. The current discussions on the need for reforms of German party 'dinosaurs' have to be understood as a framework for the flourishing on-line-activities of exactly the same political parties that complain about the continuing loss of active party members. The phenomenological transformation of party web-sites, described as a generational change from 'digital brochures' to 'on-line-magazines' to 'political portal-sites', the structural transformation into an almost integral element of modern political communication within party organizations, these are the most important findings of this brief analysis. The dialectic of 'official developments' – exemplified by the short history of Virtual Party Headquarters – and 'grass-root developments' – exemplified by the model of the Virtual Party Branch – strongly suggests the need for party reforms and the potential of computer-mediated political communication to stimulate such changes.

## NOTES

1. This study concentrates on the web-sites of the parties elected to the German Bundestag. The Virtual Party Headquarters of the Social Democratic Party (SPD), the Christian Democratic Union (CDU), the Free Democratic Party (FDP), the Green/Bündnis 90 and of the Party of Democratic Socialism (PDS) each help to exemplify specific developments of the last four years. The web-site of the Christian Social Union is excluded because of its regional bias and the 'parliamentary merger' with the sister party of the CDU. Up to now, about 40 parties maintain on-line services, much of them resembling in shape and structure the web-sites of the 'big' parties. A regularly updated list of German political parties on-line is maintained by the on-line-magazine *politik-digital* (www.politik-digital/links/parteien).
2. For further details on the technical elements of German Virtual Party Headquarters see Robert Kaiser, 'Online-Informationsangebote der Politik. Parteien und Verbände im World Wide Web', in Klaus Kamps (ed.), *Elektronische Demokratie. Perspektiven politischer Partizipation* (Opladen: Westdeutscher Verlag, 1999), pp.175–90.
3. Two examples may show the importance of domain-names for Virtual Party Headquarters: The FDP first presented a 'liberal site' (www.liberale.de), providing on-line space for the national party branch, the members of the Bundestag, the Young Liberals and the Friedrich-Naumann-Foundation. The domain www.fdp.de was concocted to fit into the general pattern of www. (party name).de In 1995 the PDS only maintained a service among private pages at compuserve.com. When trying to register its domain name the site www.pds.de was already registered by the IT-Company 'PDS – Program- and Data-Services'. Thus the PDS had to build its on-line headquarters at www.pds-online.de.
4. See, for example, Hans-Martin Tillack, 'Der Wahlkampf mit der Maus', in *Konrad*, No.1 (1998), pp.35–40; Kaiser, 'Online-Informationsangebote der Politik'.
5. Numerous journalistic tests of political web-sites focus on the levels of 'layout' and 'content', but the integration into organizational structures is often ignored. Thus such tests should only be considered as the preliminaries for serious analysis (See Angelika Eckert, 'Schlammschacht im virtuellen Bonn', in *Global-Online*, Nos.4–5 (1998), pp.58–9; Philipp Stradtmann, 'Deutschland auf dem Weg in die elektronische Demokratie? Das Internet als Mittel der politischen Kommunikation und Partizipation', unpublished MA thesis, Hannover University, 1998; and Tillack, 'Der Wahlkampf mit der Maus').
6. Analyses grounded on a solid background of political scientists covering all four levels still are hard to find. Clemens focuses on the internal organization of Virtual Party Headquarters. See Detlev Clemens, 'Wahlkampf im Internet', in W. Gellner and F. von Korff (eds.), *Demokratie und Internet* (Baden-Baden: Nomos, 1998), pp.143–56). Christian Müller concentrates on technical aspects, in 'Parteien im Internet', in Gellner and von Korff (eds.), op. cit., pp.157–70, as does Robert Kaiser, 'Online-Informationsangebote der Politik. Parteien und Verbände im World Wide Web', in Klaus Kamps (ed.), *Elektronische Demokratie. Perspektiven politischer Partizipation*. The most advanced methods are used by Rachel K. Gibson and Stephen J. Ward, 'UK Political Parties and the Internet: "Politics as Usual" in the New Media', *Harvard International Journal of Press and Politics*, Vol.3, No.3 (1998), pp.14–38.
7. Genuine Virtual Party Headquarters require the registration of a domain name on the .de-level. See Christoph Bieber, 'Digitales Glanzpapier. Virtuelle Parteizentralen im Internet', *Spiegel der Forschung. Wissenschaftsmagazin der Justus-Liebig-Universität Giessen*, No.1 (April 1996), pp.8–11, and Richard Moeller, 'A Link to the Future: German Political Sources on the World Wide Web', *German Politics*, Vol.6, No.1 (1997), pp.140–50.
8. 'The address www.pds-online.de was since 1996 used only by members of the Bundestag. Following the national convention in April 1998 there is a central project, coordinating the on-line-presentation of national, regional and local party branches' (e-mail of Ronald Friedmann, on-line-editor PDS, 9 Dec. 1998).
9. The German political landscape is usually coded as follows: red – the Social Democratic Party (SPD), black – the Christian Democratic Union (CDU), yellow – the Free Democratic Party (FDP), green – the Greens/Bündnis 90 (Die Grünen/Bündnis 90), dark red – the Party of Democratic Socialism (PDS).

10. Christoph Bieber, 'Polit-Marketing mit Megabytes', in S. Bollmann and C. Haibach (eds.), *Kursbuch Internet* (Mannheim: Bollmann, 1996), pp.148–55.
11. *Informationsgesellschaft. Chancen, Innovationen und Herausforderungen* (Bonn: Rat für Forschung, Technologie und Innovation, 1995), p.45.
12. Other ancestors of political on-line activity were a student project called 'Abgeordnete im Internet' and the web-site of the German parliament. The Bundestag launched its service at www.bundestag.de on 15 January 1996. A much more important model was the rise of on-line campaigning during the presidential elections in the USA in the same year. In Germany, most of the Virtual Party Headquarters were redesigned for the first time under the influence of this first big on-line-event. See Edwin Diamond and Robert A. Silverman, *White House to Your House: Media and Politics in Virtual America* (Cambridge, MA: MIT Press,1997); Michael Margolis *et al.*, 'Campaigning on the Internet: Parties and Candidates on the World Wide Web in the 1996 Primary Season', *Harvard International Journal of Press and Politics*, Vol.2, No.1 (1997), pp.59–79; Pew Research Center for The People and The Press, 'One in Ten Voters On-Line for Campaign '96' (1996), at www.people-press.org/tec96sum.htm; Wayne Rash, *Politics on the Nets* (New York: Freeman, 1997).
13. Claus Leggewie and Christoph Bieber, 'Demokratie auf der Datenautobahn', in *Bürger und Staat in der Informationsgesellschaft* (Bonn: Enquete- Kommission 'Zukunft der Medien', 1999), pp.131–48; Robert Kaiser, 'Online-Informationensangebote der Politik'; Christian Müller, Parteien im Internet'; Rainer Kuhlen, *Die Mondlandung des Internet. Die Bundestagswahl 1998 in den elektronischen Kommunikationsforen* (Konstanz: UVK, 1998).
14. Petra Vaske, 'Die US-Kongresswahlen '98 im Internet – ein Fallstudie über den Einsatz neuer Kommunkationsmittel im Internet' (unpublished MA thesis, Hamburg, 1998), pp.51 ff; Thomas Zittel, 'Über die Demokratie in der vernetzten Gesellschaft. Das Internet als Medium politischer Kommunikation', *in Aus Politik und Zeitgeschichte*, B42, 1997, pp.23–9.
15. Quoted in Sabine Orner, 'Brücke zum Bürger. Interview mit Anna Siebenbohm', *Insight*, No.2 (1998), p.16.
16. As quoted in Frank Patalong, 'Die Chance auf mehr direkten Einfluss während des politischen Entscheidungsprozesses', in *Das Parlament*, No.36 (1998), p.15.
17. Eckert, 'Schlammschacht im virtuellen Bonn', p.59.
18. Detlev Clemens, 'Campaigning in Cyberspace. Internet-Einsatz in amerikanischen Bundeswahlkämpfen 1996 und 1998', in *Zeitschrift für Politik*, No.1 (1999), pp.50–67; Cordt Schnibben, 'Virtuos an der Luftgitarre', in *Der Spiegel*, No.32 (3 Aug. 1998), pp.22–7.
19. See Jennifer Sullivan, 'Pretty as a … Portal?' *Wired News*, 23 July 1998, at www.wired.com/news/culture/story/13679.html.
20. Studies on the on-line services of parties within other political systems draw similar conclusions. Regarding British political parties Gibson and Ward found that: 'The parties are clearly aware of the Internet's potential to transform their modus operandi'. Rachel Gibson and Stephen J. Ward, 'UK Political Parties and the Internet."Politics as Usual" in the New Media', *Harvard International Journal of Press and Politics*, Vol.3, No.3 (1998), p.33. For party organization in the US, Margolis *et al.* (op. cit., p. 73) expect 'that party and candidate web-sites will continue to grow in number and sophistication'. For the situation in New Zealand, see Juliet Roper, 'New Zealand Political Parties On-Line: the World-Wide Web as a Tool for Democratization or for Political Marketing?', in Christopher Toulouse and Timothy Luke (eds.), *The Politics of Cyberspace* (New York and London: Routledge, 1998), pp.69–83.
21. Thomas Leif, 'Hoffnung auf Reformen? Reformstau und Partizipationsblockaden in den Parteien', in *Aus Politik und Zeitgeschichte*, B43, 1993, pp.24–33; Oscar Gabriel and W. Niedermayer, 'Entwicklung und Sozialstruktur der Parteimitgliederschaften', in Oscar Gabriel, Oskar W. Niedermayer and R. Stöss (eds.), *Parteiendemokratie in Deutschland* (Bonn: Bundeszentrale für politische Bildung, 1997), pp.277–300; Elmar Wiesendahl, 'Noch Zukunft für die Mitgliederparteien? Erstarrung und Revitalisierung innerparteilicher Partizipation', in A. Klein and R. Schmalz-Bruhns (eds.), *Politische Beteiligung und Bürgerengagement in Deutschland* (Bonn: Bundeszentrale für politische Bildung, 1997), pp.349–81; Stefan Immerfall, 'Strukturwandel und Strukturschwächen der deutschen

Mitgliederparteien', in *Aus Politik und Zeitgeschichte*, B1-2, 1998, pp.3–12; Ulrich von Alemann, R.G. Heinze and J. Schmidt, 'Parteien im Modernisierungsprozess. Zur politischen Logik der Unbeweglichkeit', in *Aus Politik und Zeitgeschichte*, B1-2, 1998, pp.29–36.

22. An intensive analysis of Virtual Party Headquarters should be designed as a long-term study and analyse the changes in site content and site acceptance. It should observe discussion areas and on-line party chat rooms, as well as monitoring the off-line effects of on-line communication on various levels of party organizations.
23. Wiesendahl, 'Noch Zukunft für die Mitgliederparteien?', pp.356–60.
24. Ibid., p.366; Ingrid Reichert-Dreyer, 'Parteireform', in Gabriel and Niedermayer, *Parteidemokratie in Deutschland*, pp.338–56; von Alemann *et al.*, 'Parteien im Modernisierungsprozess', pp.29–36.
25. Stefan Immerfall, 'Strukturwandel und Strukturschwächen', p.7.
26. This concept was developed mainly within the FDP, but other parties also discuss similar ideas of 'associated clubs' or loosely connected 'working groups'.
27. *Die Liberale*, quoted in Leif, 'Hoffnung auf Reformen?', p.31.
28. Similar developments can also be found in other political contexts. The FDP has just launched a competition for the title of the 'most wired regional party branch' (www.fdp.de/fdpbv/). Almost totally copying structure and organization of the Virtual Party Branch, an all new party was founded in July 1999. Of course, this still small group of people named 'Die Digitalen' ('the digitals') maintains a web-site at www.digitalen.de. Currently they are trying to collect 2000 signatures, the minimum necessary for official recognition as a political party.
29. Leggewie, 'Demokratie auf der Datenautobahn', p.31.

# The Politics of African America On-Line

ROHIT LEKHI

> There is no race. There is no gender. There is no age. There are no infirmities. There are only minds. Utopia? No, Internet
>
> (Advertisement for MCI Communications)

There are, broadly speaking, two views of the likely impact of the Internet on participation in modern democratic politics. The optimistic view suggests that the Internet will facilitate the increased participation and deeper engagement of citizens in the political sphere.[1] Here, the Internet is seen to offer a way of overcoming a major obstacle to political participation: namely, that the resource costs incurred by those who participate outweigh the benefits that such participation might deliver. In this way, the Internet offers a mechanism to deliver low-cost participation that is nevertheless direct, immediate and interactive. Thus, many commentators focus on the role of the Internet in generating greater levels of deliberation amongst citizens, stressing its role in building social capital through the development of electronic public spaces and horizontal communication networks.[2]

The second, more sceptical, view of the impact of the Internet suggests that it remains beholden to the same commercial and public interests that have and continue to dominate other technological media. The Internet is seen as only the latest instrument that serves to reinforce the position of already dominant social groups and political interests. Here, the issue of who has access to the Internet and who is capable of using it is seen to be the crucial factor in realizing (or not) the potential for enhanced participation.

The accuracy of these radically different views of the Internet is investigated here through an examination of African American experiences on-line. African Americans offer an extremely useful case study through which to assess the various claims in the debate over the potential of the

The author is grateful to Ricardo Blaug and Ben Rosamond for comments on earlier drafts of this account.

Internet to renew political engagement. The political crisis within post-civil rights African America is by now well documented.[3] Not only has voter turnout in federal and state elections declined to below 40 per cent, but levels of dissatisfaction with American government and society have now reached unprecedented levels. For example, less than a third of African Americans believe that racial equality will be achieved in their lifetimes.[4] Moreover, African American disenchantment with both the Republican and Democratic parties has accelerated since the mid-1980s to the extent that half of all African Americans now support the establishment of an independent political party to specifically address their concerns.[5]

If in fact the Internet does enhance participatory opportunities for citizens and signal the potential rejuvenation of interactive public forums, then it is amongst politically disengaged groups, such as African Americans, that the political benefits of this new communicative medium are likely to be most tangible. On the other hand, if dominant political and social groups and interests have captured the Internet, then the disengagement of African Americans will likely remain a central feature of their political experiences on-line.

In seeking to test these broad hypotheses, the first part of the study attempts to give some measure of the extent to which the Internet has penetrated the activities of the African American community. It seeks to understand how access to it and wider structural forces in US society and economy shape usage of the Internet within African America. The evidence presented here suggests that the majority of African Americans remain severely disadvantaged in their ability to make use of this new communications technology.

The second part of the study examines the qualitative experiences of African Americans on-line. It inspects a variety of resources made available across the Internet and assesses the extent to which these have facilitated, or are likely to facilitate, opportunities for deeper political engagement by African Americans. While there is evidence of innovation in the use of the Internet within African American politics, the conclusion is that these developments are uneven and the participatory opportunities they furnish are at best limited.

However, in the third and concluding part of the paper the question is asked whether the effectiveness of the Internet as a medium for political communication and interaction for African Americans can be assessed adequately by focusing on the impact of the Internet on ‘traditional’ political activity. An alternative way of understanding African American on-line activity is suggested. The true significance of the Internet for

African Americans may lie less in its ability to increase levels of political activity within existing institutions than in its ability to facilitate new forms of activity that either bypass those institutions or directly compete with them.

## ACCESS

The question of access has weighed very heavily in discussions of the potential of the Internet to facilitate greater democratic participation in political life. Sceptics have pointed to the fact that the Internet has been the historic preserve of an elite stratum within advanced industrial societies that is, for the most part, white, male and professional.[6] As such, its potential to deliver a socially inclusive mechanism for communicative exchange is severely circumscribed. However, those more optimistic about the Internet's potential to deliver a more informed and politically-active citizenry, point to the recent explosive growth of this medium as evidence of the inevitable democratization of access beyond these initially restricted social groups.[7]

Of course, we should be careful not to assume that the question of access exhausts the debate about the impact of the Internet on political life. As will be seen below, what social groups actually do with this new technology is equally, if not more, important. Nevertheless, even if access is not a *sufficient* condition for the effective use of the Internet in politics, it is, in a very obvious sense, a *necessary* one. Any hope of utilising the Internet for potentially beneficial political ends requires that social groups have access to it. It follows, then, that any assessment of the impact of the Internet on African American communities must begin with considerations of access. In the following review of recent data on access, access levels amongst African Americans are compared with those of whites in order to establish the extent to which, if at all, the disparities between them are narrowing.

Despite a general neglect of this subject in popular and commercial commentaries on the Internet, it is clear that African Americans are a significant presence on-line. The most reliable estimates suggest that 5 million African Americans, or 19 per cent of the total African American population, are regular users of the Internet.[8] In absolute terms, this is certainly an impressive number amongst an English-speaking global population of 128 million Internet users.[9] However, these figures notwithstanding, the proportion of African Americans who regularly use the Internet remains worryingly low when compared to the US population as a whole of whom 32.7 per cent are estimated to be regular users.[10] Compared to whites, the disparity is even greater. White Americans are now almost twice as likely to be regular users of the Internet (37.7 per cent) than are African Americans.[11]

A number of recent studies confirm these disparities across a range of access indicators. Hoffman and Novak's widely-reported 1998 study of racial differences in computer use and Internet access in the US revealed that whites are much more likely to own a home computer than African Americans (44.2 per cent versus 29.0 per cent) and also exposed disparities in access to computers at work (38.5 per cent versus 33.8 per cent).[12] In terms of Internet access, whites were more likely to have ever used the worldwide web than were African Americans (26 per cent versus 22 per cent) and were much more likely to have used it at home (14 per cent versus 9 per cent).[13] Moreover, differences between African Americans and whites were seen to persist across all income groups and all educational levels. Hoffman and Novak also concluded that while the gap in computer ownership and Internet access levels between higher-income African American and higher-income white households (above the national median of $40,000 per annum) was relatively narrow, for lower-income households (below the national median of $40,000 per annum) whites were *six* times more likely to have gone on-line anywhere (home, work or a public facility) in the past week than were African Americans.[14]

In tracking these differentials over time, Hoffman and Novak have concluded that the gap between whites and African Americans in ownership of computers and Internet use persists and, in some cases, has even intensified.[15] Thus, while access to the Internet had increased in absolute terms for both African Americans and whites between 1997 and 1998, the rate of growth was significantly higher for whites (35.8 per cent in 1997 to 49.33 per cent in 1998) than it was for African Americans (31.68 per cent in 1997 to 35.54 per cent in 1998).[16] These increasing disparities were mirrored in the reported levels of whites and African Americans who had ever used the Internet.[17]

Many of the general conclusions Hoffman and Novak arrived at are confirmed by the latest in a series of studies from the US Department of Commerce, *Falling Through the Net: Defining the Digital Divide*. This again reveals the extent of the very real disparities between African Americans and whites in their ability to take advantage of new communication technologies such as the Internet. The study reveals significant disparities between whites and African Americans in terms of household computer penetration (46.6 per cent versus 23.2 per cent), individual use of the Internet (37.7 per cent versus 19.0 per cent) and Internet access from home (26.7 per cent versus 9.2 per cent).[18]

What is of greatest interest, however, is the extent to which the disparities that are apparent between African Americans and whites are actually growing, confirming Hoffman and Novak's follow-up conclusions. This data raises serious doubts about the optimists' view that the explosive growth of the Internet will necessarily expand and equalise access. So, for example, the gap between white and African American home computer ownership actually increased by 39.2 per cent between 1994 and 1998.[19] More worryingly still, between 1997 and 1998 alone, the gap between white and African American access to the Internet rose by some 53.3 per cent.[20]

What is also revealed by more detailed analysis of these figures, however, is the wide variations in these disparities depending on household income levels. For example, the disparities between whites and African Americans in terms of home computer ownership and Internet access increase as one proceeds down the income scale. Thus, it is only in the highest household income bracket (above $75,000 per annum) that the disparity between African American and white home computer penetration rates has declined – by 6.4 per cent between 1994 and 1998. In all other household income groups below this top level, the disparity between white and African American home computer penetration rates is increasing. For households with income of between $35,000 and $74,999 it increased by 6.4 per cent; for those with income of between $15,000 and $34,999 it increased by 61.7 per cent and in the lowest income households (below $15,000 per annum) it increased by a startling 73 per cent during the same period.[21]

Unsurprisingly, the survey data reviewed above suggests that those Americans enjoying greatest connectivity to the Internet are drawn from high-income households. Moreover, this social group tends to be highly educated and in full-time employment. Conversely, the least well connected tend to be those drawn from low-income households, less well educated and lacking full-time employment.[22] Given the socio-economic profile of African Americans as a whole, it is not surprising that they are over-represented in the less well-connected category of Americans. In the case of a strong predictor of Internet access like college education, for example, African Americans are half as likely to have completed a four-year college degree than whites.[23] In employment, the jobless rates amongst African Americans have remained twice that of whites for the last 20 years.[24] In the same period, the median wage of African American men as a proportion of the median wage of white American men has remained more or less unchanged at 74 per cent.[25] Moreover, the median income of black families as a percentage of white median family income stood at 60 per cent in 1997, the same as in 1967.[26]

### *The Dangers of Socio-Economic Disadvantage in the Digital Age*

Given the evidence presented here, it is clear that socio-economic disadvantage remains a severe obstacle to the ability of African Americans to take advantage of the opportunities so far furnished by the Internet. It is also clear that such disadvantage weighs more heavily against African Americans than it does against the white population. This is in stark contrast to the now commonplace view that equalization of access is a necessary consequence of the Internet's expansion. What the evidence actually suggests is that the much-heralded potential of the Internet to deliver a medium of inclusive public deliberation remains, for the time being at least, seriously open to question. As the US Department of Housing and Urban Development bluntly acknowledged, those without equitable means of access to new communications technologies 'will be unable to fully participate in [the] nation's economic, social, civic and government life'.[27] More particularly, as another recent report argues, if African Americans are unable to take advantage of these newly-presented opportunities to foster civic engagement, they are likely to find it increasingly difficult to 'facilitate co-ordination and communication' on a collective level.[28]

The problem is not just that African Americans are unable to access and use an already in-place forum for activity and discussion, however. Inequalities in the use of the Internet may also result in the lack of opportunities to shape its technological and conceptual development. What is made possible by the Internet (and what it is not) is very much shaped by an existing community of users and the particular needs they have.[29] As a consequence, those not yet on-line may find themselves locked into a process of Internet development in which services are already pre-determined in favour of interests other than, and often quite contrary to, their own (see below).

In the case of African Americans, at least two dangers present themselves with respect to the impact of inequitable access to the Internet. First, the growing 'digital divide' between the majority of African Americans and the general population is likely to reinforce and even exacerbate the former's already severe disengagement from present and future political opportunities. As technologies such as the Internet are increasingly employed by political institutions as an important mode of political interaction and, equally, are utilized by local and national authorities in the delivery of public services, so we are likely to witness – if we have not already – the emergence of a 'digital underclass' within African America. In this case, rather than facilitating improved political participation for the vast majority of African Americans, the effect of the Internet is more likely to be quite the reverse.

The second danger brought about by inequitable access is that it is likely to reinforce already profound structural divisions within African America between a small but increasingly affluent and politically empowered middle-class and the rest. The devastating social and political effects of such internal division have been much noted in post-civil rights America[30] and the danger is that these will be further exacerbated as a result of inequitable access to new communications technologies. This is likely to result in the emergence of an information-rich elite that will increasingly come to set the agenda of African American politics on-line just as it presently does in 'real' time and space.

### *Addressing the Problem of Access*

The problem of how access might be guaranteed to the widest number has generated enormous interest in discussions of the impact of the Internet and has given rise to a variety of policy proposals and practical initiatives as a consequence.[31] In the United States, the latter have taken the form of federal and state level assistance programmes and regulatory initiatives, both of which have sought to subsidize or offer discounted service provisions to those social groups least likely to be connected to the Internet.[32] Moreover, a number of community-based initiatives have been directed towards the provision of Internet (and other information technology) services in low-income groups through public facilities such as libraries, schools and community technology centres.[33]

While it is too early to judge the success of these projects, what they already reveal is that the difficulty of guaranteeing high-quality Internet access to the widest number is a great deal more intractable than 'cyber-utopians' have tended to suggest. The imperative to expand Internet access in the United Sates remains, for the most part, commercially driven and the marked reluctance of telecommunications providers to offer high-quality access to less-profitable consumers in low-income areas is becoming increasingly apparent.[34] The very real danger is that the profit-driven imperative to enhance provision for those already benefiting from new information technologies like the Internet will frustrate attempts to address already significant disparities in access. Policy-makers have yet to resolve this conflict between, on the one hand, ensuring *commercial* competition in the provision of telecommunications services and on the other, establishing *public* policies geared towards the delivery of universal (or even near-universal) access provision.[35] Until they do, large numbers of African

Americans will be excluded from the economic, social and political opportunities that access to the Internet and other information and communication technologies is likely to deliver.

## AFRICAN AMERICANS AND ON-LINE POLITICS

When confronted with the size of the access problem in African America, it is difficult to take seriously the view that the Internet is likely to facilitate greater participation amongst otherwise marginalized social groups. However, while it certainly pays to be cautious about the many recent proclamations of a new era of political empowerment brought about by this new technology, it is equally as important not to write off existing initiatives in on-line participation and communication that, if not signifying epochal transformations, at least point to the potential for democratic renewal. While the question of access casts a long shadow over such initiatives in African America, they remain important nevertheless as indicators of the limits and possibilities of the Internet in extending participatory opportunities in the political sphere.

In the following section, we assess the extent to which initiatives in on-line participation and communication have impacted upon African American politics and society. Our aim is to consider the ways in which the Internet has facilitated, or is likely to facilitate, the deeper political engagement of African Americans across various levels of political and social life. Here, we are especially concerned to assess, first, the extent to which African Americans have been addressed as a specific constituency of interests by on-line political actors and in on-line political activities, and secondly, how African Americans themselves have sought to utilize the Internet to facilitate deeper political engagements and the advance of their own political interests.

### *Political Parties*

Political parties are increasingly seen as a primary locus of the Internet's potential to impact on politics. The ability to use the Internet to create new channels of communications between political parties and the electorate has been of particular interest. The Internet offers parties the opportunity to bypass traditional mass media in order to deliver tailored appeals to specific groups of voters with particular sets of interests – so-called 'narrow-casting'.[36]

Our analysis of a range of US political party web sites suggests, however, that the opportunities offered by the Internet to forge direct relationships with African American voters remain largely unrealized. Only the Democratic National Committee (DNC) web-site makes any attempt to address African Americans as a specific constituency of voters.[37] Through its African American 'Voter Outreach' programme, the DNC offers an 'African American newsletter' which compares the Democrat and Republican records on affirmative action, crime and poverty alleviation programmes and also offers a limited number of position papers on policy issues of specific interest to African Americans.[38] Interestingly, the Republican National Committee makes extensive use of 'positive' images of African Americans across its web-site, but fails to direct any information to African Americans as a specific constituency interest.[39] Independent parties of both the left and right similarly fail to spotlight African American constituents. The Democratic Socialists of America link to a page of interest for African Americans which in fact leads to a more general anti-racism site, while the Reform Party's site promoting a 'third political choice' in the United States has no pages directed to African American voters at all.[40]

As even this brief outline of current web-based provision indicates, the main political parties have so far failed to take advantage of the technological potential of the Internet to deliver low-cost, customized appeals to their African American constituents. For the most part, the web-based offerings of the main political parties remain oriented to little more that the provision of top-down forms of the most general and undifferentiated kinds of information.[41]

### *Civil Rights Organizations*

The great advantage of the Internet for civil rights groups is that it offers an alternative to the mainstream media as a source of information on their activities. Where such groups might otherwise struggle to find a voice within the public realm, the Internet offers a means by which they can direct their message to specific constituencies of interest in a more immediate, direct and interactive fashion than has previously been possible. African American civil right groups have a long tradition of developing and using independent media to promote their interests and to facilitate political communication.[42] The Internet would therefore seem an ideal medium through which to enable further development of such communication and interaction. Our analysis suggests, however, that while all of the major civil rights organizations have established an on-line presence through which to disseminate general information, their capacity to facilitate genuine dialogue amongst African Americans or with mainstream political actors remains for the most part limited.

In the case of the National Association for the Advancement of Colored People (NAACP), for example, those visiting its web site are offered an impressive range of informational and promotional materials in the form of 'video-casting' of annual convention speeches by NAACP leaders, pages on voter empowerment and other NAACP programmes, and the opportunity to join the NAACP on-line.[43] These certainly represent important advances in terms of the ability of an organization like the NAACP to reach an audience it might otherwise be denied if it were to rely exclusively on the mainstream media for political communication and expression. However, information dissemination and promotional activity of this sort is an almost entirely top-down form of communication. What it does not offer is the possibility of deliberation amongst that audience or of canvassing its views on any of the issues raised by the NAACP's activities.

Much the same situation prevails with respect to the on-line activities of Jesse Jackson's Rainbow/PUSH Alliance. While the web-site publicizes the Alliance's wide range of activities and again utilizes Internet-based audio and video technologies to deliver its messages and facilitate on-line recruitment of members, there is little opportunity for interaction and debate for those in search of political deliberation.[44] It is striking that the Alliance has not sought to take advantage of the opportunities of the Internet – especially given the self-proclaimed purpose of its 'Citizenship Education Fund' the aim of which is to 'promulgate the democratic principles of civic virtue in order to improve life opportunities for those citizens who are often voiceless and forgotten' and amongst whose primary objectives is to 'educate the public on the efficacy of political participation and civic responsibility'.[45]

One leading civil rights organization that has sought to facilitate greater dialogue and co-ordinated action amongst its audience is the National Urban League. The League's web-site recently underwent a radical makeover in spring 1999 and now offers detailed and attractively-presented information about its programmes, an archive of audio-visual material (and when available, live broadcasts) and a searchable database of leaders' speeches and press releases.[46] However, in addition to these examples of top-down information dissemination, the League also facilitates a co-ordinated discussion forum, the 'Urban Leaders List', that is specifically aimed at generating discussion and debate amongst African American professionals.[47]

The list is a free-to-subscribe, e-mail-based discussion forum and is tasked with developing dialogues amongst 'a virtual community of leaders who share resources and solve problems related to the development of inner-city youth, families, and communities'.[48] The listed discussions range from broad debates on the nature of race and racism in America to practically oriented deliberations that draw on resources, advice and help of African American professionals in the building of specific community initiatives. Recent examples of this type of deliberation have generated calls for communities to notify the Federal Communication Commission of their needs for investment in high-quality communications infrastructure; requests for support for an NAACP-led rally of the Supreme Court to ensure integration of law court officials; consumer information on recalled foodstuffs; and the call for a nation-wide boycott of Hollywood films by the Black Film-makers Coalition in protest against discrimination against African American technicians in the film industry.

The Urban Leaders' List is an impressive example of the possibilities opened up by the Internet for co-ordinating dialogue and debate within a national forum amongst otherwise geographically-dispersed actors. Of course, in promoting the list as an exclusive forum for 'community leaders', the League encourages self-selection amongst list participants. Thus, the majority of those who contribute to list discussions are drawn from the professional middle class, the single most active group of African American Internet users *and* already the most politically active.[49] By playing to the strengths of the current profile of Internet users in African America, a successful co-ordination of horizontal political communication and exchange is guaranteed. However, this is achieved only at the cost of enforcing already-existing structural divisions within African America whereby only that elite stratum already in possession of sufficient economic and social resources is able of contribute to and set the agenda of this deliberative forum.[50]

### *Political Mobilization and Action-Co-ordination*

Another oft-cited benefit of the Internet is the ability of users to overcome the limitations of both time and space in their communicative strategies through the near-instant delivery of information to an almost limitless number of end-users. In the political sphere, this has opened up intriguing possibilities for organizations seeking to mobilize and co-ordinate political action. Where previously the ability to affect such mobilization and co-ordination in any systematic fashion required the use of labour-intensive and/or high-cost media (for example, print and broadcast media), the Internet offers a means to realize such activities without a significant drain on the organizations' resources.

Within African American communities, the most prominent example of the use of on-line technologies in aid of political mobilization is perhaps that of the Nation of Islam and its organization of the 1995 Million Man March. The event was the largest single political mobilization of African Americans in history and made extensive use of the Internet to advertise its aims, co-ordinate the activities of organizers and disseminate information on arrangements to participants. These activities were structured through both a subscription-based electronic mailing list and the Nation's dedicated web-site for the event.[51]

While there is no analysis of the precise effect of the Internet's use in this instance, it is clear that the Nation of Islam itself has subsequently sought to expand its use of new communications technologies in the more recent development of its political strategy. The Nation is now at the forefront of implementing innovative technologies in the cause of political communication and education. Using audio and video streaming technologies, as well as more standard text-based information services, the Nation has an array of web-sites dedicated to different aspects of its work – including an on-line version of the organization's Final Call newspaper; a health education web-site; a national student association web-site; an on-line study centre and a web-page dedicated to links forged within the Islamic and African diasporas.[52] In addition, the Nation of Islam has recently sought to exploit the potential of the Internet as a medium for political communication through a strategic link-up with America Online's Black Voices Internet site. This site, in conjunction with the Final Call Online, has recently featured live interactive 'chat' forums engaging Nation of Islam Ministers in debates with the wider public.[53]

The Nation of Islam's enthusiastic embrace of Internet technologies as an integral part of its political strategy indicates the power of this new medium as an independent mechanism through which to channel the message of those on the political 'fringe'. And to the extent that it is effective in articulating its political programme to an increasingly sympathetic audience, the Nation's experiences offer a useful insight into at least one possible direction that might be taken by those who seek to exploit the Internet's potential as integral tool of political mobilization and communication.[54]

### *E-democracy*

As well as the potential to enhance opportunities for participation within existing political forums, many commentators have pointed to the Internet's potential to create entirely new political spaces or update those historical spaces that have been lost as a consequence of the increased complexity of social and political life.[55] Thus, some have suggested that the Internet offers the potential to re-enact direct forms of democratic engagement amongst citizens through the medium of electronic 'town hall' meetings and even the recreation of something akin to an ancient Athenian public sphere.[56] For those optimistic of the Internet potential to reengage citizens in face-to-face (or at least keyboard-to-keyboard) political deliberation, a number of high profile experiments in the United States are repeatedly cited as examples of the way in which this aspect of communicative technology might develop.[57]

There is no doubt that all of the examples in the literature, of attempts to reengage communities in the politics of their locality, point to a number of ways in which electronically-mediated communications can lead to a genuine growth of social capital and the enhancement of local citizenship.[58] However, what is striking about all of these initiatives is the lack of an African American voice within them. None of the most prominent examples of local initiatives in electronic democracy – including the most famous in Minnesota but also others in Palo Alto, California and Austin, Texas – have any resources, whether they be informational resources or topics of deliberation that are of specific interest to, or for, African Americans. As a consequence, attempts to explore both the possibilities and limitations of electronic interactions in actually existing political spheres have tended to bypass the specific issues that African American usage might give rise to.

Of course, it can easily be pointed out that, with the exception of Austin, all of the other prominent examples of local experiments in electronic democracy take place in areas where the proportion of African Americans amongst the general population is much lower than the national average.[59] Consequently, it is hardly reasonable to expect these experiments to raise issues of specific concern to a relatively small section of the local population. This might indeed be true. However, this still begs the question of *why* these experiments have tended to be undertaken in areas with lower-than-average African American populations. Here, the consequences of differential access come to the fore in a concrete way. Experiments in electronically-mediated citizen interaction are most likely to be adopted, of course, in those areas where on-line access rates are likely to be highest. Equally, such experimental activity is likely to exclude those areas where on-line access rates are low – precisely those areas where African Americans are found in concentrated numbers.

Of course, one might argue that the degrees of inequitable access highlighted earlier are only likely to be temporary features of Internet development in the United States and that we must assume that equalization of access is likely given the rapid pace of technological change and the cost savings this are likely to come with it. The difficulty is, however, that even if this faith in eventual equalization were justified, despite the fact that the evidence presented above suggests there are good reasons to think that it is not, in the meantime, the primary use and development of Internet technologies in the political sphere may well already have been shaped by existing groups of users. In the case of electronic 'town hall' democracy, the experiences of demographically (and ethnically) skewed groups of existing participants are likely to bear heavily in the identification of how new forms of electronically-mediated political interactions take place. However, without concrete reference to how this mediation might itself affect (or be affected by) the specific forms of political communication and interaction assumed within African America, the danger is that the African Americans will be alienated from the generalized form of this new communications technology as it is adopted within a wider public sphere.[60]

In the foregoing, we have sought to sketch out some of the possibilities and limitations afforded by African American involvement (or the lack of it) in on-line political activity. As even this brief overview suggests, so far at least, the impact of the Internet within African American politics is at best uneven and has furnished only limited opportunities for more and better participation. While there certainly are interesting examples of African American political activity on-line, these have been limited in their ideological or demographic focus and do not appear to represent a more general embrace of the Internet within African America. Moreover, where the Internet has been put to innovative use, this has invariably been the result of the efforts of political actors within African America itself. From outside African America there seems little concern to address African Americans as a specific constituency of political interest that might require and derive benefits from dedicated on-line resources.

Of course, this state of affairs can in part be explained by the immaturity of Internet development and use more generally. Despite the best hopes of 'cyber-optimists', it is still not clear how, or indeed whether, the Internet will fundamentally alter the ways in which politics is enacted. While we have hinted at the sorts of innovations that are made possible by its effective use, it is more often the case, in the present period, that on-line politics mirrors many of the features of politics in 'real' time and space. So, for example, while the Internet offers the potential to foster genuine exercises in deliberation and interactive communication, in reality that potential has been neglected by mainstream political actors in favour of strategies that reinforce top-down processes of information dissemination. Similarly, while the Internet offers the means by which to tailor political appeals and communicative and informational resources to specific constituent interests, what it in practice reinforces are already existing and, in this case, long-standing failures within 'real world' politics to address issues of primary concern to African Americans. In this way, the long-standing failure within American politics more generally to engage the concerns of African Americans simply repeats itself in the on-line activities of mainstream political actors. And here, the growing disillusionment of African Americans with mainstream political activity is only likely to be reinforced on-line.

## RETHINKING THE POLITICAL IN THE AGE OF THE INTERNET

All of this paints a rather depressing picture of the state of on-line political activity within African America and suggests that, in terms of the two broad views of the Internet's impact on politics outlined at the beginning of this investigation, we would do well to be sceptical of claims that the Internet carries with it an inherent capacity to generate more and better participation amongst the politically disengaged. Rather, much of the evidence suggests that the Internet is the preserve of already dominant social groups and political interests and that inequitable patterns of access remain the crucial determinant of the extent and type of participatory opportunities it gives rise to.

But to what extent is this conclusion premised on the particular focus adopted in this study? In other words, would the conclusions be any different if we were to understand the political as something broader than the traditional preoccupations of mainstream political actors, institutions and activities? In the case of how we understand the politics of African America this is a vitally important issue. Historically, the pre-occupations of African American politics have been much broader than the exclusive focus on mainstream political institutions and actors is able to capture. Rather, African American conceptions of the political have embraced and been articulated through an enormous variety of cultural, social and economic concerns. Indeed, this is no more than to observe that the historical exclusion of African America from mainstream political processes has required a variety of alternative mechanisms through which to express political interests and articulate political demands.[61] Moreover, and in recognition of the fact that these alternative mechanisms are a more general feature of subaltern political struggle, recent developments in social and political theory have encouraged analysts to adopt wider notions of the political in order better to understand the operation of political power across contemporary societies and economies.[62] To what extent, then, would a more expansive and diverse notion of the political alter the conclusions we have so far reached about the impact of the Internet on African American political life?

What soon becomes apparent in making this move, is that the exclusive focus on traditional notions of the political manifestly fails to account for enormous amounts of on-line cultural, social and economic activity currently going on within African America. What is also clear, however, is that the ways in which this activity is organized raises crucial political questions about the spatial division of the Internet (see below). The vast majority of African American on-line activity is not immediately accessible to the casual on-line surfer. Rather, the majority of it is self-contained within dedicated areas of interest for African Americans accessible either through payment-based proprietary systems like America Online or through publicly accessible web portals. Thus, web-sites such as NetNoir, AfroNet, MelaNet, and The Black World Today all offer entry points into an enormous set of commercial, cultural and social resources specifically targeted towards an African American audience.[63] While the vast majority of these resources are not in themselves oriented to the sphere of politics, the collective mechanisms of identity formation and interest articulation that they create have enormous potential to make an impact upon politics more broadly defined.

### *Political News and Commentary*

All of the above mentioned sites provide up-to-date news resources of specific interest to African Americans. These are often selected items of national news with specific African American orientation but they also draw heavily on news from local African American communities and on wider news stories from the African Diaspora more broadly – including Africa, the Caribbean and western Europe and most especially the United Kingdom. Political commentary is widespread on all of the sites ranging from newspaper-style ‘op.-ed.’ pieces and interviews with leading African American public figures through to more extensive analyses of the state of African American politics and society. For example, recent commentary and analysis at The Black World Today web site, currently the foremost provider of African American-oriented news on-line, covers issues as diverse as current challenges to affirmative action, afro-centric political ideology, the work of contemporary civil rights organizations, the role of the criminal justice system and the impact of the North American Free Trade Agreement on the African continent and the Caribbean.[64]

*Interactivity*

The interactive possibilities offered by the Internet, that we saw rather sparingly applied within the political mainstream, find a particular emphasis on all of the portal sites we reviewed. In each case, a huge array of chat forums, discussion lists, and message boards on any number of topics was offered by each web-site. Some sites sought to direct participants' deliberations towards specific issues of topical interest. Thus, the Afronet Discussion Messageboard sought to elicit responses and prompt discussion and deliberation around issues of black mutual respect, the rewards of working for black businesses and the means of comparing the talents of whites and blacks.[65] However, the majority of such exercises, including Afronet's own chat forum, sought only to facilitate discussions amongst African Americans rather than pre-empt their direction.[66] While these chat forums covered almost every conceivable area of African American society and culture, a number were directed specifically to political discussion. The Netnoir Black Network chat area, for example, offers participants a choice of chat room according to the specific sort of political engagement they seek.[67] Here, African Americans (the main group to which the site directs its appeal) are offered the choice of Republican, Democratic or civil rights chat rooms but also others, including one dedicated to green politics and another to issues of environmental concern. However, users of the NetNoir portal site are not confined to the current choices of chat room on offer but rather are encouraged to develop their own areas of discussion, including political ones, within the NetNoir domain. In this sense, there remains at the heart of this initiative, whatever its underlying commercial motivation, a concern that the terms and substance of deliberative interactions are determined by end-users themselves.

*Community*

The other great emphasis that runs through all of these portal sites is on 'community'. There are diverse interpretations amongst these sites of what the construction of on-line communities actually entails. These range from simply offering a virtual space within which those with common interests can interact through to much more deliberate attempts to construct social, economic and cultural resources around local areas with large African American populations. Some of these community-building facilities are limited to the top-down distribution of community information, while others allow for more decisive interactions between end-users within an identifiable geographical area. At the time of writing, many of these initiatives are at an embryonic stage of development and as a consequence, it is too early to judge how effective they might be in stimulating interaction and deliberation at the local level. However, the simple fact of their existence, in areas such as Harlem and Brooklyn in New York, the south side of Chicago and South Central Los Angeles, points to the potentially useful application of on-line resources to a concern to rebuild community, that has remained at the heart of the African American political agenda throughout the post-civil rights movement era.[68] Moreover, it is these commercially driven initiatives in community building that, at present, offer the closest approximation to the e-democracy initiatives that we earlier saw have bypassed areas where African Americans are concentrated.

### *Diaspora*

However, in addition to the focus on local-level interactions, what is also made possible by Internet technology is the ability to facilitate dialogue and co-ordinated action between those otherwise bounded by the traditional limitations of time and space. Within African America this raises intriguing possibilities with respect to the development of real and virtual links with other parts of the African Diaspora some of which are already being grasped in connection with the activities of portal sites. As already noted, much of the news content and political analysis offered by these sites is oriented to matters of diasporic, as well as specifically African American, interest. Additionally, however, the emphasis on diaspora extends within these sites to many other activities including commercial, social and cultural ones. Of particular interest in this regard, is the AfroNet portal's recent move to establish community resources for users in high-profile areas of black settlement in other parts of the world, including Brixton in London and Soweto and Cape Town in South Africa.[69] In this way, not only does AfroNet establish a valuable resource for Internet users within these specific localities but it also serves to make an active association between these communities and African America through their common existence within the Afronet domain.

## AFRICAN AMERICA ON-LINE: TENSIONS AND CONTRADICTIONS

It is clear, then, that once we accept a more expansive understanding of the political, the resources made available to African Americans through these commercially-oriented sites are of the utmost importance and give rise to a much more complex, and indeed dynamic, view of African American on-line activity than an exclusive focus on the work of mainstream actors and institutions allows for. Despite this, however, critical issues remain about the use of dedicated web portals as the favoured means of delivering communicative resources to African Americans. These issues, concerning the commercial nature of web portals and the organizational form they assume, are of central importance because they reveal the extent to which on-line activity in African America is beset with the self-same tensions and contradictions that have always lain at the heart of its political development.

The concluding part of this study, then, explores some of these tensions and contradictions and how they impact on the ways in which the political significance of the Internet in African America should be understood.

### *Politics and Commerce*

For those who champion the democratic and participatory potential of the Internet, part of its appeal is precisely that it is able to foster forms of civic and political engagement beyond what is perceived to be the detrimental control and influence of commercial interests.[70] According to this view, therefore, we should be suspicious of any attempt to realize politically favourable goals for African Americans through on-line activity driven by commercial imperatives. This is certainly an important issue. However, it is also a great deal more complex for African Americans than an either/or choice between commerce and politics supposes. The question of what sort of economic relationships are best suited to achieving African American political aims has always been a contentious one, determined historically as much by the pragmatic requirements of immediate circumstances as by fervent ideological commitment.[71] In the circumstances that the majority of African Americans find themselves in today, it is difficult not to be struck by the lack of opportunity for them to realize the benefits of on-line politics and community-building without resorting to privately financed expertize and technology.

However, while the need for a pragmatic response to the use of commercial interests for political gain is tempting, the question of control and ownership remains a particularly vexed one. Writing on the AfroNet portal site, Cinque Sengbe argues that the overriding concern for African Americans is not whether the resources that facilitate their interactions are commercial ones, but rather whether the control and ownership of these commercial resources remains in the hands of whites.[72] Pointing out that the vast majority of web portals aimed at African Americans are not owned by African Americans but rather by large media conglomerates, he argues that white-owned web portals are simply the latest means by which whites have sought to censor African American communicative interaction. As such, they have historical precedent in the constraints imposed on black-to-black communication during slavery and colonialism. Whatever one might think about the accuracy of this claim, it does go to the heart of concerns within African America about the exercise of power over communication on-line.

*The Organization of On-line Politics*

The other critical issue around which the historic tensions and contradictions of African American politics can be seen to manifest themselves concerns the organizational *form* assumed in the web portal model. The purpose of the web portal can be read in a number of ways. A benign reading might suggest that a portal simply serves to concentrate on-line resources in ways that makes them easily accessible to, and meets the specific usage demands of, a particular user-group – in this case, African Americans. Thus, according to Barry Cooper, chief executive of the Black Voices web portal, portals are an ideal way of meeting the requirements of African American users. 'Unlike non-blacks', Cooper argues, 'blacks generally do not surf the Web as a whole, but instead target Afro-centric sites and spend most of their time there.'[73]

But to what extent is this difference in usage a pre-given feature of African American on-line activity? An alternative reading of the role of African American portals suggest that, far from benign, they actually have the effect of entrenching spatial divisions on the Internet along ethnic or racial lines such that they give rise to precisely the differences in use that Cooper assumes as his starting point. At a time when African American disillusionment with post-civil rights America has reached record levels and has found expression in the widespread retreat from all kinds of engagement with the political mainstream, the organization of on-line activity into self-contained and largely isolated forums may simply serve to reinforce this process of disconnection rather than offering a means to overcome it.

In many ways, this is simply an on-line version of the historic dilemma of African American political strategy: that to realize the goal of political, cultural and economic self-sufficiency may require African Americans to abandon their faith in the universalising pretensions of American democracy. Of course, there have always been African Americans who have refused to accept the logic of this position and have sought to resolve the dilemma through inclusive mechanisms of social and political change.[74] However, in the contemporary United States, the appeal of inclusivist political strategies is clearly in decline.[75] As increasing numbers of African Americans recoil from engagement in the mainstream institutions of American democracy, so the appeal of isolationist political strategies is likely to grow. In this situation, then, we can understand the development of on-line resources exclusively servicing the needs of African America as a reaction to, and reinforcement of, its ongoing political and social disengagement in 'real' time and space.

There is, however, a third way of reading the development of African American web portals that refuses to understand their political relation to the Internet in terms of the simple dichotomy between inclusion and exclusion. Rather, a more critical reading of the complexities of African American on-line politics suggests that it does open up intriguing possibilities for the development of co-ordinated forms of activity and political representation but may *also* represent a strategic withdrawal of African Americans from the wider public sphere. So as better to understand these aspects of African American activity on-line, we can utilize Nancy Fraser's conception of the 'subaltern counter-public'.

Fraser challenges the historical origins, and thus the claims to authenticity, of the single public sphere so desired by proponents of democratic on-line culture. Recognizing that history has produced many different publics and that a number of competing publics may well produce more and better democracy, she draws our attention to subaltern counter-publics, or 'parallel discursive arenas where members of subordinated social groups invent and circulate counter-discourses, which in turn permit them to formulate oppositional interpretations of their identities, interests, and needs'.[76] She suggests that 'in stratified societies, subaltern counter-publics have a dual character. On the one hand, they function as spaces of withdrawal and regroupment; on the other hand, they also function as bases and training grounds for agitational activities directed toward wider publics.'[77]

Whether, in fact, African American on-line activity can as yet be understood in terms of 'regroupment' and the organizational form they assume in web portals understood in terms of 'bases and training grounds for agitational activities' remains open to question. There is clearly a need to flesh out the theoretical foundations of Fraser's position with more detailed and rigorous empirical work if it is to be profitably utilized in helping us to understand the current and future role of African American on-line activity. However, what Fraser offers us is a starting point from which to begin to reconceptualize the ways in which this activity is organized, ways that break with the entrenched dichotomies of integration and separation that continue to dominate current understanding of African American politics. In so doing, she offers us a mechanism through which to understand the potential of the Internet to serve the emancipatory interests of contemporary African America.

## CONCLUSION

The foregoing has traced the broad contours of the Internet's development as it has impacted upon the politics of African America and in so doing has sought to test the veracity of the two broad views of the likely impact of the Internet on politics introduced at the start. What can be concluded from this survey is that there are many reasons to doubt the Internet's potential to serve as a mechanism to enhance participatory and communicative opportunities for the vast majority of African Americans. Above all, we have seen how, far from overcoming the effects of socio-economic disadvantage, the present development of the Internet rather points to ways in which such disadvantage is reinforced and even exacerbated on-line.

It is also clear, that as well as socio-economic disadvantage political disadvantage is also manifest in much of the on-line activity of mainstream political actors and their relationship (or lack of it) to African American constituencies. Here, again, far from offering a mechanism of escape from, or transcendence of, the constraints of 'real' time and space, the character of much of African American on-line politics seems simply to mirror the pre-existing alienation of many African Americans from the political mainstream.

Given the current trajectory of African American politics in general, it seems unlikely these features of African American on-line experience will change very much in the immediate future. In these circumstances, and in lieu of simple resignation to this fate, it is, we have argued, both historically and theoretically appropriate to expand our view of the nature of African American politics and ask how such an expanded notion of the political makes itself felt on-line. Here, it was argued there are reasons to be more optimistic, although perhaps not for the reasons that optimists of the Internet's potential have tended to cite. Rather in the midst of the increasing retrenchment of contemporary American politics along racial lines, there may be good reasons for African Americans themselves to find strength on-line in concentrated numbers before seeking to engage more directly in mainstream political activity. As was shown, however, such a move carries with it inherent dangers – of isolation and the entrenchment of racial divisions on-line. It will indeed be a test of the Internet's potential to realize significant political opportunities for subaltern political groups, if it can avoid these dangers amongst African Americans and offer instead a viable means for their re-engagement with the political mainstream.

## NOTES

1. See, for example, Michael Dertouzos, *What Will Be: How the New Information Marketplace will Change our Lives* (San Francisco, CA: HarperCollins, 1997) and Nicholas Negroponte, *Being Digital* (London: Hodder & Stoughton, 1995).
2. Recent examples include, Edward Schwartz, *Netactivism: How Citizens Use the Internet* (Sebastapol, CA: Songline Studios, 1996); Ian Budge, *The New Challenge of Direct Democracy* (Oxford: Polity Press, 1996); Howard Rheingold, *The Virtual Community: Homesteading on the Electronic Frontier* (Reading, MA: Addison-Wesley, 1993); Lawrence Grossman, *The Electronic Republic: Reshaping Democracy in the Information Age* (New York: Viking, 1995); Jeffrey B. Abramson, F. Christopher Arterton and Gary R. Orren, *The Electronic Commonwealth: The Impact of New Media Technologies on Democratic Politics* (New York: Basic Books, 1988). See also B. Noveck, 'Paradoxical Partners' in this collection.
3. See, for example, Adolph Reed, Jr., 'Demobilization in the New Black Political Regime: Ideological Capitulation and Radical Failure in the Postsegregation Era', in Michael Peter Smith and Joe R. Feagin (eds.), *The Bubbling Cauldron: Race Ethnicity and the Urban Crisis* (Minneapolis, MN: University of Minnesota Press, 1995); Mike Davis, 'Los Angeles Was Just The Beginning', in Greg Ruggerio and Stuart Sahulka, *Open Fire* (New York: The New Press, 1993); Cornel West, 'Nihilism in Black America', in Gina Dent (ed.) *Black Popular Culture* (Boston, MA: Bay Press, 1992); Lou Kushnick, 'US: the Revocation of Civil Rights', *Race and Class*, Vol.32, No.1 (1990), pp.57–66; Manning Marable and Leith Mullings, 'The Divided Mind of Black America: Race, Ideology and Politics in the Post-Civil Rights Era', *Race and Class*, Vol.36., No.1 (1994), pp.61–72; Cornel West, 'The Crisis in Black America', in *Prophetic Reflections: Notes on Race and Power in America* (New York: Common Courage, 1993).
4. Michael C. Dawson, 'Globalization, the Racial Divide, and a New Citizenship', in Rodolfo D.Torres *et al.*, *Race, Identity and Citizenship* (Oxford: Blackwell, 1999), p.379.
5. Ibid.
6. Mike Holderness, 'Who are the World's Information Poor?', in Mike Holderness, *The Cyberspace Divide: Equality, Agency and Policy in the Information Society* (London: Routledge, 1998).
7. For example, recent growth in Internet use has been accompanied by a significant narrowing of gender inequalities amongst Internet users. Where only five years ago 10 per cent of all users were thought to be women, that figure now stands at 40 per cent and is forecast to rise to 45 per cent by 2001. This growth in women's representation on-line is driven by users in the US where it is estimated that the majority Internet users by 2001 will be women. (Source: Computer Economics at http//:www.computereconomics.com).
8. National Telecommunications and Information Administration, *Falling Through the Net: Defining the Digital Divide* (Washington, DC: US Department of Commerce, 1999), p.44.
9. Global Reach, 'Global Internet Statistics by Language', June 1999 at http://www.glreach.com/globstats/
10. National Telecommunications and Information Administration, p.43.
11. Ibid., p.44.
12. Donna L. Hoffman and Thomas P. Novak, *Bridging the Digital Divide: The Impact of Race on Computer Access and Internet Use* (Working Paper, Project 2000, Owen Graduate School of Management, Vanderbilt University, Nashville, TN: 1998), p.2.
13. Ibid., pp.2–3.
14. Ibid.
15. Donna L. Hoffman and Thomas P. Novak, *The Evolution of the Digital Divide: Examining the Relationship of Race to Internet Access and Usage Over Time* (Working Paper, Project 2000, Owen Graduate School of Management, Vanderbilt University, Nashville, TN: 1998).
16. Ibid., p.16.
17. Ibid.
18. National Telecommunications and Information Administration, pp.19 and 44.
19. Ibid., p.96.

20. Ibid., p.8.
21. Ibid.
22. According to the *Falling Through the Net* report, US households with incomes of $75,000 and above are more than twenty times more likely to have access to the Internet than those at the lowest income levels and more than *nine* times more likely to own a computer at home. Ibid., p.xiii.
23. The Council of Economic Advisers for the President's Initiative on Race, *Changing America: Indicators of Social and Economic Well-being by Race and Hispanic Origin* (Washington, DC: The Council for Economic Advisers, 1998), p.22.
24. Ibid., p.26.
25. Ibid. p.30.
26. Ibid., p.35.
27. See http://www.hud.gov/nnw/nnwfaqs.html
28. Benton Foundation, *Losing Ground Bit By Bit: Low-income Communities in the Information Age* (Washington, DC: Benton Foundation and National Urban League, 1998), p.6.
29. Barry N.Hague and Brian D.Loader, 'Digital Democracy: An Introduction', in (eds.), *Digital Democracy: Discourse and Decision Making in the Information Age* (London: Routledge, 1999), p.9.
30. See, for example, Norman Fainstein, 'Black Ghettoization and Social Mobility', in Smith and Joe Feagin (ed.), op. cit.; Barbara Ransby, 'US: The Black Poor and the Politics of Expendability', *Race and Class*, Vol.38, No.2 (1996), pp.1–12; William Julius Wilson, *The Truly Disadvantaged: The Inner City, the Underclass and Public Policy* (Chicago, IL: University of Chicago Press, 1987); Douglas Glasgow, *The Black Underclass: Poverty, Unemployment and Entrapment of Ghetto Youth* (New York: Vintage, 1981).
31. For recent examples see Robert H. Anderson *et. al.*, *Universal Access to E-mail: Feasibility and Societal Implications* (Santa Monica, CA: Rand Corporation, 1995), Ch.7; Benton Foundation, Ch.3; United Nations Development Programme, *Human Development Report* (New York: UNDP, 1999), pp.63–6.
32. Benton Foundation, op. cit., pp.17–19.
33. Ibid., pp.7–8 and 24–32.
34. Ibid., p.13.
35. The main plank of current federal government policy is the 1996 Telecommunications Act, representing the first overhaul of telecommunications policy since the 1930s. The Act covers all media, including all those utilising new digital technologies, such as the Internet. Section 706 of the Act charges the Federal Communications Commission (FCC) to ensure access to new communications media for all Americans in a 'reasonable and timely fashion'. So far, the FCC has sought, as the primary means of realizing this end, to encourage competition amongst telecommunication providers, through market liberalisation and deregulation. It has not sought to legislate for the provision of access to new digital media as many had initially hoped. For more detailed analysis, see Thomas W. Bonnet, *Telewars in the States: Telecommunications Issues in a New Era of Competition* (Hillsdale, NJ: Lawrence Erlbaum, 1996).
36. Paul Nixon and Hans Johansson, 'Transparency through Technology: The Internet and Political Parties', in Hague and Loader (eds.), *Digital Democracy*, p.141.
37. Democratic National Committee at http://www.democrats.org/index.html
38. African American Outreach at http://www.democrats.org/outreach/aa/index.html
39. Republican National Committee at http://www.rnc.org/
40. Democratic Socialists of America at http://www.dsausa.org/; Reform Party of the USA at http://reformparty.org/
41. For similar conclusions with respect to political parties in western Europe see Nixon and Johansson, op. cit., p.151.
42. The African American press has a long and rich history stretching back to 1827 and the publication in New York of *Freedom's Journal* in support of the abolitionist cause. Thereafter, a range of African American newspapers and periodicals, including the *Chicago Defender*, *Detroit Tribune*, *Pittsburgh Courier*, (New York) *Amsterdam News* and *The Crisis*, have been central to mechanisms of political communication across African America. Today,

there are estimated to be more than 200 local and national newspapers specifically directed to an African American audience. See James P. Danky (ed.), *African American Newspapers and Periodicals: A National Bibliography* (Boston, MA: Harvard University Press, 1999).

43. NAACP on-line at http://www.naacp.org/
44. Rainbow PUSH Home Page at http://www.rainbowpush.org/
45. http://www.rainbowpush.org/CEF/index.html
46. The National Urban League at http://www.nul.org
47. NUL Urban Leaders' List at http://www.nul.org/mlists/urban-leaders/
48. http://www.nul.org/resource.html
49. On the politics of the African American middle class, see Michael C.Dawson, *Behind the Mule: Race and Class in African American Politics* (Princeton, NJ: Princeton University Press, 1994); Marcus Pohlmann, *Black Politics in Conservative America* (New York: Longman, 1990).
50. This is not to suggest that the National Urban League is unconcerned with widening access amongst African Americans. The League has been at the forefront of recent campaigns seeking to highlight disparities in access to new information and communication resources within African America. See Benton Foundation, *Losing Ground Bit By Bit.*
51. The Nation of Islam's Million Man March web site is no longer on-line.
52. The Final Call Online at http://www.finalcall.com/; Nation of Islam Ministry of Health and Human Services at http://www.noihealth.org/; The Nation of Islam Student Association at http://noisa.noi.org/; NOI On-line Study Center at http://www.noi.org/study/Default.htm; Nation of Islam World Link at http://www.noi.org/teleport.html
53. These 'chat' forums are accessible via America Online's subscription-based, proprietary network and via the Black Voices public web site at www.blackvoices.com
54. On the growing support for black nationalist politics, see Dawson, 'Globalization', p.379.
55. See, for example, Rheingold, *The Virtual Community* and Budge, *The New Challenge of Direct Democracy.*
56. For one particularly prominent version of this view, see *Remarks by Vice President Al Gore* to the International Telecommunications Union Development Conference in Buenos Aires, Argentina 21 March 1994 (available from http://www.iitf.nist.gov/documents/speeches/032194_gore_giispeech.html).
57. Amongst the most prominent are Minnesota E-democracy at http://e-democracy.org/; the City of Palo Alto Online at http://www.city.palo-alto.ca.us/homepage.html; and Austin Free-Net at http://www.austinfree.net/
58. G. Scott Aikens, 'American Democracy and Computer Mediated Communication – A Case Study in Minnesota', Ph.D. thesis (University of Cambridge, 1997). Available from http://aikens.org.
59. In Minnesota only 2.9 per cent of the population is African American, while in Palo Alto the figure is 2.8 per cent and in Austin it is 12 per cent. (Sources: US Department of Census).
60. On the specificities of African American communication and signification, see, for example, Henry Louis Gates, Jr., *The Signifying Monkey: A Theory of Afro-American Literary Criticism* (New York: Oxford University Press, 1990) and Gregory Stephens, 'Rap Music's Double-Voiced Discourse: A Crossroads for Intercultural Communication', *Journal of Communication Inquiry*, Vol.15, No.2 (n.d.), pp.57–72.
61. See, for example, Charles P.Henry, *Culture and African American Politics* (Bloomington, IN: Indiana University Press, 1990), The Black Public Sphere Collective (ed.), *The Black Public Sphere* (Chicago, IL: University of Chicago Press, 1995) and Vincent P. Franklin, *Black Self-Determination: A Cultural History of African-American Resistance* (Westport, CT: Lawrence Hill, 1993 [second edn.]).
62. See, for example, Michel Foucault, 'Clarifications on the Question of Power', in *Foucault Live* (New York: Semiotexte, 1989); Barbara Laslett *et al.* (eds.), *Rethinking the Political; Gender, Resistance and the State* (Chicago, IL: University of Chicago Press, 1995); J. Farr, 'The Estate of Political Knowledge: Political Science and the State', in JoAnne Brown and David K. van Keuren (eds.), *The Estate of Social Knowledge* (Baltimore, MD: Johns Hopkins University Press, 1991); Claude Lefort, *The Political Forms of Modern Society* (Cambridge: Polity, 1986).

63. NetNoir at http://www.netnoir.com/; AfroNet at http://www.afronet.com; MelaNet at www.melanet.com; and The Black World Today at www.tbwt.com
64. See http://www.tbwt.com/views/
65. AfroNet Discussions at http://www.afronet.com/discussions/
66. Afro Chat and Message Boards at http://www.afronet.com/chat/
67. BlackNetwork.com – Politics at http://blacknetwork.netnoir.com/level0/view.cfm?ID=31
68. See, for example, AfroNet Communities at http://www.afronet.com/community/
69. Ibid.
70. Kevin A. Hill and John E. Hughes, *Cyberpolitics: Citizen Activism in the Age of the Internet* (Oxford: Rowman & Littlefield, 1998), p.22.
71. On the historical development of African American economic theory and practice, see Thomas Boston, *A Different Vision: Vol.1, African American Economic Thought* (New York: Routledge, 1996).
72. Cinque B. Sengbe, 'Black Sites That Are White Owned' available from http://www.afronet.com/blackorwhite.htm
73. Barry Cooper, CEO of the Black Voices web site, quoted in PR Newswire report, 'The Black Voices Career Center: The Internet's Most Effective Vehicle for Recruiting Qualified African-American Employees', 13 May 1999, available from www.prnewswire.com
74. On the tensions in African American politics around inclusive political strategies, see *Sojourners*, Vol.19, No.2 (n.d.). Special issue entitled 'What's Wrong with Integration?' featuring the following articles: Jim Wallis, 'From Integration to Transformation'; Anthony A. Parker, 'Whose America Is It? A New Generation Reconsiders Integration'; Manning Marable, 'The Rhetoric of Racial Harmony'; Delores S. Williams, 'Exposing False Distinctions'; and Harold W. Cruse, 'Stalled Out in History: The Past and Future of Integration'.
75. According to Dawson ('Globalization', p.379), 'A majority of blacks now believe that blacks should belong exclusively to black organizations … '.
76. Nancy Fraser, 'Rethinking the Public Sphere: A Contribution to the Critique of Actually Existing Democracy', in Craig Calhoun (ed.), *Habermas and the Public Sphere* (Boston, MA: MIT Press, 1993), p.123.
77. Ibid., p.124.

# Neo-Nazis and Taliban On-Line: Anti-Modern Political Movements and Modern Media

PETER CHROUST

Usually the Internet is seen as a new medium with great potential for enhancing citizenship and democracy. This essay will try to present and to reflect on some of the less well known sides of the world wide web. In this case the 'dark sides' of the Internet will not refer to web sites of sex and violence, which have attracted more attention, but rather to two political movements with a high presence in the Internet: on the one hand the neo-Nazis in Germany and elsewhere, and on the other hand the Taliban in Afghanistan.

At first glance a topic like the 'neo-Nazis and Taliban on-line' seems to combine very disparate societal movements that are neither new (the Nazis) nor very active in a modern environment (the Taliban). This contribution will show that both the neo-Nazis and the Taliban have important similarities in their structural approaches to society as well as in their presence in the Internet, but there are also of course serious differences. Because of this unusual comparison it will be helpful to sketch some of the context for the activities of the neo-Nazis and Taliban before we turn to the main issue.

## FROM 'SILENT REVOLUTION' TO POLITICAL VIOLENCE

First of all, both movements, the neo-Nazis as well as the Taliban, can be understood as fundamentalist societal movements with a specific social basis, a specific political ideology, and specific forms of organization, action and communication. According to contemporary political science, fundamentalist movements are reactions against the very complex, world-

---

The author's first reflections on this topic were presented at 'Politics & Internet: Second International Congress on Electronic Media and Citizenship in the Information Society', held in Espoo, Finland on 6–8 January 1999.

wide process of modernization, against the political and social crises and the deep changes of values and cultures connected with them.

Ronald Inglehart has researched this 'silent revolution' in several large-scale studies. In his recent study of 43 societies in four continents he writes not only about modernization, but also about 'post-modernization', which he presents as the predominant tendency of the past 30 years in the most industrialized countries, as well as the main trend of the near future. In Inglehart's words modernization is characterized by an interlinked process of industrialization, urbanization, mass education, vocational specialization, bureaucratization, mass communication and – following the German sociologist Max Weber – by a rationalization of all societal spheres with a dissolution of traditional ties. Post-modernization is marked by individualization, the loss of institutional authority and the increasing significance of non-materialistic needs such as demands for political participation or for the protection of natural resources.[1]

In the case of the original Nazism Jeffrey Herf wrote of a 'reactionary modernism'[2] which allowed for the coexistence of the ideology of 'blood-and-soil' and technical innovations like the autobahn and the Volkswagen, as well as high-tech projects like the V2 rocket plant in Peenemünde. In fact the social reality of Nazi Germany was much more contradictory than Herf's interpretation suggests. The drive for modernization under the National Socialist regime was connected with a more or less visible westernization and even Americanization of everyday life. Indicators of this include the propaganda for individual car-ownership, the increasing consumption of Coca-Cola (up to 1941), the copying of American musicals (*Revuefilme*) and the official ideology that put a primacy on building family homes.[3]

Now not only do the neo-Nazis use advanced technology in their internal and external communications, the socio-economic frame itself has changed dramatically. Meanwhile the neo-Nazis have to react to the challenges of a second wave of modernization. And, in a certain sense, the new Nazis are again – like their historical forerunners – a part of this development. So they attack the process of globalization, world-wide 'dollar-imperialism' and the threat of 'racial inundation'. At the same time they demand the protection of natural resources against the interests of 'profit' and the equal participation of women in the national struggle, both of which are post-materialist topics.

In the case of the Afghan Taliban the political situation is quite different.[4] Fundamentalist Islamism in Afghanistan was not produced by the crisis of a developed capitalist, industrialized society but in opposition to a vanquished model of repressive modernization behind a communist facade. Afghanistan was a feudal agrarian society with only a few industrial production enterprises and public services. In this sense, the appearance of the Taliban in 1994 marked the revenge of the traditional village against the modern city, which symbolized the 'immoral' and atheistic western culture. Nevertheless the Afghan Taliban could hardly rely upon historical precursors. The only legitimation of the Taliban's political thinking and acting is the Koran. But this has been surrounded with a greater political concept. This concept of rebuilding Afghan society is not laid down in detailed programmes but it becomes clear step by step. As far as can be seen, this concept is of strictly self-determined development, which tries to avoid the so-called 'disadvantages' of western-style modernization such as democratization and human rights.

This type of development incorporates western high technology into a political system that disregards human rights. In this respect the Afghan Taliban movement is similar to the earlier Nazi policy of bifurcated modernization, that distinguished between technological and social progress. Both of these regimes are characterized by a time-lag between an economic basis that is speeding ahead and an ideological superstructure that lags behind.

Nevertheless beside the different economic, social and cultural backgrounds between contemporary neo-Nazis in Germany and elsewhere, and the Taliban, there are also some evident ideological similarities. Both movements are

- anti-liberal and anti-capitalist
- anti-socialist and anti-communist
- anti-hegemonic (that is, anti-imperialist)
- anti-parliamentarian
- anti-semitic
- anti-feminist.

Both movements fight against western, especially American, cultural hegemony and against all that they term 'western decadence', such as recreational drugs and sexual permissiveness. And both movements use physical violence to achieve political change in their countries and to combat political enemies. The use of violence can itself be a pre-modern strategy against modernization.

In the case of the neo-Nazis there is one more specific characteristic that should be noted: the efforts for political participation inside the parliamentarian system. Obviously participation in voting campaigns and representative institutions is to some extent just a necessary stage in the strategy of gaining the political power. In truth the parliamentarian option is part of a long-term double-strategy, adapted to the political realities – a concession to the basic need for participation in post-modernized societies. By contrast the Afghan Taliban rejected the parliamentarian 'detour' from the beginning. They aimed directly at undivided political power through physical violence.

There is no room here to analyse other central reasons for the success of Taliban movement, which include the struggles inside the Afghan anti-communist opposition, the ethnic tensions, the external support by Pakistan and Saudi Arabia and the complex role of the Taliban in the geo-political strategies of Pakistan, Iran and the United States. Although the external support was necessary, it was not a sufficient cause for the Taliban success as a mass movement to emerge within only a few months.

## FROM POLITICAL VIOLENCE TO CULTURAL HEGEMONY

The strategy of both movements is not limited just to traditional political instruments. To break down the influence of 'western' thinking and behaviour the neo-Nazis as well as the Taliban pursue a policy of transforming everyday life.

In Germany, in France and in the US right-wing groups, think-tanks, newspapers, publishing houses and political parties have formulated and disseminated to the public various topics of what they call the 'political middle'. This development began almost three decades ago, mostly in a reaction against cultural changes that had taken place since the 1960s, and it has continued right up to the present.

In a distorted way they have appropriated the theory of 'cultural hegemony' of the Italian communist philosopher Antonio Gramsci, which they attempt to realize through manipulation of the media.[5] Such a concept envisages the building of ideological bridges from the new extreme right over the heads of moderate conservatives to the decision-makers of the political or moral majority. So, within only a few years or even only a few months, issues such as 'infiltration of society by foreigners', 'crimes by immigrants', 'abuse of social grants by immigrants', 'abortion by feminists' or the so-called 'Auschwitz lie' take over and dominate public debate for a long time. Influence in this way spreads to voting campaigns, party conventions, party programmes and legislative initiatives of the political establishment.

Gramsci developed his theory of cultural hegemony when analysing the left's defeat by Italian fascism in 1922. He argued that the left had first to achieve dominance over cultural life as a prerequisite for the political revolution that was to bring irreversible, societal change. Now it is right-wing movements that use precisely this theory to promote their ideas as the basis of their bid for power. However strange it may seem, Antonio Gramsci is well-known to right-wing cadres in eastern Germany, as an interview with a right-wing singer and songwriter reveals.[6]

Especially in eastern Germany the strategy for right-wing cultural hegemony bears the signs of a 'brown', grass-roots revolution.[7] Taking advantage of the political vacuum and societal anomie that followed the collapse of the East German state in 1989, west German right-wing groups very quickly founded branches in the former German Democratic Republic. For example the youth organization of the oldest established neo-Nazi party, the German National Democratic Party (Nationaldemokratische Partei Deutschlands, NPD) transferred their federal office to Dresden. Right-wing groups could find excellent conditions there for their ideology and propaganda. The ideal of a socially 'warm', ethnically homogeneous community (*Volksgemeinschaft*) is now retro-projected on to the defunct German Democratic Republic so as to appear as the antithesis of the 'coldness' of capitalism. The political tradition of the former East German society with its neighbourhood solidarity and absolute social security was played up as a counter to the new reality of competition, individualization and erosion of moral values.

These real everyday experiences are combined particularly among east German youth with an anti-communist attitude, which is very often a generational protest against parents and their political orientation. Although in eastern Germany young people are the main basis of all neo-Nazi groups, right-wing ideologists try to build inter-generational bridges. So young militants of the right give assistance to older persons with problems of everyday life, organize music concerts to raise funds for right-wing causes, and they act as paramilitary forces against drug-dealers and criminals from among the immigrant community to 'protect' the older generation with their fears of robbery and social misery. It is worth noting here that the proportion of foreign citizens in all eastern German communities combined (excluding Berlin) is lower than in a single west German medium-sized town like Duisburg or Dortmund. This makes for a curious resemblance between the phenomenon in some places in pre-war Germany where there was an 'anti-semitism without Jews', in that now eastern Germany has a strong xenophobia despite being almost devoid of foreigners.

The next steps in the 'brown' cultural revolution are the establishment of 'free zones' (*befreite Zonen*), where right-wing, mostly male, young people dominate the public sphere to the exclusion of any other political behaviour and skin colour. In concentric circles they first conquer single buildings (such as pubs, youth centres and bookshops), then neighbourhoods, streets and complete quarters as in Cottbus or Frankfurt an der Oder on the Polish border. Fighting against drug-dealers and 'foreign criminals', the right-wing 'storm-troopers' hunt punks, coloured political refugees or just 'social deviants' like homosexuals or handicapped citizens. 'Cleansing' streets, playgrounds and neighbourhoods from drugs and crime, the right-wing paramilitary groups attack persons whom they accuse of being the perpetrators of these crimes. The aim is to achieve 'ethnically cleansed' villages and cities – like the 'Jew-free' (*judenfrei*) communities under National Socialism. To a certain extent east Germany is the laboratory for a greater experiment: the transfer of a new political strategy to the whole of Germany.

This strategy of German neo-Nazis is not unique, as a comparison with some other countries demonstrates. In France the Front National (FN) tries to redirect cultural life and the collective memory in communities where they win power. Thus in Southern Orange the local FN mayor banned left-wing books from public libraries and ordered instead publications propagandizing the 'Auschwitz-lie'. Such a campaign aims at breaking political taboos and also the 'cultural hegemony' of the left, which in the view of the FN has dominated France since the 1920s. The movement of Jean-Marie le Pen was one of the first European right-wing parties to come out with xenophobic propaganda against coloured immigrants, playing on inferiority feelings among modernization's losers. This policy culminated in the slogan 'Les français d'abord' ('French people first').

Another example of the right-wing politicization of everyday life can be found in Belgium, where the 'Vlaams blok' received in some local elections (e.g. in Antwerp) the greatest share of the votes. The struggle against the infiltration of the suburbs and against crimes by immigrants from the Maghreb and Asia is one of the central issues for this very successful party. The slogan of the Vlaams blok, 'Eigen volk eerst' ('One's own people first'), is a copy of their French counterparts.

At the beginning of the 1990s an equivalent of the French slogan was also adopted by the 'Deutsche Volks-Union' ('German People's Union'), when agitating against European Monetary Union. The diffusion of this slogan testifies to ideological exchange and real international contacts between the 'national' groups. It should be mentioned, that the German 'Republicans'

(*Republikaner*), another established right-wing party, the Front National, the Vlaams blok and other parties like the Italian post-fascist 'Allianza Nazionale' are in close co-operation in the European parliament. Of course, the new media facilitate communication between the new right in various European countries. Further a leading cadre of the French Front National asserted (1996) an identity between their policy and the programme of the right-wing presidential candidate in the US, Pat Buchanan.[8]

The particular constellation of political, social and intergenerational factors, supported by strong and clever efforts at political propaganda, has produced a dominant trend in east German society within the last decade, where today it is 'cool' to be right-wing – and more and more normal for a great part of east German youth. Like the younger generations in other industrialized countries too, young east Germans are interested in computers, video-games and the Internet. Precisely these new media play an important role in the modern propaganda of right-wing groups, as will be shown in the next section.

In Afghanistan the Taliban aim to transform everyday life by physical violence so as to roll back 'western' influence and Marxist relicts, particularly in education, professional life and the mass media. The extreme brutality of the Taliban's policy of Islamization may result from an imagined double threat: from the former communist regime and from western civilization. Therefore Afghan women probably are the predetermined victims of the Taliban's oppression: girls in classrooms, women in lecture-halls and in offices symbolized the communist 'heritage' as well as the influence of westernization, which merged at this point into a single phenomenon. So the Taliban's fight for cultural hegemony in their own country includes simultaneously campaigns against foreign forces and attacks against members of their own population.

These selected examples show that the confrontation of modernization and fundamentalism is more complex than Samuel Huntington implied in his account of the 'clash of civilizations'.[9] The 'cleavages' not only result from a cultural struggle between nations or greater cultural spheres but also can arise out of conflicts inside each society.[10]

Now it is time to turn to the function and impact of the Internet in the plans for cultural hegemony by neo-Nazis and Taliban.

## PUBLIC SPHERE AND POLITICAL HYPER-TEXT

Both the neo-Nazis and the Taliban have a high presence on the Internet. Even allowing for the enormous differences in economic and social development between highly industrialized societies like Germany, France or the US on the one side and Afghanistan on the other side, the new media play a distinguished role also in the political propaganda and communication of the *opponents* of modernization and globalization. The fundamentalist movements like the neo-Nazis and Taliban in extremely disparate societies have obviously accepted that the path towards cultural and political hegemony today leads over the information superhighway.

That explains why the Taliban invest financial resources and manpower in their presence on the Internet. That most of the Afghan population have no electric light and even are illiterate, let alone have access to the world wide web, is not such a paradox as it first seems.

The presence of the neo-Nazis and Taliban on the Internet creates a new three-dimensional public sphere. Going beyond the first two dimensions of the printed media and radio and television, the world wide web enables a thicker structure of political networks through a system of electronic links. Now not only is it possible to have communication from some to many (by newspapers, radio, television), but also from many to many and even from all to all (Internet-users). Consequently an open medium like the Internet endangers established information hierarchies.

The use of the Internet in right-wing political organizations causes additional problems. Strictly hierarchical organizations like the German neo-Nazi groups have to balance the needs for mass propaganda and high attraction for young users against the needs for more effective internal communication and for 'fire-walls' against investigations by intelligence services. So realities outside the web are also reflected in the virtual reality of the Internet. For example, skinhead meetings with a right-wing background are often announced on the web for mobilizing more participants, while internal communication between the different levels of leadership of the organization is achieved behind closed electronic doors. Access to the centres of power and internal information pools is blocked by passwords and the necessity for several guarantors. Nevertheless the publicly accessible web sites are informative enough about many relations and sufficient for political analysis.

Of course, the Afghan Taliban in their fight for cultural hegemony are confronted with other tasks and questions, but they also face similar problems to those of the neo-Nazis. A political movement originating from the Afghan refugee camps and Koran schools in Pakistan seems an unlikely user of high technology in their internal and external communication. Afghanistan is a society with one of the world's highest proportion of illiterates, with an infrastructure that has been almost completely destroyed by the years of fighting. So who is likely to take part in the electronic public sphere? Who reads the voluminous web sites of 'Taliban On-line'?[11]

In fact, it is unlikely that the Internet is much used outside the Taliban leadership for internal communication. But in the longer term the basis of religious education, even when it is rudimentary and doctrinaire, could be fertile soil for the spread of this new medium. As states like Malaysia, the United Arab Emirates and others demonstrate, such a development is no contradiction. Also the flat or non-hierarchical structure of the Taliban, which is emphasized in several reports, could be 'compatible' with the sometimes anarchic Internet.

In this respect the decision of the anti-modern Taliban to use the web right now – despite the actual restrictions – could be very far-sighted. Limited access to the 'Taliban Online' will probably be just a problem of transition. As experiments in Africa and Asia (for example as financed by the Grameen Bank in Bangladesh)[12] show, there will be possibilities for public access in so-called 'Cyber-Kiosks' to the Internet through telephone exchanges or by portable satellite phones in the near future. Such concepts not only allow public Internet access to the population in the countryside. Of the same importance is also the web-based access of rural producers to national and international markets, the escape from the tyranny of local money-lenders and the chance for an autonomous economic life for women by managing the cyber-kiosks.

Up to now, the main purpose of 'Taliban On-line' seems to be external public communication with the new political and information elites of the Islamic 'freedom-fighters' in Afghanistan, communications within the Islamic world and worldwide propaganda for the ideas of the Taliban movement. For the purposes of external communication, electronic links lead within a few seconds from the home-page 'Taliban On-line' to all Islamic countries and political movements – up to and including the KLA fighters in Kosovo.

The example of the Taliban shows that even a society with the lowest economic resources is not condemned to remain an electronic 'have-not'. Thanks to their own worldwide networks, Afghan students living in London or elsewhere are able to be web-masters for the daily updated home page of the Taliban army fighting some thousand miles away, though they admit to difficulty in regularly updating material. This fact is like an inversion of the new global electronic economy, where, for example, young Indian women work in south Indian call-centres for European airlines, or in the Indian silicon valleys where highly qualified specialists work for German insurance companies. Because of the economic dynamics of the new media itself, the monopoly in using the Internet exclusively by the first world has been broken.

In the public sphere of the world wide web the former technological 'have-nots' appear for the first time as equal communication partners in the electronic agora. To a certain extent the virtual community of the Internet emancipates its users from many of the real limitations outside the net. The long-term consequences for the relationship between North and South, East and West – and within each society – are potentially revolutionary.

Despite its current limitations the new third dimension of the public sphere enlarges the scope for political publicity by overcoming time and space. Within the general universe of neo-Nazi web sites, the Internet permits an electronic tour within a few minutes from a right-wing German rockband to the 'Thule-Net' or the North-American 'White Aryan Resistance', from the 'Zündel-Site' via the 'Jewish Joke Center' (now apparently defunct) to the 'Stormfront' web-site or to the French 'Front National'.[13]

Paradoxically national borders, which are one of the central concerns in right-wing ideology, lose their importance for right-wing groups on the Internet. Instead this medium establishes a world-wide electronic network which supports the creation of an international right-wing culture. This comprises members of the American Ku-Klux-Klan as well as German skinheads or French academics wanting to revise the written history of the Second World War. In opposition to the new world-wide 'hyper-bourgeoisie'[14] the Internet promotes the rise of their political opposites as 'hyper-nazis' or 'hyper-fundamentalists'.

Of course, even before the Internet age there existed transatlantic communications between German and North-American neo-Nazis. For example lots of propaganda material concerning the 'Auschwitz-lie' has been printed since the 1960s by the German-American Gary Lauck in Nebraska because of the more liberal laws there and distributed in west Germany. Conversely US-American right-wing journals like *White Aryan Resistance* published full pages of advertisment for German revisionist literature, videos and Nazi militaria.

Nevertheless the Internet leads, beside a growing community of active communicators, to an acceleration of political communication on the right. As consequence the transmission of ideological topics from the new right or neo-Nazi groups to the political centre is presumably easier. But there are also certain unintended side-effects: a growing pool of information among web participants *outside* the right-wing organizations about their programmes, profiles and activities.

And with the growing international communication on the web political leaders, even right-wing ones, find it difficult to maintain the aura of their authority. So, for example, when young, right-wing, German women chat on the Internet about the 'machismo' of male neo-Nazi leaders, such topics can be discussed merely a few hours later in the US or elsewhere by anyone with the requisite linguistic competence.

Meanwhile internal communication using the new media on the right-wing scene seems to have become so normal that it is mentioned for example in the first US movie dealing with American neo-Nazis. The only old person in this film, the ideological mentor and secret commander of a Californian Neo Nazi-group is made to say that their internal communication is 'anyhow [realized] on the Internet'.[15]

The Internet creates – in the cases both of the neo-Nazis and the Taliban – a political hyper-text which goes beyond traditional political communication. This hyper-text is more than the sum of thousands of right-wing or fundamentalist news items, articles and electronic letters. This daily increasing and changing communication can be read as a collective anti-modern answer to the challenges of modernization and post-modernization. Unlike in the traditional media, this electronic text is written by thousands of writers, even when in organizations like the neo-Nazis and the Taliban probably some of the material is edited.

Very often to this political hyper-text also belong the (electronic) voices of political opponents: the home-pages, networks and chat-rooms of anti-fascist German students, American 'hate watchers' or British feminist organizations which publicize the human rights situation in Afghanistan.

The enormous advantages of using the Internet cause contradictory problems for movements like neo-Nazis and Taliban. On the one hand this new medium opens – even for a few people with a low budget – a global audience, an enormous field for political propaganda. On the other hand the presentation on the web and the links to other similar, friendly organizations make the national and international networks public. By this medium underground structures become partially public, co-operation via the Internet leaves electronic traces. This facilitates observations by, for instance, the counter-intelligence services, even though the German services apparently do not lay great stress on observing the activities of both of these movements on the Internet.

## THE INTERNET, POLITICAL BEHAVIOUR AND POLITICAL ACTION

To right-wing groups the Internet not only serves as an electronic mail-box. It also enables the distribution of ideologies for political training of the cadres – and for reaching interested people outside the real network. For example one of the voluminous right-wing web-sites, 'Stormfront', contains in the German version a detailed handbook on the Nazi version of the 'third way', on 'free zones', on 'political action', on 'the age of the end of parties' and on the question 'how to organize?'.

The theoretical construct of this third way is quite similar to the concepts of the so-called social revolutionary wing of the early Nazi movement, which was presented by the brothers Gregor and Otto Strasser, and of ideas from national bolshevism, propounded by Ernst Niekisch in the Weimar republic. Both currents of ideas proclaimed a path for economic and political development that was very different from both capitalism and communism. Without the web probably most Internet-readers would never had heard about these political theories. Probably they also would never have tried to read a 60-year-old book from a Romanian fascist leader. The Internet article on the third way offers a biography of the founder of the Romanian fascist Iron Guard, Corneliu Zelea Codreanu,[16] as a heroic model. Codreanu had killed 'a traitor' (in truth, a prefect) and was not sentenced by the judge because of the latter's openly declared sympathy for the young fascist murderer. In the Internet story the case of Codreanu becomes a pleading for the right to use might against the 'reactionary system'. The Romanian regime failed to bring in a sentence because of the pressure of popular opinion and to avoid riots. In the eyes of the web-site author, the regime still had its political power, but it had already lost its moral authority among the majority, that is its cultural hegemony. The author concludes: 'This kind of counter-power is stronger than thousands of machine guns, TVs or electronic bugs.'[17]

To the neo-Nazi groups the web serves as an electronic transmission belt for changing public and private everyday life. An anti-authoritarian gesture, a raw protest against political correctness becomes a public event. So articles contain biting and sexist invectives against feminist-inspired orthographic reforms in the official German language. Adapting the skinhead music shout 'oi', words like *Deutschland* and *Euthanasie* (euthanasia) are changed to 'Doitschland' and 'Oithanasie' in the right-wing web-sites. Even computer terms, which in Germany are commonly used in English, are 'Germanized', for example 'home page' becomes 'Heimat-Seite'. Home pages and right-wing web texts are frequently marked with '88', which is a cypher for the repeated eighth letter in the German alphabet, that is 'h', 'HH' standing for 'Heil Hitler'. With such cyphers individuals and groups can project 'key-words' into the public sphere of the Internet without infringing existing laws. New linguistic terms and behaviour patterns can be sown on the Internet and taken up by young users much more quickly than before.

The fight for cultural hegemony is not only a struggle over language. The right-wing counter-culture which is shown on the web includes material goods too – and encouragement for using them in a certain manner. The Internet offers right-wing literature, posters, compact discs, music videos, video-games and T-shirts that are popular among young people, especially males, even when they are not intrinsically associated with the right. In Germany such offers also today have the touch of a subversive protest against established political culture. They still have the aura of taboo-breaking which itself is fascinating for young people, irrespective of contents and context. For example, in east German classrooms order forms for right-wing literature and fashion accessories are circulated openly. Because of peer group pressure, the pupils mostly demonstrate support for the neo-Nazis by ordering right-wing goods as a way of provoking teachers.

The electronic entrepreneurs of the neo-Nazi scene use this ambivalent attitude very intelligently in their offers. So their virtual warehouse catalogue lists side by side offers for publications on the 'Auschwitz lie' and clothes like 'Pitbull' T-shirts.

Dealing with the hegemonic strategy of a counter-culture consequently leads to the main point of difference between current neo-Nazis and the grass-roots movements of the 1960s, from whom the right-wing groups copied some cultural techniques. In this context it should be remembered that the first experiments in using personal computers for social and political communication were made in the west-coast 'future-labs' in the post-'flower power' age. Computer freaks and rural communities tried to create networks by electronic media. What in the 1960s and 1970s was enthusiastically called TV – or electronic – democracy[18] now returns to a new, fundamentalist, counter-culture. The new phenomenon today is not only the ideological shift from left or liberal to right-wing and anti-liberal attitudes, from a sometimes naive belief in human progress to a fanatic intolerance. One of the most important differences between the counter-culture 30 years ago and the current right-wing and fundamentalist groups today is the intention of the former movement to develop separate, autonomous and non-hierarchical spheres which anticipate a concrete societal utopia. In contrast to this model the neo-Nazis and the Taliban aim at complete control and rule over the whole of society by eliminating all opponents.

A further distinction between both grass-roots movements is the role and the acceptance of physical violence as an instrument for gaining political ends. Finally, a new point is also that the monopoly over control of high technology has broken down in the process of globalization. Now the electronic have-nots also increasingly take part in the virtual global village. Despite the fact that leadership of this community still largely comes from the northern hemisphere, this is a new quality that will change the web structure in future.

Up to now, the relations between presence and communication on the Internet and real political action are not quite clear. As the community networks in the US and other countries teach, there is no possible sustained and living Internet presence for political movements without a real basis in social life. International Internet campaigns, such as against regimes disregarding human rights, have always been accompanied by, and did not replace, social movements. In this respect, the Internet merely reflects political life in front of the screen, even though a few active people might be able to create a 'virtual' social movement as well.

As is known from political research on activism, first of all individuals who are not very tightly linked with the institutions of political life find it easier to agree with unconventional means of political communication, such as signing a manifesto, taking part in a meeting and so on. So it could be expected that young people in particular would be inclined to new forms of political participation such as the Internet offers. Commonly women are also disproportionately represented in this group of unconventional citizens. Up to now, the image of a high-tech medium seems to scare women away from using the Internet as an instrument for political chat-rooms and voting campaigns. But as many experiences in schools and universities show, this restriction may well be just a transitional phenomenon.

Actually the terms of political action and of participation itself have been changed by the Internet. As shown above, the authors of right-wing web sites in particular intend to redirect everyday behaviour so as to achieve cultural hegemony. On the other hand, participation in Internet-based community networks or in electronic voting campaigns requires more than the traditional role of the citizen.[19]

Scenarios of a 'cyber-war' launched by left-wing web terrorists, such as the RAND corporation's analyst David Ronfeldt has developed, seem at present not very realistic.[20] Much more realistic seems the future of an Internet access to a greater public also in the developing countries, which could lead to a higher presence of social and political conflicts on the web. So the 'electronic struggles' between movements like the neo-Nazis and Anti-Nazi groups, or between the Taliban and human rights watchers will become more common on the Web.

Already there are worrying signs of this. Some German neo-Nazis who name themselves 'Anti-Antifa' publish lists and circulars of 'wanted' left-wing persons on the Internet. A very troubling case became public in 1999 when the homepage of 'Davids Kampfgruppe' (David's combat-group) published the detailed personal profile of a young man living in south-west Germany. Beside identification marks his name, home address and the address of his workplace was announced on the web, even the bus route he took to work. The 'wanted' circular was accompanied by comments like: 'You can catch him on the way from the bus stop to the firm.' And: 'Anyone able to build letter bombs should urgently send one to him.' For proof of his death a reward of 15,000 Deutsche Mark was offered.

The reason for this Internet-based appeal was that the target is allegedly 'hunting Nazis and hanging about with Russians'.[21] 'Russians' here means families who returned to Germany in recent years after they had lived in Tsarist Russia and the Soviet Union for two centuries. Incidentally this terminology marks a change in right-wing ideology. While in the Second World War the Nazis called this population 'Volksdeutsche' and tried to settle them in places such as the occupied 'Generalgouvernement', in order to replace murdered Jewish people, the new radical right names them 'Russians' and sees them as enemies. The same mechanism of ethnic denigration is applied to persons returning from Poland. Obviously the circle of '*volkisch*' exclusion has become definitely tighter. Under the conditions of current German multicultural society the traditional right-wing views of patterns of ethnicity have changed. It is also worth mentioning in this context that this appeal used the term Nazis instead of neo-Nazis.

In this case the author of the 'Davids Kampfgruppe' web page murder appeal could be uncovered by the Federal Secret Service. He was a young skinhead who had recently been freed from prison on parole. Because right-wing web-sites like the 'Stormfront' web site are often managed by servers in the US punishment in German courts is very difficult. But the experiences of attempting to ban right-wing groups and parties in recent years show that there is no problem for them in creating new groups bearing different names within days. Actually, the new media shorten the time needed to create a new home page to a few hours. So the number of right-wing home pages increased between 1998 and 1999 from about 200 to about 300.

## CONCLUSION AND COUNTER-STRATEGIES

This inquiry has shown how the movements of both the neo-Nazis and the Taliban reject the process of globalization and its 'negative' consequences, particularly in the sphere of culture. But in a very contradictory manner both movements take part in the global political network – and actively use the very symbol of high-tech globalization for their own political propaganda and communication.

To counter them it will be necessary to search for a realistic political and societal strategy to respond to both of these fundamentalist phenomena in the public sphere. Of course, actions such as the 'appel de la vigilance' of Pierre Bourdieu and dozens of French intellectuals against the growing influence of the Front National in French society are necessary.[22] But, equally, manifestos like this are no more adequate in themselves than were the million candles lit in Germany against the neo-Nazis' xenophobic violence some years ago.

In addition to such forms of symbolic politics, it seems more likely that an effective answer over the long term will have to be found in developing the spirit and behaviour of civic society in everyday life. Permanent efforts to achieve will have to take place in families, class-rooms, lecture-halls, offices, factories – and media like the Internet. However influential the Internet may become, it cannot in itself provide an answer to the threat of right-wing groups without being backed by some active commitment from society at large.

## NOTES

1. Ronald Inglehart, *Modernization and Postmodernization* (Princeton, NJ: Princeton University Press, 1997).
2. Jeffrey Herf, *Reactionary Modernism. Technology, Culture, and Politics in Weimar and the Third Reich* (Cambridge: Cambridge University Press, 1984).
3. Hans-Dieter Schäfer, *Das gespaltene Bewusstsein. Deutsche Kultur und Lebenswirklichkeit 1933–1945* (Munich: Hanser, 1981).
4. William Maley (ed.), *Fundamentalism Reborn? Afghanistan and the Taliban* (London: Hurst, 1998).
5. Joseph A. Buttigieg (ed.), *Antonio Gramsci. The Prison Notebooks* (Chicago, IL: University of Notre Dame Press, 1991).
6. *Süddeutsche Zeitung*, 23 Nov. 1998.
7. Bernd Wagner, *Rechtsextremismus und kulturelle Subversion in den neuen Ländern. Studie* (Berlin: Zentrum Demokratische Kultur, 1998).
8. Martin A. Lee, *The Beast Reawakens* (Boston, MA: Little, Brown, 1997), p.370.
9. Samuel P. Huntington, *The Clash of Civilizations* (New York: Simon & Schuster, 1996).
10. Stein Rokkan *et al.*, *State Formation, Nation-Building, and Mass Politics in Europe. The Theory of Stein Rokkan, Based on his Collected Works* (Oxford: Oxford University Press, 1999).
11. See the 'Taliban Online' portal: http://www.ummah.net/taliban
12. David Bornstein, *The Price of a Dream. The Story of the Grameen Bank* (Chicago, IL: University of Chicago Press, 1997).
13. For a link list of right-wing web-sites, see
'Stormfront': http://www.stormfront.org/german.htm
'Thule-Net': http://thulenet.com

'White Aryan Resistance': http://aryan.com
http://www.crusader.net/index.html
http://www.nizkor.org/hweb/orgs/american/war (antiracist Web-Site with links to other right-wing groups)
'Zündel-Site': http://www.webcom.com/~ezundel/
'Hate Directory' (Hate Watch): http://www.bcpl.net/~rfrankli/hatedir.htm
http://www.hatewatch.org
http://www.adl.org (Anti-Defamation League)

14. Denis Duclos, 'L'hyperbourgeoisie internationale', *Le Monde Diplomatique*, Aug. 1998.
15. Film *American History X*, directed by Tony Kaye, 1998.
16. Corneliu Zelea Codreanu, *Eiserne Garde* (Berlin: Brunnen, 1939; reprinted Munich: Colectia Omul Nou, 1972 (5th edition)).
17. http://www.stormfront.org/german/htm
18. N. Johnson, *How to Talk Back to Your TV Set* (Boston, MA: Little Brown, 1970); Michael Shamberg, *Guerrilla Television* (New York: Holt, Rinehart & Watson, 1971); Michael Rossman, *On Learning and Social Change* (New York Random House, 1972); Monroe E. Price, *Cable TV: a Guide for Citizen Action* (Philadelphia, PA: Pilgrim Press, 1972).
19. Douglas Schuler, *New Community Networks. Wired for Change* (Reading, MA: Addison-Wesley, 1996); Steven E. Miller, *Civilizing Cyberspace. Policy, Power, and the Information Superhighway* (Reading, MA: Addison-Wesley, 1995).
20. John Arquilla and David Ronfeldt, *Advent of Netwar* (Santa Monica, CA: Rand Corporation, 1996). Also D. Ronfeldt and Ian O. Lesser (eds.), *Countering the New Terrorism* (Santa Monica, CA: Rand Corporation, 1999).
21. All quotations from *Süddeutsche Zeitung,* 14 July 1999.
22. *Le Monde,* 14 July 1996.

# The Internet in Indonesia's New Democracy

DAVID T. HILL and KRISHNA SEN

The most abiding image of the Indonesian struggle for independence from the Dutch is that of the steely-eyed young (usually male) revolutionary (*pemuda*), his long black hair tied back in the red-and-white colours of the Indonesian flag, clutching a sharpened bamboo spear. The image of the *pemuda* still adorns public memorials across the archipelago, representing the romantic revolutionary youth.

In May 1998 the *pemuda* were again out in force on the streets of Indonesia, long-haired, and nationalism's familiar red-and-white still around their forehead. But for the students who spear-headed the fall of the former general, Suharto, after 32 years in the presidency, '[I]nstead of fighting with bamboo spears, swords, guns or tanks, they used banners, placards, the mass media and the Internet'.[1] The movement to overthrow Suharto 'was the first revolution using the Internet'.[2]

The question addressed here is not whether this new vector of communication, with anarchic freedoms built into the technology, *caused* the erosion of a structure of political control that had been maintained for three decades in part by a complex structure of propaganda and censorship. It will always be difficult to pin down such an historic change to one or even a small number of factors. We look instead at the Internet as one of the instruments used by groups opposed to Suharto's 'New Order' to communicate publicly, but beyond the state's control. But this deliberate use of the technology needs to be seen within a more complex process of the emergence of an Indonesian 'public sphere' on the Internet.

Habermas's theorization of the public sphere is widely cited in recent critical understanding of the relation between media and politics. The argument, that industrialization and the attendant commercialization of the media eroded the 'public sphere' where citizens as collectives could formulate and express their opinion, has been taken up repeatedly in the

This study is part of a larger research project on the Internet in Indonesia that is funded by an Australia Research Council grant.

theorizations of democracy in the west.[3] It is easy to see the Internet as a foil to commercial and state-controlled media – a medium not owned by anyone and so where everyone can speak – and thus a space where public opinion can be formulated, debated, expressed without being overwhelmed by commercial or state intervention. Whatever the situation in the advanced capitalist democracies, in Suharto's Indonesia, a public sphere, or in Hewison and Rodan's more limiting (but also more clearly located in the Southeast Asian context) term 'political space',[4] was obviously highly restricted. Print and audio-visual media were strictly censored and increasingly concentrated in the hands of a small coterie of powerful commercial interests. The Internet arrived in Indonesia already valorized as a 'technology of freedom', and became the space where frustrations and aspirations – not all political, and certainly not all 'democratic' – excluded from state and commercialized platforms, could be expressed. This account starts, therefore, with an examination of the ways in which the Internet in the 1990s became rapidly anchored into urban Indonesia's economic, political and cultural practices. For that made possible the targeted use of the medium in both the overthrow of Suharto's authoritarian rule and since then in the efforts to institutionalize electoral democracy in Indonesia.

## THE INTERNET IN INDONESIA[5]

Driven by the promise of information-led economic development, the Indonesian government, like many others in the region, facilitated the establishment and expansion of the 'Net' throughout the country. In 1986 the National Research Council (Dewan Riset Nasional), under B.J. Habibie, then Minister for Research and Technology (and subsequently brief successor to President Suharto), recommended the development of science and technology information services. Over subsequent years this policy crystallized into the design for the information Network, IPTEKNet, connecting major universities, research centres and government instrumentalities. IPTEKNet began offering global Internet access in June 1994, and remained the major non-commercial Internet provider for the research sector.[6]

Indeed much of the groundwork for the 'information superhighway' in Indonesia was laid by what one industry executive dubbed 'Habibie's kids', the generation of foreign- and locally-trained technologists who benefitted from Habibie's 'grand vision' of a high-technology Indonesia, leapfrogging into the twenty-first century. In the 1980s they staffed the universities and research centres like the Agency for the Assessment and Application of

Technology and the Indonesian Aeronautics and Space Institute, both chaired by Habibie, promoting the concept of, and subsequently trialing, the Internet. In the mid-1990s the same people established the first commercial Internet companies. IndoInternet (known as Indo.Net) and RADNet commenced services to the public in mid-1995. At the close of the year there were five commercial Internet Service Providers (ISPs). A year later 22 ISPs were listed with the Directorate-General of Tourism, Post and Telecommunications.[7] By May 1997, on the eve of the Asian financial crisis, the government had issued permits to 41 ISPs, of which 32 appeared to be operational.

With IPTEKNet increasingly accessible to academic staff in the major universities, and with the progressive appearance of private commercial ISPs in the metropolitan areas of Java, the Internet was developing a public profile in Indonesia. Businesses which recognized the commercial imperative of acquiring new technologies found highly skilled young technicians staffing the emerging ISP companies who were able to provide the know-how to get middle and large national and multinational companies linked into the Net. Concurrently, the technological advances were improving the speed and efficiency of Internet communication. In 1994 the connection speed from Indonesia via IPTEKNet, the sole provider, was only 64 Kbps (Kilobytes per second). In 1995 this had increased tenfold to 640 Kbps, and by October 1996, it exceeded 7Mbps (Megabytes per second).[8]

The economic potential of the Indonesian market for Internet technologies was evident. In 1997 the country was included by the *Inter@ctive Week* as one of the 'Emerging 20' nations offering 'a plethora of untouched opportunities for expanding the Internet'. The Latin American, Asian and Eastern European countries listed were noted for having 'two qualities that make them extremely attractive to U.S. equipment providers: All are in their technological beginnings and all are headed by governments that realize the vital need for advanced communications to sustain an economy in the new Internet frontier.'[9]

The exact number of Internet users in Indonesia is notoriously difficult to establish. At the close of 1995 there were estimated to be 15,000 Internet users in the country. A year later the estimate stood at about 40,000 subscribers.[10] In these early years, industry insiders, like Henri K. Sumartono from RADNet, predicted an annual growth of 100 per cent, between 40–50 per cent of this in the government or university sectors, which had access to non-commercial service providers (like IPTEKNet).[11] In the year after the Asian financial crisis, which hit Indonesia in July 1997, the growth in subscription numbers slowed and remained at about 85,000 through 1997–98.[12] However, by June 1999, at the time of the first post-Suharto general election, a deputy chairperson of the Indonesian Association of Internet Service Providers (APJII) estimated that there were 200,000 Internet subscribers, a fivefold increase in the two-and-a-half years since the end of 1996.[13] Even with this constant growth since its introduction in 1995, Internet subscribers still only account for a minute 0.1 per cent of the country's 210 million inhabitants.

Subscription numbers, however, provide only a very incomplete picture of the extent of Internet usage. The APJII official cited above emphasized that within subscribing companies many staff would use the service, and within a home, several members may use the same subscription, raising the number of people with access to the Net substantially above the total of financial subscribers. In Indonesia the practice of sharing passwords and accounts seems common. And estimates that each copy of a newspaper reaches about six readers indicated that the mere 200,000 subscriptions could be providing access to thousands, even hundreds of thousands more.

More importantly, the provision of public access points puts the technology within reach of people who could not afford a computer or even a telephone connection. In 1996 PT Pos Indonesia (the postal service privatized in June 1995) joined with Telekom (formerly the state monopoly and the largest telecommunications company in Indonesia) and the Telecommunications Technology College (STT Telkom) to establish the ISP, Wasantara.Net, to offer Internet services through local nodes in every provincial capital and other major cities. Pos Indonesia had been using Internet internally from about 1988 but around 1993 it began exploring the possibility of offering public Internet services, developing plans for *Warpostron* (electronic mail kiosks) at post offices, parallelling existing arrangements for long-distance fax and telephone facilities.

The popularity of public access Internet emulated an earlier boom in public telephone and facsimile services, through the government-owned and private '*wartel*' (*warung telekomunikasi*, telecommunication kiosks) which began to dot the Indonesian urban landscape in the mid-1980s. By the early 1990s there were 25,000 public phones and 800 *wartel* around the country,[14] with the latter, particularly, used frequently for semi-public political communication.[16] Expansion of the *wartel* continues.[16] Many *wartel* added Internet to their existing telecommunications facilities, and adopted the name '*wartelNet*' (Internet telecommunication kiosks). As numbers grew, the West Java branch of the Association of Indonesian Telecommunication Kiosk Managers (APWI) even established their own mailing list to provide support for *wartelNet* proprietors and customers.[17] By the end of 1998,

Wasantara.Net was accessible to subscribers in more than 100 cities and towns throughout the archipelago[18] with public access points in most provincial centres.

A cursory search of Internet directories shows over 50 commercial public access points (in addition to Wasantara's kiosks), mostly cafes or university campuses in major cities like Jakarta and Surabaya, or the tourist destination of Bali. But increasingly they are springing up in shopping malls or bookshops, across the country in provincial towns like Malang, Manado, Semarang or Palembang.[19] In Yogyakarta, there were three *warNet* at the end of 1996, and more than 20 by mid-1999. According to *Infokomputer*, Indonesia's premier computer magazine, 'The mission of these [cyber] cafes and restaurants is always the same, that is, to enable the introduction and expansion of the Internet through different sections of the community.'[20]

A questionnaire e-mailed at random to two dozen *warNet* in September 1999, indicated a wide range of average daily users. In Ubud, Bali, one small café had less than ten users daily, another had 60, while still others had 50–80. A West Jakarta 'Internet corner' had between 10 and 20, while a chain of four *warNet* in Bogor had between 30 and 60 at each location. Our observations in Yogyakarta in 1996 suggested that most clients of the *warNet* were young Indonesian males. These were not Jakarta's ' mobile-phone and McDonalds'[21] crowd who had become iconic of Asia's new urban middle class in the early 1990s. The *warNet* users in Yogyakarta rode in on buses and motor bikes, and even on bicycles, ate in the cheap road-side stalls, the *warung,* from which the *warNet* had derived their nick-name. Prior to the financial crisis of 1997, hourly rental rates in Yogyakarta *warung* could be as little as Rp 5,000 an hour, that is just under US$2 at the pre-crisis exchange rate. Their counterparts in Jakarta charged two to three times that amount. A profile of the Jakarta's six Internet Cafes in early 1997 and usage figures from our own random survey suggest, also, that these were on the whole less busy than many of their provincial counterparts. The *warNet* seem to be much more a phenomenon of the larger provincial centres like Yogyakarta or Bandung where there is sufficient technological and educational capacity to create a market for the Internet but not the level of wealth required for widespread personal ownership of computers or private access to phone-lines. In Jakarta, too, most of the Internet cafes were located in areas where they might easily reach high-school students, young office workers and families.[22]

A recent prediction from the deputy chairperson of APJII that Internet users would grow by one million per year may be overly optimistic if one is thinking of numbers of subscriptions. What is clear is that the growth of public access Internet points, such as the *warNet*, has opened up the net to a substantial population beyond those formally subscribing to a commercial ISP, and indeed into income groups where the Internet would not reach but for the *warNet*. It is worth noting, however, that vast majority of the urban population are excluded from Internet access in a country where the minimum daily wage remains below the hourly rental rates at the *warNet*.[23]

By the end of 1996, the Internet had a presence in the media, commerce and in politics well beyond what the actual numbers of connections might suggest. Within a year of its launch in Indonesia, government, business and political radicals were all talking about the Internet. Major daily newspapers, such as *Kompas*, *Media Indonesia*, and *Republika* devoted regular sections or columns to Internet and associated computer technologies. Businesses were being assured of its marketing potential,[24] with the Internet offering a smorgasbord of on-line information on everything from employment services, medical advances, education and culture, to travel and music.[25] E-mail addresses were adorning the name cards of political activists as well as company directors. Viewers could participate via modem in television game-shows. Readers could respond immediately and anonymously to opinion polls on various hot political issues, which appeared on web-sites, like that of the cyber-magazine, *Tempo Interaktif*.[26] The Internet had been embraced by the technophilic developmentalists in the New Order government, personified by B.J. Habibie, by big business, and also by students and the professional middle classes.

## THE FINANCIAL CRISIS

When the collapse of the Thai financial sector and the floating of the Thai baht in July 1997 started to impact on other economies in the region, the ramifications were dramatic for Indonesia. Within twelve months of the commencement of the crisis the rupiah depreciated by more than 80 per cent, the inflation rate for 1998 rose to around 13 per cent.[27] The economic crisis increased the rising opposition to President Suharto. But the economic impact was not uniform in all sectors of the economy.[28]

The drastic fall in the value of the rupiah drove up the price of all imported computer and Internet hardware, making it more difficult to upgrade infrastructure. The crisis posed problems for the ISPs who had to pay for their bandwidth (about 40 per cent of their operational cost even before the crisis) in US dollars, while receiving their subscription income in the devalued rupiah.[29] Although the ISPs generally attempted to maintain their subscription fees at the pre-devaluation prices to avoid an exodus of customers, government increases in the cost of timed telephone calls (including connections to the ISP) effectively drove up the costs to the consumer of Internet access. But the Net, by now embedded in the commercial and political life of significant sections of the Indonesian population, did not shrink substantially under the economic strain. The increased cost of new imported materials enhanced the market for the local repair and maintenance of computer hardware. For ISPs, the customer base continued to grow. For instance, IndoInternet (one of the oldest ISPs in operation), lost about 60 subscribers each month in the first half of 1998 about 40 of whom were foreigners presumably leaving Indonesia in the face of the impending political crisis. But at the same time the company was registering 180–200, mostly Indonesian, new subscribers a month.[30] The ISPs' organization, APJII, attempted to minimize use of expensive international gateways by maximising mutual exchange of domestic Internet traffic between Indonesian providers, via the 'Indonesia Internet eXchange' (iIX).[31]

Through 1997–98 as the economic crisis and political turmoil deepened, the industry managed to present the Internet as both a political and economic solution to the nation's ills. The print news media generally, and computer industry-linked publications in particular, repeatedly pointed to the Internet as the single most important medium of unfettered communication both within the nation and internationally. An article in *Infokomputer*, some weeks after the fall of President Suharto, stated 'Thanks must be given to the ISPs who did not cut or censor the content of Internet traffic. Thus, the idea of people's power that originated in the Philippines could reverberate through some of the chat rooms and mailing lists like *apakabar* and KdP'[32] (both discussed later).

Similarly, as businesses faced dire times they were urged to reconsider their communication practices in order to economize. Industry analysts sought to promote e-mail and the Internet as cheaper alternatives to long-distance telephone and fax contact. Companies were encouraged to do more direct marketing of goods and services on the web, advertising more economically on the Internet rather than in the conventional form of print, radio and television. The messianic zeal of some of these promotions is evident in the opening lines of one such article: 'In the midst of the economic crisis today, every company and every family is forced to economize in all activities. Nonetheless, the one activity that we cannot do without is communicating. Communicating, whether within the company or within a family, is the life-blood … A company without communication will fail.'[33] The rest of the very same article is given over to promoting the Internet as faster and cheaper than all competing modes of communication such as fax and telephone, particularly at a time when prices of international calls were rising rapidly, while the ISPs continued to offer Internet services at pre-crisis prices.

The pessimistic assessments that emerged in international academic debates about the Internet technology had no resonances in Indonesia at all. The security arm of the New Order government, including the military and the Department of Information which was largely responsible for government propaganda and censorship, had proved entirely incompetent in using the new technology.[34] The period of economic and attendant political crisis in 1997–98 only further embedded the Internet within large sections of the urban Indonesian middle class. The Internet became simultaneously the locus of a critique of dirigism – a proof that the state (qua New Order) could not and should not impede free and international movement of goods and ideas – and a space in which to articulate the anti-statist, pro-free market and freedom of speech arguments.

## 'TECHNOLOGIES OF FREEDOM'[35]

The newest communication technologies are often valorized in discourses of political reform. In 1989 the ability of Chinese dissidents to occupy Tiananmen Square for as long as they did has often been seen as a credit to satellite television's capacity to transport dramatic footage to viewers in western democratic nations. A decade later, the Internet seemed to have enabled Indonesian activists to work against the Suharto regime. There is little doubt that the Internet had given opposition groups in the closing years of the Suharto regime the ability to control and direct their message internationally and domestically with far greater precision, through 'broadcast' to news groups and chat groups, or through 'narrowcast' to specific targeted individuals, within split seconds. There is also little doubt that there was some overlap between the students who used the *warNet* in Yogyakarta and Bandung or at their universities in Jakarta and those who stormed the parliament on the eve of Suharto's resignation. However, the points of translation between virtual freedom and constitutional, electoral democracy are neither direct nor essential. If the Internet has provided a space for like-minded citizens of the world to come together in defiance of powerful capital and powerful governments, then it has done so even-handedly – giving as much to liberal democrats struggling against dictators and moderate nationalists seeking self-determination as to right-wing racist and religious extremists of every variety.

The jury is still out on the progress of democratization in Indonesia and whether or not Internet will, in the final analysis, act as a means of protecting citizens' democratic rights against the state. There is no point in speculating; so this acount now turns to focus on two issues: (i) the establishment of e-mail news groups by student radicals in the last few years of the Suharto regime designed to act as alternative sources of news and information; and (ii) the continuing significance of the Internet in the formation of 'public spheres' in post-Suharto Indonesia.

Analysts of Indonesian politics have repeatedly pointed to the mechanisms for limiting public discourse through the New Order period. But beyond government intervention specific to the New Order there is a general perspective to be derived from Habermas's much cited conceptualization of a public sphere at the heart of any democracy. In conceptual terms Habermas's public sphere 'is the space within a society, independent both of state power and private, corporate influence, within which information can freely flow and debates on matters of public, civic concern can proceed'.[36] One of the precedents of such a sphere for Habermas was a small group of literary and political intellectuals who read newspapers and debated issues in the coffee houses of London in the eighteenth century. For him the main twentieth-century culprit in the erosion of a public space is television – a less discursive, more centralized system which has replaced the pluralist, critical public press as the main source of political and social information and ideas.

Habermas is taken up mainly in three ways (though not necessarily self-consciously) in media studies. First, there is empirical research on audiences which show the growing importance of television over the print media; secondly, structural and textual analyses of televison which reproduce Habermas's pessimistic view of television as a centralized system of 'knowledge control';[37] and finally political economy perspectives of media which suggest increasing concentration of ownership of not only television but also the print media.[38] While the nature of televisual communication and its relation to public accountability in democracy remains an open question, there is clear empirical evidence to suggest the spread of television in Indonesia in the 1980s and early 1990s, as well as a growing concentration of newspaper ownership over the same period. This has been demonstrated elsewhere.[39] What we want to take up here is the possibility of thinking of the Internet in Indonesia precisely in terms of Habermas's eighteenth-century example of the public space which is simultaneously a source of information and a coffee-shop. It is not entirely flippant to suggest that the 'cyber cafes' and their Indonesianized counterpart, *warNet*, and the 'chat rooms' are all, in part, references to that important function of sharing information, opinion, gossip in a way that is simultaneously public but unstructured, un-institutionalized, un-edited. In the context of 1990s Indonesia, marked by an unrepresentative political system and highly restrictive media, the Internet was able to become the space where privately experienced and mounting grievances could be publicly voiced and evolve into collective public opinion.

## NETWORKS OF DISSENT

The e-mail discussion list 'Indonesia-L', popularly known as *apakabar* ('how's life?'), moderated by John MacDougall in Maryland in the United States was the first Net-based activity to become central to political communication between the critics of the New Order inside and outside of Indonesia. The list's content, a mix of 'hard news' on Indonesia from papers and broadcasts from around the world, as well as a variety of commentaries, opinions, snippets of political gossip, mainly in Indonesian language, not only uncensored but also unedited, established *apakabar* as a valuable means of disseminating their materials amongst many activists in the non-governmental organizations. Around the end of 1995, MacDougall estimated that the number of identifiable recipients of *apakabar* material was about 13,000, with the majority of them Indonesians living in Indonesia, followed by Indonesians living or studying abroad.[40]

Around the same time several articles in the mainstream national print media drew attention to *apakabar*, especially to the speed with which politically sensitive news got posted on the list. The weekly *Gatra* wrote, for instance, that news of the arrest and release of some prominent political activists was on *apakabar* within hours, but could not make the local papers until the following morning.[41] Increasingly too, *apakabar* was cited in the Indonesian print media as a source of information, particularly on activities of opposition groups. The list's web-site was popular amongst the clientele of the *warNet,* as they spread across the cities. When the first Internet cafes opened in Yogyakarta six weeks after the 27 July riots[42] in Jakarta, one of the owners estimated that about 40 per cent of Indonesian clients sought out *apakabar* and consulted it regularly. The two privately-owned Internet cafes in Yogyakarta kept information on hand to assist those customers who wanted help to connect to *apakabar*. While *apakabar* remained important as a meeting place for diverse ideas and information, beyond the control of state censors, from early 1996 a variety of political organizations within

Indonesia started their own mailing lists, most of them cross-posting with each other and with *apakabar*.

To the extent that defiance of state control over information flow was a political purpose in itself, *apakabar* was serving a specific political purpose. But the first Indonesian political group to establish its own particular political presence on the net was PIJAR (The Centre for Information and Reform Action Network), an organization established by student activists as a 'mechanism for democratic struggle' in September 1989. PIJAR pursued its aim of social and political justice through a programme of publications, education and training, and public advocacy. Its print periodical, *Kabar dari PIJAR* [News from PIJAR] (KdP) was one of a number of unauthorized publications that circulated amongst students, mainly in Jakarta. After the banning of three prominent newsweeklies in June 1994 for their critical stance on various government policies, there was a heightened public interest in underground publications such as *Kabar dari PIJAR*, (which for two months appeared daily) because of their continued ability to remain critical at a time when the government was winding back freedom of speech. In July 1995 KdP editor Tri Agus S. Siswowihardjo was charged with insulting the president in an article in the magazine, and spent two years in jail. Office bearers of another underground publication *Independen* were also jailed around the same time for spreading 'hostility, hatred and contempt' towards the government in their unlicensed publication.[43] *Independen* had been established by a group of working journalists and students to counter 'the atmosphere in the Indonesian press of repressive control by the government and the dictates of a small group of owners of capital'.[44]

Early in 1996 *Kabar dari PIJAR* went on-line as a mailing list, called KdP-Net, which made it possible for PIJAR to distribute its messages much more easily to non-governmental organizations outside Jakarta, to expatriate Indonesians and to international human rights groups. Like many of the formal and underground publications going on-line in the early years of the Internet in Indonesia, PIJAR used a server outside Indonesia, provided by the Association for Progressive Communication in the United States. The underground periodical *Independen* also appeared on-line, on the same server around the same time. *Tempo*, the once highly successful mainstream journal banned in 1994, appeared with far more radical content as *Tempo Interaktif* in March 1994. *SiaR-list*, closely connected to both *Independen* and *Tempo*, started with the aim of becoming an 'alternative news agency' trying to reproduce what its founders saw as standard journalistic practices which were being corrupted by censorship and propaganda of the New Order government.

This is by no means an exhaustive list of opposition groups in the closing years of the New Order, driven from the mainstream media and making their case on the Net. By 1999 there were hundreds of mailing lists relating to Indonesia.[45] The reform movement spawned its own collection of sites dedicated to political change in Indonesia; KdP-Net and SiaR are only the oldest and longest surviving of them. In any case, the importance of these groups is not in how, or whether, individually they constituted a challenge to the Suharto regime or to the mainstream news media (which were also going on-line at the same time) but rather in the ways they functioned together as a forum in which to discuss, question, and supplement what was formally defined as news. News stories that journalists wrote but could not get printed in newspapers regularly got posted on one or more mailing lists. Letters to editors which could not be printed whether for editorial policy or through lack of space could easily be accommodated on a bulletin board. The on-line news groups were a constant reminder that censorship could be got around and much that could not be said in the formal media whether for state-imposed restriction, or commercially or politically driven editorial policy or simply lack of page space, could be circulated on the Internet. On the Net, also, the user did not have to be limited to a particular source of news (a particular paper), one web page was necessarily an entry point to another. That web-sites such as PIJAR's were linked to a variety of international human rights organizations, is only to be expected. But in our surfings we found also connections that appeared not to be politically motivated – for instance, in late 1996 an Indonesian government department page was linked to the then illegal and highly politicized *Tempo Interaktif* site!

This technological faculty of the Net to interconnect across the world was actively used in the final days of the Suharto regime by the student demonstrators. 'Bypassing the government-controlled television and radio stations, dissidents shared information about protests by e-mail, inundated news groups with stories of President Suharto's corruption, and used chat groups to exchange tips about how to resist repression by the governemnt's troops. In a country made up of thousands of islands, where phone calls are expensive, the electronic messages reached key organizers.'[46] When the students occupied the parliament in the days before the resignation of Suharto, Abigail Abrash, of the Robert F. Kennedy Memorial Centre for Human Rights in Washington, was able to receive reports which appeared to come from 'someone [who had] brought a lap-top inside Indonesia's parliament building, and went on-line while [the Parliament was] surrounded by armed troops'.[47]

The Internet's function as a weapon against state censorship became largely redundant by the end of the New Order. In the closing days of Suharto's rule, state censorship had collapsed. Even private television, largely owned by Suharto's family members, had joined the anti-government fray and all media regulations were ignored. Apart from state television (TVRI) and state radio (RRI), the new Habibie government exercised relatively little direct control over the content of the news media. But the cyber Networks remain important. In the year from the fall of Suharto KdP-Net's membership went from 3,000 to 3,800. There were probably two reasons for this. First, the political public in Indonesia has remained uncertain about the long-term security of the newly-won media freedoms. In this context the Internet is something of an insurance against any closure of access to uncensored information. Secondly, and for our purposes, more importantly, the Internet has become a significant public space of political discourse, whose extent and immediacy simply cannot be matched by print or broadcast media. For even without government censorship they are still restricted through commercial requirements and the physical limits of space and time.

## PUBLIC SPACE FOR A NEW POLITICS

Political parties, which emerged within the formal structures of electoral democracy in Indonesia after Suharto, did not, however, embrace the Internet as the informal semi-underground opposition to Suharto had. In June 1999 only nine of the 48 parties contesting Indonesia's first free and fair election since 1955 had their own web-sites. Most of their constituencies, the overwhelming majority of voters did not have access to Internet, were not the young university students and graduates who had posted to news-groups, designed web pages and filled the *warNet*. The Democratic People's Party (PRD), with its base in the radical student movement, used mailing lists like SiaR and KdP-Net but did not even come close to winning a seat.

None the less, the role of the Internet in the political process permeated the general understanding and institutionalization of democracy in post-Suharto Indonesia. The upper house of the parliament, MPR, itself mounted a web page in a self-conscious move to improve public accessibility of an institution which, in the New Order, had largely become simply a means of re-anointing Suharto. A statement placed on the page detailing ways of accessing information starts thus:

> A lack of understanding amongst the community regarding the MPR … is very disappointing. On the other hand, the expansion of education and improvements in living conditions have made the greater proportion of our population increasingly sensitive, perceptive and critical.
>
> One way of containing and channeling the interests of such a community is to publicize and communicate widely about the activities carried out by the People's Consultative Assembly (MPR). And the development of communication technology itself demands that the activities of the MPR be published and communicated by the fastest information services … .[48]

The above statement specifically mentioned that the MPR page could be accessed from the *warNet* around the nation, and it invited all citizens to post criticisms and complaints against either individual members or parliamentary policy, detailed in the web. On the eve of Indonesia's historic elections in 1999, making clear the connections between politics on the city streets and the information highway, Onno Purbo, one of the pioneers of the Internet in Indonesia called on 'the community to make use of the Internet to convey their thoughts to the People's Consultative Assembly/House of Representatives (MPR/DPR), in order that they may not come face to face with the troops'.[49]

While the Internet had no direct impact on the ballot, it was important in the public scrutiny of the election and thus in the legitimization of its results. The National Electoral Commission (KPU) had its site on which it provided full transcripts of all electoral legislation, regulation and forms.[50] After election day, the site carried a running tally of the results in Indonesian, English and Japanese, broken down not only to specific provinces but even to district level. In the first week or so of counting, television news reports did provide national statistics with provincial breakdowns of the major parties, sometimes on an hourly basis. But the KPU web page offered a range and depth of statistical information and recorded the unfolding detail with a speed that could not be matched by any other medium. Many of the country's news media also included election sites on their web pages, carrying more detail than was being published or broadcast – some of these hyper-linked to the Electoral Commission. A variety of non-government organizations, such as API (the Almanac of Indonesian Political Parties), provided independent information on the 141 official political parties registered with the Department of Justice, and specifically the 48 authorized parties which fielded candidates in the elections.[51]

The Internet was not central to the game plan of any of the political parties in Indonesia's first serious experiment with electoral democracy since 1955. But this historical event in the life of the Indonesian nation was most fully displayed on the Internet for the world to watch.

## CONCLUSION

The limitlessness of the net, quite literally, is able to haul up the information that the rest of the media simply cannot contain. Political speeches that appear only in sound-bites and quotes in other media appear in full on the Internet sites of those same newspapers. Polling surveys which are summarized in the daily papers are available on the paper's web pages even as they unfold. To some extent that very quantity makes the information qualitatively different – less mediated through concerns about editorial policy, advertising space and even conventional understanding of reading and viewing habits that shape the older media. The newness of the medium and its technological capabilities at this point of time in Indonesia free it from constraints and conventions that tie the older media.

However, it is not the technology but its particular articulation into the political work of democratization in Indonesia that is of most interest here. Set up with the precise purpose of opening up the limits of political communication in Indonesia, the dissident networks built on the Internet during the last years of Suharto, as a foil to the formal media, remain significant as a means of bringing into public discourse a diversity of voices. More importantly it is their mode of address – conversational, dialogic, non-hierarchical – that distinguishes some of these groups from the formal news media. The full elaboration of this mode of address of contemporary Indonesia's Internetworks still needs to be written. For the moment we want to suggest only that, while this mode of address is made possible by the Internet, it is in no way essential to this new communication technology. A flourishing public space underpinning a new democracy in Indonesia may emerge from the web of political conversations on the net but only if there is a continued and conscious commitment from the participants to maintain an autonomy from the state, and capital. And equally importantly the Indonesian sector of the information superhighway needs to remain a *Network*, not split up into sectarian communities of special interest. The state of the technology in Indonesia offers possibilities of enormous discursive openness but technology alone will not secure such a public space.

## NOTES

1. Hanny Agustine, 'Internet Replaces Bamboo Spears in Fight for Freedom', *The Jakarta Post*, 8 June 1998, p.7.
2. W. Scott Thompson quoted in David L. Marcus, 'Indonesia Revolt was Net Driven', *Boston Globe*, 23 May 1998, reproduced in Edward Aspinall, Gerry van Klinken and Herb Feith (eds.) *The Last Days of President Suharto* (Clayton: Monash Asia Institute, 1999), pp.73–5.
3. Jürgen Habermas, *The Structural Transformation of the Public Sphere* (Cambridge, MA: Polity, 1989).
4. Kevin Hewison and Garry Rodan, 'The Decline of the Left in Southeast Asia', in R. Miliband and L. Panitch (eds.) *Socialist Register* (London: Merlin Press, 1994), pp.235–40.
5. For a discussion of the first years of the Internet in Indonesia, see David T. Hill and Krishna Sen, 'Wiring the Warung to Global Gateways: The Internet in Indonesia', *Indonesia* (Cornell University), No.63 (April 1997), pp.67–89, from which some of the following detail is drawn.
6. Information on IPTEKNet is taken from <http://www.iptek.net.id/background.html> (downloaded 31 Jan. 1997), with a comprehensive list of member organisations given on <http://www.iptek.net.id/member.html>. The authors are indebted to Mr Tri Kuntoro Priyambodo, Network Manager of GAMA-Net, the Gadjah Mada University Internet facility, for information of the university sector's early development of Internet technologies. Interview, Yogyakarta, 18 July 1996.
7. A list of commercial Internet Service Providers, sourced to the Directorate General of Tourism, Post & Telecommunication, appeared on <indonesia-l@igc.apc.org>, 16 May 1996.
8. Onno W. Purbo, 'Ceramah Ilmiah: Komunikasi Internet dan Dunia Pendidikan' (pp.43–7), in *Duta Wacana menyongsong Budaya Teknologi*, (Dies Natalis ke34, Duta Wacana Christian University, Yogyakarta, 31 Oct. 1996. A kilobyte is a thousand 'bytes'; a megabyte is a million 'bytes'.
9. Quotations from 'The Emerging 20 Nations', on the CyberAtlas site, http://cyberatlas.internet.com/big_pictur…graphics/print/0,1323,5911_150661,00.html sighted on 5 Sept. 1999.
10. 'Bisnis Internet Service Provider: Harus kreatif'', *InfoKomputer*, Sept. 1996, pp.132–4.
11. Estimates given by Feraldi W. Loeis of RADNET, interview, Jakarta, 18 November 1996.
12. Estimate totalled from figures in Rahmat M. Samik-Ibrahim, 'Indonesia-102: The Internet Service Providers', http://www.tjt.or.id/rms46/imho-eisp.html, with number of permits given in Indonesian Internet Service Provider Association (APJII) , 'D. Profile', on http://www/apjii.or.id', both sighted 17 May 1997. See also 'Penyelenggara Internet Bentuk Konsortium', *Kompas Online*, 9 April 1998.
13. The figures of 200,000 and one million, given by Didi Apriadi, Director of the ISP, PT Elga Yasa Media, and a deputy chairperson of the Indonesian Association of Internet Service Providers (APJII), are cited in M.M.I Ahyani, 'Internet Fails to Woo Most Political Parties', in *The Jakarta Post*, 29 May 1999, posted on *The Jakarta Post.com*, at http://www.thejakartapost.com:8890/iscp_render?menu_name=hitlist_details&id=215349, sighted on 21 Aug. 1999.
14. Naswil Idris and Marwah Daud Ibrahim, 'Communication Scene of Indonesia', in Anura Goonasekera and Duncan Holaday (eds.), *Asian Communication Handbook* (Singapore: Asian Mass Communication Research and Information Center, AMIC, 1993), pp.59–86. Statistics from p.63.
15. For instance, the first detailed account of the 27 July 1996 military-backed assault on the headquarters of the opposition Indonesian Democracy Party (PDI) in Jakarta reached the Gadjah Mada University campus in Yogyakarta by fax. The disturbances had started sometime before dawn. By 11 a.m. a three-page fax from the Jakarta Legal Aid Institute was circulated to various student groups and NGOs in Yogyakarta. On the 27 July incident, see Damien Kingsbury, *The Politics of Indonesia* (Melbourne: Oxford University Press, 1998), pp.137–8.
16. For example, in Bandung the 40 *wartel* in 1990 had tripled to 120 by 1997 according to

'Tentang Wartelnet', at http://wartelnet.melsa.net.id/tentang.htm, sighted 21 August 1999, quoting an unnamed article from *Pikiran Rakyat* daily newspaper of 5 April 1997.

17. 'Tentang Wartelnet'.
18. Sentot E. Baskoro, 'Peranan Internet dalam Reformasi Indonesia', *Info Komputer On-line*, 10 July 1998, <http://www.infokomputer.com/analisa/100798-1.shtml, sighted 19 Dec. 1998.
19. After discounting double entries, three searches (conducted on 25 Aug. 1999, via at http://cybercaptive.com/, http://netcafeguide.com/asiaINDO.htm and http://ernst.larsen.net/cafeguide/asiaINDO.htm, and http://www.cybercafe.com/country3.asp) identified 53 Internet cafes as listed in Indonesia. Cross-checking this list with other oral sources suggests these account for only a tiny fraction of the commercial public Internet access points.
20. 'Mengejar Internet sampai ke Kafe', in *Infokomputer Online*, Feb. 1997, located via http://www.infokomputer.com, sighted 1 Sept. 1999.
21. See Richard Robison and David Goodman (eds.), *The New Rich in Asia: Mobile Phones, McDonalds and the Middle-Class Revolution* (London: Routledge, 1996).
22. 'Mengejar Internet sampai ke Kafe'.
23. Personal communication from Vedi Hadiz, an expert on the Indonesian labour movement (15 Sept. 1999). According to Hadiz the minimum daily wage in Jakarta is about Rp 5000, and considerably lower in all other areas.
24. For example, an advertizement for Fujitsu Internet Web Servers in *Kompas*, 10 July 1996, p.17, stated 'The Internet has changed the parameters of marketing. For half the cost of a full page advertisement in a national newspaper, you can have your own World Wide Web (WWW) server and address and audience of millions.'
25. See, for example, "Sartono Tawarkan Cari Pekerjaan Lewat Internet", *Kompas*, 26 Sept. 1996, p.3; "Memanfaatkan Jaringan INTERNET", *Media Indonesia*, 3 Sept. 1996, p.14; "Kanker di Internet", *Media Indonesia*, 1 Sept. 1996, p.18; "Indonesian Artists Leap onto Internet", *Jakarta Post*, 28 June 1996, p.2; "Data Pendidikan Indonesia Dapat Diakses di Internet", *Kompas*, 11 Nov. 1996, p.20.
26. *Tempo Interaktif* was an incarnation of the country's most prestigious news weekly print magazine, *Tempo*, banned by the Suharto government in June 1994 in a highly controversial and contested crackdown banning three outspoken news publications.
27. J. Soedradjad Djiwandono, 'The Rupiah – One Year After Its Float', in Geoff Forrester (ed.), *Post-Soeharto Indonesia: Renewal or Chaos?* (Bathurst: Crawford House Publishing, 1999), pp.144–52, particularly p.150.
28. For instance, US embassy assessments using consumer price index resulted in different assessment of poverty depending on the how food was weighted in the calculation. 'Studies that used the increase in the general consumer price index (up 78 per cent in 1998) concluded that poverty increased to … close to 18 per cent (meaning from about 22 million before the crises to about 36 million persons in 1998, out of a population of 200 million). However, studies that focused on the increase in food prices (up 118 per cent in 1998), which account for a large share of purchases for low-income households, concluded that the increase in poverty was larger' at nearly a quarter of the population. Embassy of the United States of America, 'Indonesia Economic Trends 1999 – Signs of Life', on http://www.usembassyjakarta.org/econ/trends 99-2.html sighted on 2 Sept. 1999.
29. 'Para ISP Makin Terengah-Engah', *Info Komputer Online*, June 1998, at wysiwyg://148/http://www.infokomputer.com/0698/bisnis/bisnis.shtml, sighted on 27 Jan. 1999.
30. 'Para ISP Makin Terengah-Engah'.
31. 'Para ISP Makin Terengah-Engah'.
32. Sentot E. Baskoro 'Peranan Internet dalam Reformasi Indonesia', in *Info Komputer Online*, June 1998, at wysiwyg://148/http://www.infokomputer.com/100798-l.shtml, sighted 19 Dec. 1998.
33. P.M Winarno, 'Peran Internet di tengah krisis', *Info Komputer Online*, 13 April 1998, on http://www.infokomputer.com/analisa/130498-1.shtml, sighted on 19 Dec. 1998.
34. See our discussion of HANKAM-Net, the propaganda home-page of the military, in Hill and Sen 1997, pp.81–2.
35. Ithiel da Sola Pool, *Technologies of Freedom* (Cambridge, MA: Harvard University Press, 1983).

36. John Corner, *Television Form and Public Address* (London and New York: Edward Arnold, 1995), p.42.
37. See especially Douglas Kellner, *Television and the Crisis of Democracy* (Oxford: Westview, 1990).
38. For a review of some of these works see Corner, pp.41–9.
39. See Krishna Sen and David T. Hill, *Media, Culture and Politics in Indonesia* (Melbourne: Oxford University Press, 2000).
40. Information provided by John MacDougall via e-mail, 19 Jan. 1997.
41 Ini Milik MacDougall', *Gatra*, 2 Dec. 1995 on <apakabar@clark.Net> 28 Nov. 1995.
42. See note 15 above.
43. The Suharto government required all periodicals to obtain a government publication licence (SIUPP) without which they were regarded as illegal. Neither *Kabar dari PIJAR* or *Independen* held, or would have been likely to be issued with, this permit. In addition, *Independen* was published by the Alliance of Independent Journalists (AJI), an independent rival to the government-backed Indonesian Journalists' Association (PWI), which all journalists were formally obliged to join.
44. *Suara Independen*, 'Tentang Tujuan Kami', http://www.gn.apc.org/independen/info.htm sighted on 14 Sept. 1999.
45. Budi Rahardjo gives the figures of 240 mailing lists on his *Indonesian homepage*, sighted 20 Aug. 1999, which has a hyper-link to the list, *Milis*, where there were 268 mailing lists (http://indonesia.elga.net.id/milis.html sighted 3 Sept. 1999). However, quite a number of these appear to be inactive or with incorrect URLs.
46. Marcus, p.73.
47. Marcus, p.74. This observation also appears in Sentot E. Baskoro, 'Peranan Internet dalam Reformasi Indonesia', which appears to draw heavily on the Marcus article.
48. 'Wasantara Net Suguhkan Layan Cepat Informasi Kegiatan BP MPR', sighted 14 Sept. 1999.
49. Onno Purbo quoted in Ahyani.
50. http://www.kpu.go.id/ sighted 29 Aug. 1999.
51. http://almanakparpol.org/ sighted 29 Aug. 1999.

# The Electronic Republic? The Role of the Internet in Promoting Democracy in Africa

DANA OTT and MELISSA ROSSER

## INTRODUCTION

> The general belief holds that representative government is the only form of democracy that is feasible in today's sprawling, heterogeneous nation-states. However, interactive telecommunications now make it possible for tens of millions of widely dispersed citizens to receive the information they need to carry out the business of government themselves, gain admission to the political realm, and retrieve at least some of the power over their own lives and goods that many believe their elected leaders are squandering.[1]

Since the earliest conceptualization and discussion of politics and the political, communication has held an equally prominent position, both in terms of its necessity for political ideas to be transmitted and replicated and as a tool by which political actors seek to ensure the predominance of their ideas through improved methods of communication. In the *polis*, as conceived by Aristotle, direct communication among and between all the political actors in the system was an attainable ideal. The growth of larger and more geographically diverse states necessitated the development of alternative modes of interaction as societies moved from direct political interaction to representative political action. Those chosen to represent the interests of others in the political system have historically used a variety of methods to obtain information about their constituents' preferences, including physically touring their districts periodically, reading letters from constituents and polling their constituents about key issues. All these methods can be time-consuming and costly to employ, limiting the frequency with which they can be used and by extension the quality of

---

The views presented in this study are those of the authors alone and should not be interpreted as reflecting those of the United States Agency for International Development or the Academy for Educational Development.

information which can be regularly obtained. However, the changing nature of communication ushered in by the dawning of the age of electronic communications and the concomitant decline in the costs of communication on a global scale have profound implications for political interaction among representatives and their constituents, and for economic and political development throughout the world. This study focuses explicitly on the impact these changes may have on political communication and potentially on the formation and maintenance of democratic political regimes in Africa.

## I: THE ROLE OF INFORMATION IN PROMOTING DEMOCRATIZATION

> Now as in the past it is difficult to separate the quality and cast of political life from the methods of communication that sustain it. But behind the changes wrought by technology, organization, and the scale of politics, there is also a certain sameness. Linked to the communication structures which characterize a society, and in fact inseparable from them, are numerous face-to-face relationships. Much of the political business of the world is still done in such situations, and it would indeed provide a mistaken view of the communication process to concentrate on machines and organizations to the exclusion of the face-to-face groupings which are a prominent feature of all political systems.[2]

Writing over 30 years ago, Richard Fagen cautioned against reading too much into the impact of technological developments such as radio and television on political communication and ultimately on the conduct of politics. He argued that, while technology does matter in the functioning of a political system, there are more elemental relationships of power in political communication that are unaffected or barely affected by the development of enhanced methods of communication. One-to-one interactions remain a critical part of the political process. In other words, the political elite will always be small enough to remain relatively unaffected by changes in communications. This article argues that while it is certainly true that actual decision-making in a political system (even a democratic one) may remain concentrated at the level of a few individuals, the complexity of information which those individuals use to engage in decision-making processes (especially constituency feedback) is equally important and *is* subject to influence by the changing nature of communications. As electronic communication enables citizens to directly and instantaneously convey their wishes to their representatives and to communicate with one another and the outside world with ever decreasing costs, the nature of political interaction is likely to change. There are several possible consequences for democracy, both positive and negative, that can be highlighted:

In what Lawrence Grossman calls the 'Electronic Republic', the power of individual citizens is increased in two major ways: through greater access and through greater influence. There is *greater access* to those who represent the individual in the political system, and to information about issues, decisions and pending legislation that might affect the individual. There is *greater influence* both as an individual who can more easily communicate his or her views on a topic directly to elected representatives, and indirectly through easier access to issue advocacy organizations and the media.

In Africa, where in the 1990s democratic reforms are off to a slow and shaky start in many states, the indirect effects of electronic communication are often the most critical. Easy access to international advocacy organizations and international media outlets has been especially important for organizations to maintain international pressure on regimes with a questionable commitment to liberal ideals and democratization. Human rights organizations in Africa, for example, have been quick to embrace the Internet as a means of thwarting government attempts to suppress information about rights violations, using their electronic link with large international human rights organizations to quickly publicize abuses and repressive practices. This has become known, in the literature, as the Zapatista effect (after the experience of the rebels in Mexico's Chiapas who used electronic communication to gain international leverage against the national government of Mexico).[3] Furthermore, the ease and affordability of publication on the Internet has already, in some cases, effectively circumvented government censorship and control of national media. There have been instances of newspapers publishing on-line in defiance of a government ban (in Liberia and Zambia, for example), as well as journalists obtaining vital information from the Internet that had been concealed from the public by the national government, as in Nigeria under military rule. By contributing to free speech and the free flow of information, electronic communication has clearly exhibited the potential to augment the power of the African citizen *vis-à-vis* the state, with beneficial effects for liberalization and democratization initiatives.

In addition to empowering the individual, there are other, more subtle implications of this shift in public power for elected representatives in Grossman's 'electronic republic'. For representatives, this could mean the transformation in the definition of their role. The more traditional conception of the representative is someone who is selected to represent his or her constituents by considering the facts surrounding various issues and making carefully reasoned decisions on that basis with the interests of the constituents in mind. The 'new' representative is merely a proxy for his or her constituents, adding up the constituency responses on a given issue and voting accordingly. The electronic media has given a larger percentage of constituents than ever before the ability easily and quickly to transmit their opinions on public policy issues to their representatives. The danger is that whereas a representative is supposed to consider what is best for his or her district as a whole (including all members of the district), a proxy is constrained to represent the majority viewpoint. This dominance of a majority faction could have serious repercussions in the African context where ethnic minority populations might be vulnerable to total political disenfranchisement under such a system. Yet, at the same time and in the same vein, the opportunity costs of participation for individuals and civil society organizations are reduced by advances in electronic communication. Electronic access could also potentially erase disparities of distance and geography, minimizing the rural–urban distinction that has had significant political implications in Africa in the past. It is too early to tell which condition might prevail in the African context.

Aside from these direct consequences, Grossman sees as an additional consequence a power shift in the electronic republic:

> The big losers in the present-day reshuffling and resurgence of public influence are traditional institutions that have served as the main intermediaries between the government and its citizens: the political parties, labor unions, civic associations, even the commentators and correspondents in the mainstream press.[4]

By empowering ordinary citizens to participate more directly in their political system, Grossman argues, electronic communications increases the role of citizens in the policy-making process at the expense of the political 'middlemen' who have historically provided the forum by which ordinary citizens could make their interests on specific issues known through interest aggregation and representation. Not only this, but electronic communication and participation in politics may eventually lead to a more direct democracy in which general participation is increased, with both positive and negative consequences. In larger democracies such as the United States, there is a potentially troubling outcome:

> As the political system grows ever more responsive to majority impulses, and the legislative and executive branches feel increased pressure to bend to the public will, the judiciary remains the branch of government in the best position to serve as a brake upon the people … In the electronic republic, the judiciary will have the increasingly difficult and sensitive role of protecting the rights of unpopular minorities and thwarting the popular will when it gets out of hand … Protecting the essentially anti-majoritarian doctrine of judicial review will become the key to preserving democracy in the electronic republic and preventing it from succumbing eventually to a popular tyranny or a demagogic leader.[5]

In other words, the concern expressed by James Madison, one of the main writers of the *Federalist Papers*, in the early days of the United States' democracy over controlling the effects of a 'majority faction' may once again become a problem in an electronic republic.[6] That this issue could become a concern even in the United States where strong legal barriers exist to this 'tyranny of the majority' has significant implications for the political impact of electronic communications in the many African countries where factionalism is already a problem and only weak safeguards exist against majority domination. While such a possibility exists, given the relative lack of widespread access to electronic communication in Africa in comparison to the advanced industrialized countries, it is quite unlikely that the Internet will increase individual participation to such an extent that it will bring a tyranny of the majority. In fact, it is possible that electronic communication could have the opposite effect in Africa, where interest aggregation and social organization historically have been severely hindered by the lack of infrastructure and poor methods of communication. National interest group formation could in the short term, at least, be facilitated by the spread of electronic communication.

Contact with international advocacy networks through e-mail and the Internet has already been shown to bolster the power of interest groups in developing countries, by providing a ready source of skills, experience, and information from which local advocacy organizations can draw to more effectively promote the interests of their fellow citizens.[7] Given the low levels of literacy in Africa and the inexperience of the average African citizen with political participation, thanks to electronic communication, the 'middle men' could actually become more important to African democratization rather than less as Grossman hypothesized for the advanced democracies like the United States.

In terms of the role of electronic media in promoting democratic outcomes, it has been well established that radio and television can have significant impact on political participation in developed countries.[8] The case is less clear for the impact of the Internet on political participation. A recent study by Bruce Bimber on the impact of the Internet on the 1996 Presidential elections in the United States argues,

> The most 'wired' of political participators did make some use of the Net to communicate with their elected officials, but for the most part traditional means of communication were still much more important … Where mobilization is concerned, political organizations appear to have made little widespread use of the Internet as a tool of communication and persuasion yet. Although the Internet may already be significant as a passive information resource about public life … it is still far from transforming active political communication on a wide scale.[9]

Bimber deliberately targeted his survey at those individuals most likely to be involved in political activity and still found that the Internet was not as prominent in their political activity as the literature would predict. It could be argued, however, that in the United States, where many avenues to political participation already exist and where the opportunity cost of participation is quite low, the Internet does not provide sufficient 'added value' to make it a better alternative than more traditional methods of political communication. This is obviously not the case in Africa where avenues of political participation have been quite limited and the costs of participation have traditionally been prohibitive. Still, Bimber shows that we might be well advised not to overstate the potential impact of the Internet on fostering better or more political participation.

It has also been argued that the impact of electronic media on democratization can be distinguished by its potential range versus print media, particularly in the developing world. Radio and television have long provided a source of information for the millions of people who are illiterate and/or unable to afford the cost of newspapers. But the Internet provides an interactive component that radio and television lack. As Graeme Browning and Daniel Weitzner note,

> The Internet's greatest strength, however, is its ability to support simultaneous, interactive communications among many people. Unlike the telephone, which primarily supports one-to-one communications, or radio and television, where information flows in

> only one direction, from a single source to an audience that can only listen passively, the Net allows information to flow back and forth among millions of sources at practically the same time.[10]

The implication is that millions of people can be exposed to a medium in which they have an active role to play and can influence political as well as other outcomes. However, like newspapers, active use of the Internet requires literacy which limits access in Africa, parts of which have illiteracy rates as high as 80 per cent.[11] Perhaps more troubling, access to the Internet will likely require literacy in English, for the most part, to enjoy the benefits. For French- and Portuguese-speaking African countries, this is yet another hurdle on top of the financial and infrastructure constraints that many African countries already face to widespread Internet connectivity. Newspapers in Africa have traditionally been utilized primarily by the elite and urban population. It is possible that Internet access in many African countries will merely cement and potentially expand these disparities, despite the best efforts of international aid donors and others. This possibility is explored in greater depth in sections III and IV. The next section gives a brief overview of the current state of electronic communications in Africa.

## II: ACCESS TO THE INTERNET IN AFRICA

Electronic communication is not a new phenomenon in Africa. Radio and television have played a significant role in political life in most African countries since independence. Radio and television ownership and use continue to expand even as the Internet begins to make inroads into Africa.

It is an astounding fact that where the Internet barely existed in Africa even five years ago, today 51 of the 54 nations in Africa have some form of Internet access in their capital cities. Over the past six months, the number of computers in Africa that is permanently connected to the Internet has grown at twice the average world rate. But as Mike Jensen notes: 'Nevertheless Internet access in Africa has been largely confined to the capital cities, although a growing number of countries (currently Angola, Benin, Botswana, Ghana, Kenya, Mozambique, Namibia, Tanzania and Zimbabwe) do have points of presence (POP) in some of the secondary towns, and South Africa has POPs in about 70 locations.[12] Jensen notes that access costs are generally higher in Africa than elsewhere, and Aden argues that this may be related to the profit margins of the telecommunications sector in African countries, where the revenue per subscriber line is twice as high as in Europe.[13]

Aden argues that the two greatest impediments to the development of electronic communication in Africa are insufficient infrastructure and regulatory barriers. Infrastructure limitations include such problems as scarce and/or poor quality telephone lines, unreliable power supplies, outdated equipment, and a lack of knowledge and training. Consider, for example, that Africa has the lowest density of telephone lines per inhabitant in the world. Large urban areas in Africa have on average 1.6 telephone lines for every 100 inhabitants, compared with an average teledensity of 45 in Europe.[14] In rural areas, the teledensity rate drops as low as one per every 1,000 inhabitants. Regulatory barriers include government monopolies on telecommunications, high access rates for telephone service, and legal disincentives to foreign investment. The result is that

> in the majority of cases national telecom operators are also guided by policy-makers with less background in telecommunications technology and its value for development. These politicians often perceive telecommunications as a trivial public utility; sometimes as a utility for 'high officials'. The guidance of policy-makers has made telecom operations management inefficient and unconfident in decision-making. Such arrangement has blocked visions towards deregulation and increased conflict in adopting the most appropriate deregulation and privatization models based on national situations.[15]

There are numerous efforts under way by donors and other organizations to remedy some of these deficiencies in partnership with African governments, non-governmental organizations and the private sector. To improve the prospects for wider access to information and communication networks on the African continent, international development assistance initiatives strive to address numerous complex issues of use in African countries including poor telecommunications infrastructure; government regulation and censorship; poor knowledge about the opportunities for economic and social development afforded by information technologies, especially among policy-makers; the prohibitive cost of hardware and connection for individuals and organizations; and a lack of technical expertize, training capacity, and requisite skills for using the Internet.

Lack of adequate infrastructure may actually be the easiest to surmount as new technologies such as satellite communication and cellular and radio systems become less costly and more widespread. Many African countries have already developed and adopted national communication development plans aimed at developing the underlying infrastructure required for low-cost telephone services and global Internet access. Regional cooperative agreements and partnerships with commercial ventures have resulted in a number of infrastructure-building projects across the continent. The Common Market for Eastern and Southern Africa (COMESA) and the East African Co-operation (EAC) have launched initiatives to improve communications infrastructure between neighbouring African countries. The national telecoms in Senegal, Ivory Coast, Ghana, Togo, Gabon, Benin, Namibia, Nigeria, Burkina Faso, Cameroon, Niger, Guinea, Angola, and South Africa have all contributed to the construction of an MCI Worldcom coastal marine fiber optic cable, which will considerably lessen the problems of transmission capacity via the Internet and increase the speed of access when it is activated in 2001. RASCOM, the pan-African satellite consortium, jointly owned by the African telecoms, has announced plans to launch its own satellite for transmitting telephone, data, and television signals across Africa. The infrastructure investments made by South Africa's telecom in its efforts to become a hub for Africa's Internet traffic benefit all the surrounding countries in the region and boost interregional communication.

The infrastructure boom will not, by any means, solve all the problems of access on the continent. More difficult obstacles include reaching rural areas, overcoming the problem of illiteracy and restructuring the policy environment to decrease costs. Neither African governments nor the private sector can hope to accomplish these things on their own. Market forces dictate a concentration on investment where markets are large enough to guarantee a return. Thus, rural areas are largely neglected by the projects undertaken by multinational companies. In addition, traditions of over-regulation, high tariffs on ICT equipment, and artificially high profit margins enjoyed by the national telecommunications industry persist, creating internal resistance to deregulation and privatization of telecommunications services within national governments. The involvement of international donors is critical in these areas.

The United States Agency for International Development's (USAID) Leland Initiative is but one example of a multifaceted donor effort to assist African countries with overcoming policy and access obstacles to Internet connectivity. The Leland Initiative is a five-year $15 million project, active in 22 African countries. Assistance is initially directed at providing technical and material support in the setting up of national Internet gateways and is contingent on the host government's willingness to liberalize the telecommunications sector to allow private sector Internet service providers, to adopt cost-based tariff-setting for Internet services, and to allow the unrestricted flow of information. Leland also has supported Internet training and awareness-building to over 1,200 USAID grantees in Africa. The project has recently shifted to a second phase of involvement that includes working to develop local Internet training capacity within African countries through a training of trainers workshop, thus far in Mali and Madagascar, and helping to establish secondary city connectivity in eight to ten African countries beginning with Guinea.

Other USAID projects complement Leland Initiative activities and promote the use of the Internet for development in a number of specific sectors through training, technical assistance, and investments of hardware. The Southern Africa Regional Telecoms Restructuring Project works with telecommunications ministries and regulatory bodies in the southern Africa region for reform of the telecommunications sectors that will improve service delivery, support policies that promote private investment in the industry, and ultimately lower communication costs across the region. The Greater Horn of Africa Initiative is connecting Ministries of Agriculture and Foreign Affairs to the Internet. The GLOBE Program and the Education for Development and Democracy Initiative (EDDI) concentrate their efforts on hooking up schools across the continent. The GLOBE projects links United States' schools with schools in Africa for interactive environmental monitoring projects. EDDI funds will be used to hook up 100 African universities, 1,000 primary and secondary schools, and 100 pilot community information centres. The Africa Trade and Investment Project promotes the use of the Internet to support business linkages between Africa and the US and now includes a component to broaden secondary city access in South Africa and Tanzania.

The World Bank and many agencies in the United Nations system have also assumed a very proactive role in helping to bring Africa into the information age. The World Bank has been the primary contributor to the multi-donor InfoDev fund to support information and communications technology (ICT) projects in developing countries. In Africa, the InfoDev fund has supported a $1.2 million project to create an African virtual university, using satellite technology to offer distance education courses in 12 Anglophone African countries, seven Francophone African countries, and three Lusophone countries. Through InfoDev, the World Bank also provided awareness-building workshops on the Y2K problem in Africa and has made funds available to help critical sectors beat the Millenium Bug.

In addition to the InfoDev projects, the World Bank has made it a priority to incorporate information technology into its existing sectoral programmes, supporting applications of ICT, for example, in the health sector, environment projects and public administration reform efforts in several African countries. The United Nations Economic Commission for Africa (ECA) is coordinating a sub-regional effort to promote connectivity awareness under the African Information Society Initiative (AISI) framework. ECA supports five sub-regional development centres (SRDC) to stimulate electronic networks of various stakeholders in African economic and social development. SRDC's in Niger, Morocco, Zambia, Cameroon, and Rwanda link sector experts, non-governmental organizations and private sector institutions to exchange information and facilitate communication. In addition, the ECA and UNESCO, in conjunction with the International Development Research Centre (IDRC) and the International Telecommunications Union (ITU) have undertaken efforts to increase rural accessibility through community telecenters. The United Nations Development Program (UNDP), United Nations Environmental Program (UNEP), United Nations Industrial Development Organization (UNIDO), the United Nations University (UNU) and the United Nations Institute for Training and Research also have ICT activities which include training, creating learning and policy networking programs, supporting telecenters, and providing ICT equipment to ministries, universities, and other organizations.

A few international projects are trying to address the problem that illiteracy poses for access to information and communication technologies, particularly the Internet. Both USAID/Mali and the Pan African News Agency (PANA) have sponsored initiatives that make the Internet available to the national press and radio broadcasters. These projects will, at least, allow rural inhabitants the information benefits of Internet connectivity, however indirectly. A more direct approach is that of the Centre National d'Études des Telecommunications (CNET) in France. CNET is providing technical assistance with vocal interfaces which, if successful, would allow direct access to information services by illiterates. The pilot project is being conducted in Mali under the auspices of a five-year co-operation agreement with UNESCO.[16]

The list of projects funded by other bilateral donor organizations, multilateral development organizations and foundations is much more expansive that can be presented here.[17] However, there are several web sites that provide links and comprehensive overviews of ongoing projects, including BellaNet and Information Systems in Developing Countries. The next section explores the relationship between electronic media and democratization in Africa in greater detail.

## III: DEMOCRATIZATION AND THE INTERNET IN AFRICA

Is access to the Internet related to the formation of representative political systems in Africa and elsewhere? Kedzie makes a strong case for a global linkage between democracy (as operationalized by New York's Freedom House) and interconnectivity, which he defines as access to e-mail. Using sophisticated statistical analysis, he finds a strong, positive and causal relationship between interconnectivity and democracy; a relationship that is stronger in his model than more traditional causal variables for democracy such as per capita Gross National Product and education. These findings are very significant, and the implications for the larger global efforts to promote are potentially quite dramatic.

However, a few caveats to the analysis conducted by Kedzie are also in order. Specifically, Kedzie chooses a measure of interconnectivity (e-mail) that is likely to have the strongest impact on democracy. As he himself notes: 'e-mail, but not necessarily the other services [such as Internet], offers the specific capability that is hypothesized to have dynamic implications for democratization: multidirectional discourse across borders in a timely and inexpensive manner, unbounded by geographic and institutional constraints'.[18] While e-mail capability is certainly the most sought after and most common form of connectivity in the African context, other aspects of the larger 'Internet' also have great potential to enhance democracy in Africa – particularly access to information from a variety of sources other than the state. While e-mail is certainly a major component of the electronic media, it does not capture other components of Internet access that may also be worth examining, such as the number of Internet Service Providers (ISPs) in a country or the cost for monthly access.

A closer examination of Kedzie's data for Africa specifically reveals a more ambiguous picture than the overall analysis presents. A scatterplot of the regression line for the Africa region presented there shows a strong cluster of data points at the lower end of the scale. This means that countries with *less interconnectivity* tend to be *less democratic* (as defined by Freedom House scores). However, there are also a significant number of countries that are more democratic but have low interconnectivity. The number of countries which could be classified as having medium or high interconnectivity is very small, which does not allow for verification in the African context of the positive nature of the relationship between interconnectivity and democracy that Kedzie claims. In other words, neither democratic nor authoritarian countries in Africa appear to have much interconnectivity. As a result it is unclear from this data whether increases in interconnectivity will necessarily result in greater democracy in Africa.

Considering the persistently high illiteracy rates in Africa, it is unlikely that a significant percentage of Africans will be able to use the Internet as an interactive communication tool in the near future. What is perhaps more important for Africans is the presence of alternative sources of information (such as independent and national radio) which have the capacity to disseminate knowledge from the Internet to a broader audience. None the less, a quantitative analysis was undertaken to examine these relationships more systematically and determine if any correlation could be found.

The dataset used in this analysis was compiled using data from several sources, including *Africa South of the Sahara*, *The World Media Handbook*, Freedom House annual country performance reports, Mike Jensen, and UNESCO *Statistics on Education*. A database codebook listing data sources and years for which the data was collected is attached in the Appendix.

In 1997, the only measures available widely for Africa which measured access to the Internet were the number of Internet service providers in a country (ISP) and the average monthly fee paid by users of the Internet in a country (MONTHFEE). Correlations were run between these measures and measures of political and economic freedom. For political freedom, three measures from the Freedom House index were used. The first, FREEDOM, is an overall measure of freedom that ranks countries into one of three categories; Free, Partly Free, and Not Free. It is calculated using the sub-indices of political rights (POLRIGHT) and civil liberties (CIVIL) that rank countries using a seven-point scale. Economic freedom (ECONFREE) is also calculated by Freedom House using a series of sub-indices measuring several economic dimensions such as corruption, regulation, and taxation. It is important to note that with both of these indices, higher scores indicate *less* freedom. In 1998, other measures of Internet access became available and these were employed in the analysis as well. A measure of Internet density (INTDENS), calculated by dividing the population of a country by the number of Internet users was used, as was a calculation of average local toll rates in a country. In addition, two dummy variables were used to measure whether having a government ISP monopoly (ISPMONOP), or having secondary city access to the Internet outside the capital had any relationship to political and economic freedom. While data on the number of Internet service providers in a country (ISP) were available for both 1997 and 1998, data on monthly fees (MONTHFEE) were not and were therefore dropped from the analysis for 1998.

The findings of the analysis are displayed in Tables 1 and 2. Preliminary results show that, at least in Africa, measures of Internet access are increasingly correlated with the presence of political democracy and economic freedom. Perhaps the most interesting finding is that in less than two years (using data from early 1997 and from late 1998), there has been appreciable strengthening of these relationships. From Table 1 we see a negative but not statistically significant relationship between measures of political freedom and the number of Internet service providers. This means that as the number of ISPs increases, political freedom also increases (because lower scores mean higher freedom). This holds true for all three political freedom measures. One year later, in 1998, we see a strengthening of these relationships such that there is a statistically significant relationship between the measure of civil liberties (CIVIL) and the number of Internet service providers (ISP). For the measure of economic freedom, the results are even more dramatic. In 1997, there was already a significant relationship between the measure of economic freedom (ECONFREE) and the number of Internet service providers (ISP). By 1998 this relationship was very significant (see Table 2). As the number of ISPs increases, so does economic freedom. In some ways this is not unexpected as we typically associate economic liberalism with the proliferation of competition. But it is interesting that the relationship is verifiable in this context.

Interestingly, the measure of average monthly fees for 1997 (MONTHFEE) was not significantly correlated with any of the measures of economic or political freedom. It was, however, significantly correlated with the measure of ISPs. Again, we would expect that as the number of Internet service providers increases that the average monthly fees would decrease as a result of the competition for customers. The data support this conclusion for the African context.

For the new variables that were added for the 1998 analysis there were some very interesting findings. Specifically, both Internet density (INTDENS) and secondary city access (SECOND) are strongly associated with all the measures of political freedom. Internet density is also very strongly associated with the measure of economic freedom (ECONFREE). This tells us that there is an association between counties which have high Internet density (meaning that there are relatively more Internet users) and political and economic freedom. It should be noted that Jensen's measure uses the number of population per Internet user, which means that declining population per Internet user is the indicator of increased access. There is also a clear association between access outside the capital city (SECOND) and political freedom, meaning that countries that have such access are more likely to be democratic than those who do not. Secondary city access was also strongly positively correlated with the presence of increased

TABLE 1

CORRELATIONS BETWEEN DEMOCRACY AND THE INTERNET IN AFRICA, 1997

| 1997 data | ISP Number of Internet Service Providers | MONTHFEE Monthly fee for Internet Access |
|---|---|---|
| FREEDOM Overall Freedom Measure | –.243 | –.295 |
| POLRIGHT Index of Political Rights | –.187 | .208 |
| CIVIL Index of Civil Liberties | –.208 | .154 |
| ECONFREE Economic Freedom Rating | –.328* | –.116 |
| MONTHFEE Monthly fee for Internet Access | –.421* | ... |

*Note*: * significant at the .05 level.

TABLE 2

CORRELATIONS BETWEEN DEMOCRACY AND THE INTERNET IN AFRICA, 1998

| 1998 data | ISP | INTDENS | ISPMONOP | SECOND | LTOLL |
|---|---|---|---|---|---|
| | Number of Internet Service Providers | Internet Density – Population per User | ISP Monopoly Dummy variable | Secondary City Access | Local toll |
| FREEDOM Overall Freedom Measure | –.245 | .307* | –.072 | –.347* | –.101 |
| POLRIGHT Index of Political Rights | –.241 | .360* | –.150 | –.321* | –.040 |
| CIVIL Index of Civil Liberties | –.302* | .507** | –.079 | –.300* | –.130 |
| ECONFREE Economic Freedom Rating | –.499** | .668** | .257 | –.291 | .115 |
| LTOLL Local toll | .086 | –.054 | .169 | –.086 | ... |
| SECOND Secondary City Access | .620** | –.354* | –.394** | ... | ... |
| ISPMONOP ISP Monopoly Dummy variable | –.578** | .065 | ... | ... | ... |
| INTDENS Internet Density – Population per User | –.368* | ... | ... | ... | ... |

*Note*: ** significant at the .01 level; * significant at the .05 level.

numbers of ISPs, and negatively correlated with the presence of an ISP monopoly (ISPMONOP). The measure of local toll rates (LTOLL) was not significantly associated with any other variables in the analysis.

What does all this information tell us? The statistical data, although preliminary, suggests that there is a measurable link between political and economic freedom and access to the Internet in Africa. It must be remembered, however, that association is not the same as causation, and it is beyond the scope of this analysis to determine whether such a causal link exists. Some would argue, in fact, that the causal arrow might point in the other direction, namely that political and economic freedom are, in fact, promoting the Internet, rather than the converse. At the present time we can say with confidence little more than a relationship exists between these variables and is growing stronger. Clearly the Internet has a substantive role to play in the process of democratization and economic development. Considering the relative newness of the Internet to Africa, our ability to determine its impact on other development sectors is still in its infancy. However, the available data suggest that we might want to focus greater attention on this area to try and further explicate the relationships and determine if and how we can use the Internet to achieve our other development goals. In the light of these findings, section IV offers conclusions and recommendations about the role of the Internet in political life in Africa.

## IV: THE INTERNET AND THE PROMOTION OF DEMOCRACY IN AFRICA

> The information revolution could help level the international playing field in terms of opportunities for social and economic development. However, if appropriate care is not taken, the same revolution instead could lead to increasing disparities in incomes and information access, across regions, countries, areas within countries, income groups, communities and individuals … Donors should strongly encourage the development of electronic networking in Africa in directions which will reduce discrepancies between areas and social groups.[19]

There is no doubt that the Internet has the potential to profoundly influence the economic and political development of African states, and affect their role in the global economic and political system as well. To what extent those effects will be positive and sustainable will depend on a myriad of factors, some predictable and others not. This analysis has attempted to address only the narrowest of issues within this broader spectrum;

specifically, whether there is in fact an association between the expansion of the Internet and political and economic development in Africa.

Four conclusions and broader implications can be drawn out from the material presented here.

First, at present, there is statistically significant evidence that the presence of Internet is related to the presence of political and economic 'freedom' in Africa. Second, the Internet is becoming increasingly available to larger proportions of the population in Africa through such initiatives as public Internet kiosks or cafes, and through donor supported initiatives to provide government and civil society access, improved infrastructure for connectivity, and appropriate regulation to foster Internet expansion. Third, the Internet appears to hold great potential to improve access to information in Africa. In particular, great benefits can be derived through ongoing efforts in distance learning and other similar methods. Education in and of itself is a great need in Africa, but using electronic technologies to further that goal also has the additional benefit of ultimately enabling more Africans to gain access to the Internet by increasing overall literacy.

The political and economic implications of this access for Africans are not yet clear. While preliminary studies in the United States (one of the most wired places on earth) show little impact on the Internet on political participation, it could also be argued that there are already sufficient opportunities to provide political input in the United States and the Internet gets lost in this larger array of choices. In Africa, on the other hand, there are very few opportunities and it is possible that the Internet could become a major tool by which non-governmental organizations and citizens exert political influence. While the data here suggest that the presence and growth of the Internet in Africa will lead to more opportunities for political interaction, at this juncture there simply is not enough evidence to make any determinations about the magnitude of impact that the Internet might have on these processes.

Fourth, a critical issue for the spread of Internet technology across Africa will continue to be the question of access. At this time, access remains limited in many Africa countries to urban elites who gain access either through universities or non-governmental organizations. Fagen argues that stripped of all the complexity, the basic question that must arise in any discussion of the impact of these new technologies on communication is 'Who shall control the new instruments of communication, and for what purposes shall they be used?'[20] In Africa, this question may have to be answered at two levels. On the one hand, initiatives by USAID such as the Leland Initiative, along with efforts of other donors, might allow African nations to become players in the international system by enabling them to access the information they require to do so. On the other hand, such efforts may also widen the gap between haves and have-nots, or deepen existing cleavages within individual African countries, creating the potential for political instability if specific efforts are not undertaken to address the problem. Despite the flurry of donor activity, telecommunication projects aimed at rural communities still account for a small percentage of overall networking activity. Approximately 95 per cent of internationally funded projects benefit urban areas.[21]

## FINAL CONCLUSIONS

This examination has argued that the Internet offers great potential to the political and economic development process in Africa. Access to alternative sources of information, as well as the capacity to overcome the limited availability of print media, have the potential to strongly affect the political *status quo* in much of the continent. At the same time, if access is limited to traditional advantaged groups in Africa, there may be negative consequences resulting from the cementing of economic and social inequalities. How the Internet can promote political and economic development in an equitable way remains to be seen. At this time, we can only say that linkages between measures of access to the Internet and political and economic freedom in Africa exist and are getting stronger. The full implication of these linkages for those who would promote the Internet as a means to encourage democratization is not yet clear. The reality is that whether Africa is prepared or not, the Internet exists and will continue to expand and change to meet the needs of its global users. The challenge for Africa, and for those who care about it, is see that the Internet is used in a positive and sustainable manner, both within and without.

## NOTES

1. Lawrence K. Grossman, *The Electronic Republic: Reshaping Democracy in the Information Age* (New York: Penguin, 1996) p.6.
2. Richard R. Fagen, *Politics and Communication* (Boston, MA: Little, Brown, 1966) p.3.
3. Harry M. Cleaver, 'The Zapatista Effect: The Internet and the Rise of an Alternative Political Fabric', *Journal of International Affairs*, Vol.51, No.2 (1998), pp.621–40 and at http://lcweb2.loc.gov/const/fed query. html.
4. Grossman, *The Electronic Republic*, p.16.
5. Ibid., pp.162–3.
6. James Madison, *Federalist Papers: Federalist No. 10*, From the *New York Packet*, Friday, 23 Nov. 1787, at http://lcweb2.loc.gov/const/fed query.html.
7. Kathryn Sikkink and Margaret E. Keck, *Activists Beyond Borders: Advocacy Networks in*

*International Politics* (Ithaca, NY: Cornell University Press, 1998).

8. See, among others, Darrell M. West, 'Air Wars: Television Advertising in Election Campaigns, 1952–1992' (Washington DC: Congressional Quarterly, 1993); and Shanto Iyengar, Donald R. Kinder and Benjamin I. Page, *News That Matters: Television and American Opinion* (Chicago, IL: University of Chicago Press, 1989).
9. Bruce Bimber, 'The Internet and Political Participation: The 1996 Election Season', paper prepared for delivery at the 1997 Annual Meeting of the American Political Science Association, Washington, DC, 28–31 Aug. 1997, p.2.
10. Graeme Browning and Daniel J. Weitzner, *Electronic Democracy : Using the Internet to Influence American Politics* (Wilton, CT: Online, 1996).
11. UNESCO/USAID Global Education Database. 1999, at http://cdie.usaid.gov/esds.
12. Mike Jensen, 'African Internet Status', July 1999, p.1, at http://www3.sn.apc.org/africa/afstat.htm.
13. Lishan Aden, 'Electronic Communications Technology and Development in Africa', 1995, at http://www.sas.upe nn.edu/African_Studies/ASA/lish.html, p.5.
14. O'Coeur de Roy, 'The African Challenge: Internet, Networking, and Connectivity', *Internet Activities in a Developing Environment*, No.5 (1997), p.883.
15. Aden, 'Electronic Communications Technology and Development in Africa', p.6.
16. UNESCO. 'Multipurpose Community Telecenters', at http://www.unesco.org/webworld/public_domain/mct.html.
17. For an extensive review of current donor activity in the area of information and communication technology in Africa, see Mike Jenson, 'A Summary of International ICT Development Projects in Africa', 1998, at http://www3.wn.apc.org/africa/projects.htm. Most of the information in this segment is drawn from this source.
18. Christopher R. Kedzie, 'African Connectivity, Problems, Solutions and Actions: Some Recommendations from INET'96', paper presented at the 1996 Annual Meeting of the Internet Society (INET), at http://wwww.nsrc.org /Africa/regional-reports/iNet.txt.
19. Etienne Baranshamaje, Eugene Boostrom, Vidoje Brajovic, Masud Cader, Robert Clement-Jones, Robert Hawkins, Peter Knight, Robert Schware and Hugh Sloan, 'Increasing Internet Connectivity in sub-Saharan Africa: Issues, Options, and the World Bank Group Role', draft paper, 29 March 1995 (Washington, DC: The World Bank), pp.6–7.
20. Fagen, *Politics and Communication*, p. 150.
21. Mike Jenson and Don Richardson, 'Wireless Weaves to Lessen the Gaps in Rural Telecommunication Coverage in Africa', in *UNESCO, The First Mile: Advancing Telecommunications for Rural Development through a Participatory Communication Approach* (Rome: United Nations Food and Agriculture Organisation, 1998).

## APPENDIX A

## CODEBOOK FOR AFRICA CONNECTIVITY DATASET

| Variable Name | Description | Source | Years |
|---|---|---|---|
| COUNTRY | All African Countries | N/A | 1997–98 |
| YEAR | Year | N/A | 1997–98 |
| FREEDOM | Summary figure for overall Freedom House ranking; 1=Free, 2=Partly Free, 3=Not Free | Freedom House | 1997–98 |
| POLRIGHT | Political Rights score as assigned by Freedom House | Freedom House | 1997–98 |
| CIVIL | Civil Liberties score as assigned by Freedom House | Freedom House | 1997–98 |
| ISP | Number of Internet/Email Service Providers | Mike Jensen | 1997–98 |
| MONTHFEE | Rate (USD) per month for Internet Subscription – (Note:where more than one provider exists, the lowest rate for individuals was selected) | Mike Jensen | 1997 |
| ISPMONOP | Dummy variable for presence of ISP monopoly | | 1998 |
| INTDENS | Internet Density – population per Internet user | Mike Jensen | 1998 |
| SECOND | Dummy variable for secondary city Internet access | | 1998 |
| LTOLL | Not Significant | | |
| ECONFREE | Summary ranking of Economic Freedom calculated by Freedom House | Freedom House | 1998 |

# Tibet, Democracy and the Internet Bazaar

JOHN BRAY

In the western imagination, Tibet has often been seen as a land of mystery, protected by high mountains from unwanted intruders, but the greatest barriers were political rather than geographic. The political barriers were highest in the nineteenth and early twentieth centuries when Tibet closed its borders to westerners – but not to Indians or Nepalis – for fear of being sucked into the vortex of European imperial expansion. In the early years of the twentieth century British officials were reduced to gathering gossip in the bazaars of Darjeeling and Kalimpong to supplement unreliable intelligence on India's nearest northern neighbour.

The political barriers were lowered – if not removed – from 1904 onwards, only to rise again when Tibet was absorbed into the People's Republic of China (PRC) in 1951. The failure of the Lhasa uprising of 1959 led to the Dalai Lama's flight to India. During the 1960s and 1970s, when the PRC went through the traumas of the Cultural Revolution, Tibet was more closed than it has ever been. Since 1980 Tibet has again been open to tourists, journalists and now aid workers, but – like the PRC as a whole – it scarcely enjoys freedom of information.

Political obstacles may still exist, but now there is a new electronic bazaar. According to figures provided by the Altavista database, the number of English-language worldwide web pages dealing with East Asia rose from 2.2 million to 9.1 million between February 1997 and June 1999. In the same period, the number of web pages relating to Tibet rose from 39,060 to 212,980, an increase of more than 400 per cent.[1] The topics covered ranged from politics and religion to tourism, postage stamps, rare breeds of dog and fictional flying lamas. Real Tibet may face all sorts of problems: cyber-Tibet flourishes.

Tibet advocacy groups in the West hope that this abundance of information on Tibet, and the speed of e-mail communications, will help promote democracy. For example, the Canada Tibet Committee home page cites Christopher R. Kedzie on the liberating impact of the Internet:

> The use of email embodies specific characteristics with dynamic implications for democratization. Affordable and quick access to information, unbounded by geographic or institutional restrictions is a critical component for the development of democracy.[2]

However, problems arise not just because of the questionable quality of much of this information but – still more – because of its uneven distribution. This survey analyses the extent to which the Internet assists the national and international political debate on Tibet, and the obstacles that still remain.

## THE IDEOLOGICAL DIVIDE

Tibet's political future is contested between the PRC government in Beijing and the Dalai Lama's government-in-exile in Dharamsala (northern India). For many years the two sides have argued in speech and on paper: now they have taken their dispute to the Internet. The Internet does not change the nature of their arguments, but it does provide them with a new platform from which to express their positions

One of the most authoritative recent expositions of Beijing's position is the *White Paper – New Progress in Human Rights in the Tibet Autonomous Region* (issued on 20 February 1998), and this is available on the Chinese government's web-site (www.chinaguide.org/WhitePapers) as well as through the Chinese Embassy in Washington (www.china-embassy.org). Another source of official views is *China's Tibet* (www.tibet-china.org), and this includes sections on history and politics; tourism and landscape culture and art; Tibetan Buddhism; science; technology and education; and women and children. News updates reflecting the official view appear in the Xinhua News Agency (http://info.xinhua.org).

The Tibetan government-in-exile presents its position on its official web-site (www.tibet.com), which is managed by the Tibet Office in London, and through affiliated institutions such as the Tibetan Centre for Human Rights and Democracy (TCHRD – www.tchrd.org). With the help of American volunteers, Dharamsala has now established an e-mail network to facilitate communication between the scattered Tibetan refugee communities in India.

The two sides contest almost everything about Tibet. The areas of dispute include the legitimacy (though the word is rarely used) of the pre-1951 Tibetan government; the role of Tibetan Buddhism; the boundaries of Tibet; human rights; the most appropriate form of democracy; and the history – as well as the future – of Tibet's relationship with China.

## THE VIEW FROM DHARAMSALA

Tibetans acknowledge that their country was not scientifically or technologically advanced in the period before 1951, but claim that it nevertheless enjoyed a special status – and therefore legitimacy – because of its religious affiliation. In 1946 the Tibetan National Assembly summarized this view in a letter to President Chiang Kai-shek's Kuomintang government in China:

> There are many great nations on this earth who have achieved unprecedented wealth and might, but there is only one nation which is dedicated to the well-being of humanity in the world, and that is the religious land of Tibet which cherishes a joint spiritual and temporal realm.[3]

The exile government's web-site expresses the same view with sections on the latest news; the status of Tibet, including articles on human rights and the environment; the government of Tibet; and Tibetan culture, with a particular emphasis on Tibetan Buddhism.

The official Tibetan view of the country's past relationship with China is that it stemmed from a personal *mchod yon* ('priest/patron') relationship between the Dalai Lama and the Chinese Emperor, and that this lapsed following the collapse of the Manchu dynasty in 1911. Dharamsala's web-site insists that 'a study of Tibet's history reveals that, contrary to Chinese Communist claims, Tibet at no time became an integral part of China'. The site includes reproductions of Tibetan bank notes as visual evidence that the Tibetan government exercised the functions of an independent government between 1911 and 1951.

The debate about Tibet's political future is complicated by different interpretations of the boundaries of 'Tibet'. Dharamsala's online map of 'Tibet at a glance' shows all three traditional Tibetan provinces – U-Tsang, Kham and Amdo – inside the country's borders. By contrast, when Chinese official sources refer to 'Tibet', they usually mean the Tibet Autonomous Region (TAR) rather than other ethnic Tibetan areas in the neighbouring Chinese provinces of Qinghai, Sichuan, Gansu and Yunnan. According to Chinese population figures, there are as many Tibetans in these provinces as there are within its borders – approximately 2.3 million each in 1994.[4]

The Dalai Lama's thinking on democracy is outlined on the web-site in the *Guidelines for Future Tibet's Polity and the Basic Features of its Constitution,* which were originally issued in 1992. The document reviews the history of the exile government's constitutional experiments, starting with a draft constitution which was promulgated by the Dalai Lama in 1961, and 'based on the principles of modern democracy'. Looking forward, the Dalai Lama asserts optimistically:

> It will not be long before the Chinese find themselves compelled to leave Tibet. When this joyful occasion comes … the present totalitarian system, dubbed centralised democracy, will have to give way to true democracy under which the people of all the three provinces of Tibet, namely U-Tsang, Kham and Amdo, can enjoy freedom of thought, expression and movement. My hope is that Tibet will then be a zone of peace where environmental protection becomes the official policy. I also hope that Tibetan democracy will derive its inspiration from the Buddhist principles of compassion, justice and equality.

*The Guidelines* lay down outline procedures for the appointment of an interim President and a Constituent Assembly. The principal features of the constitution include adherence to the United Nations Universal Declaration of Human Rights, the renunciation of violence and use of military force, and the establishment of a two-chamber parliament.

## THE VIEW FROM BEIJING

Beijing's political claims on Tibet are based on a combination of historical interpretation; denunciations of the pre-1951 Tibetan political system; affirmation of the present democratic system; and economic development. When official documents refer to 'Tibet', they almost always mean the TAR.

Beijing's historical claims, as presented online in the *White Paper* and other documents, are unequivocal. Tibet was 'officially incorporated into the domain of China's Yuan dynasty in the mid-13th century'. Since then it has been 'under the jurisdiction of China's Central Government as an inalienable part of China's territory'. However, before 1959 it was 'a society of feudal serfdom characterized by the merging of politics and religion and the dictatorship of the clergy and nobility'. Recently, economic and social development has been speeded up, thus promoting the cause of human rights.

The *White Paper* and *China's Tibet* both emphasize the democratic nature of the current political system. For example, the politics section of *China's Tibet* describes how 91.6 per cent of the total electorate voted in the 1993 elections for people's congresses at various levels. It says that ethnic Tibetans account for 99.92 per cent of township level deputies; 92.6 per cent of country-level deputies, and 82.44 per cent of the Sixth People's Congress of the TAR. The TAR enjoys autonomy in a variety of areas including the right to draft self-government ordinances and the right to independently plan local economic undertakings.

Despite Tibet's 'exceedingly primitive and backward foundation', the region's economic development is one of its main achievements, according to the *White Paper*, and it cites improvements both in industry and agriculture. Health and educational resources are available to all and, thanks to the government's initiatives, the region enjoys religious and cultural freedom: 'The essence of traditional Tibetan culture is a component part of Chinese national culture and the government has always attached great importance to protecting and developing it and helping it flourish.'

Government sources offer no room for compromise on Beijing's basic position: that Tibet is an integral part of China, and has been for centuries.

## THE VIEW FROM LHASA

The view from the streets of Lhasa – or from the fields and pastures of rural Tibet – is less readily available on the Internet. Chinese official sources are correct in pointing out that large numbers of Tibetans have reached senior office in the TAR, including a number who come from the much maligned clergy and former nobility.[5] Tibetans inside Tibet are to be found on both sides of the ideological divide. No doubt most struggle to survive and to flourish as best they can, regardless of ideological niceties. Nevertheless, the evidence of the last 15 years shows continuing attachment to the Dalai Lama – despite official denunciations – and to the ideal of independence.

In 1987 and 1988, following a period of comparative political liberalization, Buddhist monks and nuns led a series of demonstrations in Lhasa to demand Tibetan independence. The ideas that they expressed showed that they were capable of adapting information from a variety of sources to fit Tibet's particular circumstances. One of the most interesting documents produced in this period was an 11-page block-print produced by a group of monks from Drepung monastery near Lhasa. The text was called, 'The Meaning of the Precious Democratic Constitution of Tibet', and began by affirming that:

> ... we will not always have to remain under the foreign Chinese invaders; possessing the right to self-determination in accordance with international law, there is no doubt that we will be able to enjoy the splendour of all religious and political freedoms.

It argued that the country's future democratic government should adopt both religious and secular principles, and made clear that there was no question of a return to the past:

> Having completely eradicated the practices of the old society with all its faults, the future Tibet will not resemble our former condition and be a restoration of serfdom or be like the so-called 'old system' of rule by a succession of feudal masters or monastic estates.[6]

Instead, it would be necessary 'to build political and social organization on the basis of the cooperation and support of the broad masses of Tibet'.

Predictably, the Chinese authorities have denounced all such writings as 'splittist'. The compilers of the Drepung manifesto were arrested and condemned to lengthy prison terms, and the government has invested much time and effort in propagating the official version of Tibet's history and its relationship with the Chinese motherland. For example, in 1996 the government launched its 'Patriotic Education Campaign' in monasteries and schools in the Tibet Autonomous Region, and this has since been extended to Tibetan monasteries and schools in Qinghai province.[7] The campaign denounces the Dalai Lama as:

> … a conspirator, the chief of the splittist movement aspiring for Tibetan independence, the unequivocal tool of the western forces inimical towards China, the main source of all disturbances in Tibetan society, and the biggest stumbling block to the establishment of normal religious discipline in Tibetan Buddhism.[8]

It would scarcely be necessary to make these assertions so emphatically unless the authorities believed that large numbers of Tibetans thought otherwise.

All these political questions must be seen against a background of social and economic change. In some rural areas the post-1980 reforms have enabled Tibetans to reassert something approaching their pre-1950 lifestyles.[9] In Lhasa and other larger towns, the situation is very different. Tibetans feel increasingly marginalized in an urban economy dominated by Chinese migrants, and this has led to the emergence of previously unheard-of social problems, including widespread prostitution.[10]

Many of these problems are shared with other developing societies. It will be hard to find equitable solutions without genuine popular participation in government, and that will require a more open – and more informed – political debate than has yet been heard in Lhasa.

## THE NEW TIBETAN INTERNET BAZAAR

The absence of real democratic debate within Tibet raises the question whether Tibet's international sympathizers can use the Internet and other tools to draw attention to the most important issues from abroad. The answer will depend on who is writing on the Net – and who responds.

### *Politics, Religion and Fantasy*

By 1998 more than 143 million people worldwide were using the Internet, and that figure was expected to rise to more than 700m by 2001.[11] However, although these users were widely distributed across the world, there was still a marked imbalance in favour of the developed countries of the West. In 1998 the typical Internet user was still a western, middle-class graduate who could read and write English. Similarly, it can be assumed that the Tibetans most likely to communicate through the Internet are educated members of the diaspora – typically the children of the refugees who left their homeland with the Dalai Lama in 1959. It is difficult to generalize amidst the enormous variety of web sites, but inevitably the majority reflect the interests of these two categories of people – separately and in alliance.

The *Geocities* guide to the Web offers a special section of 326 Tibet-related links (www.geocities.com/Athens/Academy/9594/links.html). The first page makes a political statement by displaying the Tibetan flag (proscribed in the PRC) along with the slogan 'Free Tibet!' Two main categories dominate the 326 references: religion and politics, with the former predominating. For example, under the letter 'A', the viewer is offered sites relating to: 'The Art of Tibetan Sand Painting'; 'The Arya Tara Homepage'; 'The Asian Classics Input Project'; 'Astrology by Jhampa Shaneman', and the 'Asynchronous School of Buddhist Dialectics'. The more political sites under the letter 'A' are Amnesty International and the Australian Tibet Council.

From a political point of view, the western preoccupation with Tibetan religion is both an advantage and a disadvantage. In principle, greater awareness of Tibetan Buddhism should lead to greater awareness of the country of Tibet, and some political activists have come to the Tibet issue by that route. Professor Robert Thurman of Columbia University offers himself as an example of this trend. Thurman is a former Buddhist monk and initially was interested solely in Tibetan religious teachings, but then broadened his view:

> I thought Tibet had done me the kindness of preserving the dharma from ancient times in India and handing it to me ... I woke up to how

> callous that was about 15 years ago and decided that I could try to repay their kindness by helping to get the world's attention focused on this massive injustice.[12]

However, other writers have expressed concern that a narrower preoccupation with religion, and especially with Shangri-la fantasies of Tibet, may serve to divert attention from the realities of contemporary politics. Writing in 1992, before the Internet began to play a significant role, Tibetan historian Tsering Shakya declared: 'It is a paradox that, while Tibet receives overwhelming sympathy and expressions of concern from individuals, nevertheless the Tibetan political struggle remains marginalized and on the periphery of the international agenda'.[13] He noted that no trade unions or similar bodies had taken up the Tibetan cause and suggested that all too often the Tibet issue was not taken seriously because 'the politics of Tibet are seen as how to preserve a dying civilization, whether it is best to preserve it in jam jars or museums'. He concluded 'If the Tibetan issue is to be taken seriously, Tibet must be liberated from both the Western imagination and the myth of Shangri-la.[14] Two years later Donald Lopez expressed a similar view:

> Fantasies of Tibet have in the past three decades inspired much support for the cause of Tibetan independence. But those fantasies are ultimately a threat to the realization of that goal … To the extent that we continue to believe that Tibet prior to 1950 was a utopia, the Tibet of 1994 will be no place.[15]

Many of the 'New Age' sites on the web appear to justify Lopez's concern that Western Tibet aficionados are more concerned with a fantasy or 'virtual' Tibet than the reality. This raises the danger that many of the Tibetans' would-be allies elsewhere in the world will see the Tibetan cause as a purely western preoccupation, partly generated by Walt Disney and on the same level of seriousness as other Hollywood creations. On the other hand, people who are originally attracted to Tibet by the fictional attractions of Shangri-la may subsequently gain a deeper awareness of its contemporary realities. Concern for Tibet has created some strange political and cultural alliances and, as will be seen, the Internet has played a role in cementing them.

In any case, New Age messages are far from being the only Tibet-related voices on the Internet. The web also provides access to up-to-date news and other sources of information.

*A Source of News and Analysis*

The Internet makes it easy to consult mainstream news sources such as the BBC, the *New York Times* and *The Times of India*: many of these provide significant – albeit intermittent – coverage on Tibet. In addition, there are now a number of specialist Internet sources:

- The *World Tibet Network News* (WTN) is the brainchild of the Canada Tibet Committee (www.tibet.ca). It provides regular compilations of news articles on Tibet from sources such as Reuters, Xinhua (the official Chinese news agency), the *Washington Post* and advocacy groups such as the UK-based Free Tibet Campaign. These are sent free of charge by e-mail to subscribers four or five times a week. Some 8,000 articles dating back to 1992 are available on WTN's archives. Three out of its five editors are Tibetans, and they draw on an international network of voluntary news monitors.
- The *Tibet Information Network* (TIN) is a London-based news and research agency, founded by Robert Barnett in 1987. Unlike WTN, TIN compiles its own news updates – some 40 a year. These focus on developments inside Tibet, which tend to be poorly covered in the mainstream international media, and draw on a network of official and unofficial sources in Tibet, Nepal and India. TIN news updates are sent to subscribers by e-mail and, after a short interval, posted on the organization's web-site (www.tibetinfo.net). TIN also produces longer, hard-copy research publications on topics such as education and the Chinese government's Patriotic Education Campaign. TIN's mandate is solely to provide information: it does not adopt any particular political line.
- The *Voice of Tibet* is based in Oslo and part-financed by the Norwegian government as well as other charitable foundations. It produces daily 30-minute Tibetan-language radio programmes on short-wave, and these are broadcast to reach Tibet in the evening . The broadcasts can now be downloaded from the organization's web-site (www.vot.org).
- Certain academic institutions have woken up to the significance of the Web, and these include the Australian National University (ANU), where Dr Matthew Ciolek runs the *Tibetan Studies WWW Virtual Library* (www.ciolek.com/WWWVL-TibetanStudies.html).[16] The library was established in January 1995, and includes cross-references to web-sites on – among other topics – 'Art, Theatre and Music', 'Human rights', 'Language, Literature and Software', and 'Travel and Tourism'.

In all these cases the Internet 'interacts' with other media. For example, WTN draws on articles in the print media and extends their audience via the Internet. Similarly, material sent out by organizations such as TIN via the Internet may contribute to articles in mainstream print publications, such as the *Guardian* (London), as well as specialist periodicals such as the New Delhi-based *Tibetan Review*. The overall result is that material which might otherwise reach no more than a narrow audience is now more widely distributed.

*Linking Advocacy Groups*

One of the main ways that news is distributed is through national and international Tibet support groups, many of whom provide translations of significant news items for their local audiences. The Internet provides a cheap and efficient means for these groups to co-ordinate and share information. Each national group's web-site typically offers links to other related organizations both in-country and abroad.

The US-based *Tibet Online Resource Gathering* (Tibet ORG) group has set itself the task of helping co-ordinate the online resources of the various national and international Tibet support groups. On its own web-site (www.tibet.org) the group explains that it aims to 'counteract the disadvantages Tibetans face in their struggle against the vast resources of the Chinese government' and believes that it can 'level the playing field by leveraging the Internet's ability to harness international grassroots support for Tibet's survival … '.

Tibet ORG's web-site includes links to the web pages of a wide range of support organizations. The major US-based organizations include *International Campaign for Tibet, International Committee of Lawyers for Tibet* (www.tibeticlt.org), *The Committee of 100 for Tibet* (www.tibet.org./Tibet100) and *Tibet Fund* (www.tibetfund.org). International links include dozens of support groups – each with their own angle on Tibet – in countries ranging from Germany and France to Russia, Japan and South Korea. In countries such as France and Germany there are often half a dozen or more Tibet support groups. Non-English resources on Tibet are available in 15 European and Asian languages – with the conspicuous absence of Tibetan and Chinese. Tibet advocacy web-sites also typically offer links to non-governmental organizations with a broader geographical remit such as Amnesty International or Human Rights Watch.

*Campaigns*

These links make it easier to co-ordinate national and international campaigns, including boycotts. One example is the US-based Tibetan Rights Campaign (TRC) whose web-site calls for support in a campaign involving Recreational Equipment Inc. (REI).[17] The organization explains that it is only seeking a boycott of REI goods made in China, and not REI as a whole. TRC claims an earlier success in persuading the Puget Consumers' Co-operative, the largest natural food store in the US, to discontinue carrying anything made in China until Tibet is freed.[18] However, while such activities may have a certain symbolic value, it is questionable whether they have a significant impact on policy either in China or the US. For US consumers, the link between Tibetan human rights and Chinese-made sports goods may seem a little tenuous.

Letter-writing campaigns appear to be more effective, although they are more likely to have an impact on western leaders than the Chinese. The Internet makes it much easier to co-ordinate such campaigns both by advertizing them and, in many cases, by making it possible to send off the letter straight from the keyboard, either by fax or by e-mail. The combined US Tibet lobby has ensured that Tibet remains a significant item – even if not the decisive one – on the agenda of the US in its relations with China.[19]

The controversy between April and June 1999 over a proposed World Bank loan to China provides a recent example of the potential impact of the Tibet lobby. On 27 April the Tibet Information Network (TIN) published an online article about a World Bank-sponsored resettlement project in Haoxi Prefecture in Qinghai province. The project was to resettle some 58,000 poor farmers on more fertile land. Most of the settlers were Chinese or members of the Hui, Tu and Salar communities, but they were to move to areas that traditionally had been populated by Tibetans or Mongolians.

TIN's story was picked up by Tibet advocacy groups across the world, and their supporters issued hundreds of letters to their respective governments and to World Bank President James Wolfensohn calling on them to use their influence to have the project cancelled. The campaign had particular resonance in the US where, as the *New York Times* commented, it helped create an unusual but perhaps appropriate alliance comprising Senate Foreign Relations Committee chairman Jesse Helms and the Beastie Boys pop group, both of whom were opposed to the project.[20] By the end of May US Treasury Secretary Robert Rubin announced that the US was 'inclined to oppose' the project.[21]

The eventual outcome was a compromise. The World Bank's Board of Executive Directors approved the project on 24 June, but said that no funds would be made available in Qinghai until the board decided on the results of a review by an independent Inspection Panel. In the Bank's press release, Wolfensohn commented that the project had been 'particularly grueling' in the light of criticisms in regard to the Bank's handling of environmental and minority issues in China.[22] The panel has yet to report, and the board's decision was therefore no more than a partial victory for the Tibet lobby. It is highly unlikely that it could have achieved as much impact as it did without the co-ordinating power of the Internet.

The World Bank Qinghai affair therefore points to the power of the Internet in western capitals. However, to make a real impact on Tibet, the medium will have to influence policy in China. That is likely to prove much more problematic.

## CHINA: FIREWALLS AND DEMOCRACY WALLS

Access to the Internet in the PRC is limited in comparison to most western countries, but growing rapidly. In early 1999, the number of Internet accounts in the PRC was only two million; by the following July the figure had doubled to four million; and it was expected to reach ten million by the end of the year 2000.[23] At least three people commonly use each account, and the Internet is already beginning to have a political and social impact.

### *Pro-democracy Activists*

Like the Tibet lobby, China activists have been quick to see the potential of the Internet as a means of spreading information and ideas, both inside and outside China. Examples of web-sites concerned with Chinese democracy include the Hong Kong Voice of Democracy (www.democracy.org.hk); Silicon Valley for Democracy in China (www.svdc.org), and Human Rights in China (HRIC – www.hrichina.org). In 1999 international China activists chose to commemorate Tiananmen by setting up a 'Virtual Democracy Wall' for posting comments relating to Chinese politics (http://books.dreambook.com/vead/tiananmen.html). They made much of the fact that they enjoyed freedom of speech – or writing – on a virtual wall, even if not on real walls made of bricks and mortar inside China.

It does not necessarily follow that Chinese activists are interested in or sympathetic to Tibet. As American scholar Warren Smith points out:

> While many Chinese have since learned to discredit much party propaganda, most still accept without question the CCP's version of Tibetan history and China's role in Tibet. Many Chinese, even

'democratic' Chinese, respond to criticism of China's Tibet policy with a litany of the supposed horrors of Tibet's pre-liberation social and political system.[24]

Smith's observation applies particularly to Chinese brought up in the PRC, but even overseas Chinese are liable to cast a sceptical eye at the Tibetan cause. For example, in two articles published in the Chinese Community Forum (a US-based e-mail magazine – www.china-net.org) in March and April 1998, Bevin Chu wrote that the Dalai Lama was a 'petty tribalist' because of his unhealthy pre-occupation with Chinese migration into Tibet and his 'obstinate campaign of ethnic separatism'.

Nevertheless, both in the PRC and abroad, some Chinese democracy activists have begun to make common cause with their Tibetan counterparts. This is reflected on their web-sites. For example, HRIC's web-site carries articles on human rights and political prisoners in Tibet, and offers links to Tibet-related sites such as the Free Tibet Campaign in the UK, and the Tibetan government-in-exile. Similarly, Hong Kong Voice of Democracy carries a report dated December 1998 on a PRC attempt to jam Voice of Tibet radio broadcasts. The report was prepared by Reporters sans Frontières in Paris, and distributed by the International Freedom of Expression Exchange (IFEX) in Canada – a typical example of the Web's interconnections.

Wei Jingsheng, a veteran of the 1978/79 democracy wall movement who was forced into exile in 1997, has been particularly outspoken on the subject of Tibet. In an interview published on the on-line *China News Digest*, he explained that he gained a particular insight into the Tibetan situation through his friendship with a Tibetan girl, the daughter of a veteran communist activist.[25] He said that both Tibetans and Chinese have been 'oppressed by the violent regime of the Communist Party', but added that the Tibetans had 'suffered from an extra layer, that of ethnic oppression'. Chinese should therefore 'try to seek the truth about the Tibet problem, instead of placing total trust in the propaganda of the Communist Party'. At best it would take years to remove the ill-feeling between the two peoples. In theory, one long-term outcome might be Tibetan independence, but there would be no 'absolute need to separate' if true democracy could be achieved.[26]

Wei's original insights came from his personal connections, but another prominent dissident, Xu Wenli (leader of the fledgling China Democratic Party) attributes changing attitudes to external news sources: 'Access to the World Wide Web, along with broadcasts into China by VOA [Voice of

America], Radio Free Asia and the BBC is providing accurate news for a growing number of Chinese on Tibet's problems'.[27] Xu points out that the 'government is using guns and cannons to solve its ethnic problems, but that policy is fueling pro-independence sentiment in Tibet'. The solution is for the CCP to loosen its control and allow Tibet to decide its own future in democratic union with China.

Neither Wei nor Xu can be considered representative of Chinese popular opinion, but their views suggest that Chinese attitudes towards Tibet are not inflexible – and that the Internet, along with other media, may play a role in changing them.

### *The Chinese Government's Reaction*

The Chinese authorities' response to the challenge posed by the Internet has been ambivalent at best. On the one hand, officials recognize the importance of free flows of information for economic development. On the other, they are fully aware of the medium's potential for subversion. They have reacted by trying to contain what they regard as the malign influence of the Net, but with limited results.

China has enacted sweeping legal restrictions on the use of the Internet. Would-be account-holders have to seek permission from the Ministry of Public Security, and it is an offence to use the Net for such activities as 'inciting hatred or discrimination among nationalities or harming the unity of nationalities'; 'openly insulting other people or distorting the truth to slander people'; and 'injuring the reputation of state organs.'[28] Online discussions of the need for political reform in Tibet would certainly be included in one or other of these categories.

In January 1999 Lin Hai, a Shanghai software engineer, was sentenced to two years in prison for sending a list of 30,000 e-mail addresses to a US-based pro-democracy Internet news letter.[29] However, despite Lin's fate, many Internet account holders still fail to register or to obey the law in other ways – and these include many proprietors of the new cybercafés currently springing up across China. In practice, the law acts as no more than a partial deterrent.

The same applies to the government's attempts to use technology to censor the net. In principle, Chinese users are supposed to access the web through one of four government-controlled networks: the government uses these to screen out undesirable web-sites, such as *Penthouse* and the *New York Times.* In practice, Internet users find ways of circumventing these networks, and instruction manuals telling them how to do so are readily available. Similarly, publishers of dissident newsletters try to cover their tracks by sending articles to foreign colleagues who then 'rebroadcast' their material en masse to Chinese e-mail addresses.

The Chinese government is not yet ready to admit defeat. However, whatever technical or legal means it employs, the sheer volume of information will make the Internet increasingly hard – indeed impossible – to control. The Chinese Communist Party's view of Tibet's history may be deeply entrenched in the minds of China's citizens, but alternative points of view are becoming more and more widely available via the country's computer networks.

## OUTLOOK FOR NETWORK DEMOCRACY IN TIBET

Cybercafés are common in the streets of Beijing and Shanghai, and they have now reached the streets of Lhasa – along with a proliferation of karaoke bars. Government-imposed barriers to the free flow of electronic information may therefore be gradually eroding, even in Tibet. But at best, this will be a long process.

In the long run the greatest obstacles may not be legal, but economic and educational. Internet access fees cost some US$50 a month in the PRC. Quite apart from the costs of the equipment, this kind of money is well beyond the resources of most Tibetans – even in the towns. Shortage of computers is another factor, especially in the countryside. However, the most important issue is lack of education. In the early 1990s 73.3 per cent of all Tibetans – and 84.2 per cent of Tibetan women – were illiterate.[30] Without literacy skills it will be impossible to use the computer. Without a knowledge of English, it will be impossible to make the most of the Internet's international networks.

The United Nations Development Programmes's most recent *Human Development Report* emphasized the potential humanitarian benefits of new information technology, but at the same time emphasized the continuing obstacles:

> Geographic barriers may have fallen for communications, but a new barrier has emerged, an invisible barrier that, true to its name is like a world wide web, embracing the connected and silently – almost imperceptibly – excluding the rest … The network society is creating parallel communication systems: one for those with income, education and – literally – connections … ; the other for those without connections … .[31]

The overwhelming majority of Tibetans lack connections, in every sense.

Nevertheless, it would be wrong to underestimate the power of the Internet in two important respects. First, for all the Chinese government's attempts at censorship, it is becoming an increasingly important means of sharing information inside the PRC. Even if only a few Tibetans are 'connected', they will find means of sharing what they learn with other people, and it would a mistake to underestimate their ingenuity in finding ways of doing so.

Secondly, and for the present more importantly, the Internet provides a means whereby otherwise obscure news from the markets and bazaars of Tibet can be broadcast cheaply and efficiently across the world to everyone who wishes to listen. Such information in turn provides a basis for more informed discussion of Tibet both within governments and in international institutions such as the World Bank and the United Nations.

The e-mail and the web page may one day join the blockprint and the street song as standard mediums of Tibetan political expression. That day has yet to arrive, but the Internet already makes a difference.

## NOTES

1. Information supplied by Dr Matthew Ciolek of the Australian National University (ANU). See the ANU's Asia Web Watch: www.ciolek.com.Asia-Web-Watch/tables/table-003.htm.
2. Cited on the World Tibet Network News web-site: www.tibet.ca.wtnnews.htm.
3. Cited in: Melvyn C. Goldstein, *A History of Modern Tibet, 1913–1951* (Berkeley, CA: University of California Press, 1989), p.542.
4. For a detailed discussion see: Steven D. Marshall and Susette Ternent Cooke, *Tibet Outside the TAR. Control, Exploitation and Assimilation: Development with Chinese Characteristics* (Washington, DC: The Alliance for Research in Tibet, 1997. Published on CD-ROM).
5. For a detailed analysis see: Victoria Conner and Robert Barnett, *Leaders in Tibet: A Directory* (London: Tibet Information Network, 1997).
6. Cited in Ronald D. Schwartz, *Circle of Protest: Political Ritual in the Tibetan Uprising* (London: Hurst, 1994), p.127.
7. For a selection of translated documents relating to the Patriotic Education Campaign see: Tibet Information Network (TIN), *Political Campaigns. Documents and Statements from Tibet 1996-1997* (London: TIN, 1998. Background Briefing Papers No. 30); TIN, *A Sea of Bitterness. Patriotic Education in Qinghai Monasteries* (London: TIN, 1999. TIN Briefing Paper No.32).
8. Patriotic Education Book 1, June 1996. Cited in the preface to *Political Campaigns: Documents and Statements from Tibet 1996–1997.*
9. For an optimistic assessment of a community of nomads in western Tibet, see M.C. Goldstein, 'Change, Conflict and Continuity Among a Community of Nomadic Pastoralists. A Case Study from Western Tibet, 1950–1990', in Robert Barnett (ed.), *Resistance and Reform in Tibet* (London: Hurst, 1994).
10. TIN, *Social Evils. Prostitution and Pornography in Lhasa* (London: TIN, 1999. TIN Briefing Paper 31).
11. United Nations Development Programme (UNDP), *Human Development Report 1999* (New York: UNDP, 1999), p.58.
12. Rodger Kamenetz, 'Robert Thurman doesn't look Buddhist', *New York Times Magazine*, 5 May 1996. Also available on the newspaper's web-site: www.nytimes.com.

13. Tsering Shakya. 'Of real and imaginary Tibet', *Tibetan Review* 27, No.1 (Jan. 1992), pp.13–16.
14. Ibid.
15. Donald S. Lopez. 'New Age Orientalism: the Case of Tibet', *Tibetan Review* 29, No.5 (May 1994), pp.16–20. See also D.S. Lopez's recent book which develops these themes: *Prisoners of Shangri-la.* (Chicago, IL: University of Chicago Press, 1998).
16. Ciolek is of Polish origin and compares the Internet with the role of the BBC during the Second World War. During the Warsaw Uprising of August/September 1944, the BBC picked up messages broadcast by the Polish resistance on weak, home-made transmitters. It then re-broadcast them more loudly and more clearly so that the messages would be received by other insurgents using equally weak receivers. He argues that the Internet can have a similar impact by 'rebroadcasting' narrowly circulated information to a global audience.
17. The appeal is posted on: www.tibet.org/Activism/Action/rei.html.
18. Ibid.
19. For a review of recent US policy on Tibet, see: Barry Sautman, 'The Tibet Issue in Post-Summit Sino-American Relations', *Pacific Affairs,* Vol.72, No.1 (1999), pp.7–21.
20. David E. Sanger, 'A Stick for China, a Carrot for Tibet's Lobby', *New York Times,* 11 July 1999.
21. Paul Lewis, 'US May Try to Stop Loan Seen As Bad for Tibetans', *New York Times,* 30 May 1999.
22. 'World Bank Approves China Western Poverty Reduction Project', World Bank Group news release No. 99/2282/EAP (www.worldbank.org/html/extdr/extme/2282.htm).
23. Reuters, 'China's Internet Users Double to Four Million', 15 July 1999.
24. Warren Smith, *Tibetan Nation, A History of Tibetan Nationalism and Sino-Tibetan Relations,* (Boulder, CO: Westview Press, 1996).
25. 'The Tibet Issue, as a Chinese Dissident Sees It', *Tibetan Review* Vol.33, No.3 (March 1998), pp.13–17. The *China News Digest* interview was published in Chinese on 25 Jan. 1998.
26. Conrad Richter, 'Wei for Respecting Tibetan Wish for Independence', WTN, 14 Feb. 1999. Reprinted in *Tibetan Review*, Vol.33, No.3 (March 1998), pp.6–7.
27. 'Chinese Democrats Make Common Cause with Tibet', *Tibetan Review,* Vol.32, No.12 (Dec. 1998), pp.28–9. Reprinted from *Christian Science Monitor*, 19 Nov. 1998.
28. Charles D. Paglee, *Chinalaw Web – Computer Information Network and Internet Security, Protection and Management Regulations.* Approved by the State Council on 11 Dec. 1997, and promulgated by the Ministry of Public Security on 30 Dec. 1997. www.qis.net/chinalaw/prclaw54.htm.
29. 'China Poised to Hunt Down Anti-government Material Online', Associated Press, 2 Feb. 1999. Carried on Freedom Forum Online: www.freedomforum.org.
30. Catriona Bass, *Education in Tibet* (London: Zed Books, 1998), p.206.
31. World Bank, *Human Development Report 1999*, (New York: Oxford University Press, 1999), p.63.

# Conclusion

PETER FERDINAND

So how far has the Internet transformed politics up to now? Is the glass half-full or half-empty? It is certainly possible to point to particular events in democracies that would not have happened without the Internet playing an important role. The election of Ventura as Governor of Minnesota in 1998, for instance, is usually credited to his campaign, which was chiefly based on the Internet. And slightly more generally, Stromer-Galley has shown various ways in which campaign professionals in the United States have adopted some techniques that would not have been possible without the Internet. Already campaigning has been affected by these innovations.

On the other hand the basic impression that follows from these papers is that the glass is not even yet half-full. Even in the United States, where Internet penetration is still very much greater than in any other country, commentators are still awaiting the first signs of real transformation. People predict that the presidential election campaign of 2000 will be the first to be heavily influenced by the Internet, just as they said about the 1996 election. Other commentators agree. Bimber, for instance, notes that television did not come to exercise its full influence on American politics until the 1960s and 1970s. Even allowing for differences between the impact of the Internet and of television upon society, it would be unrealistic to see the full effect of the Internet for some years.[1]

In any case, as the Internet comes to play a bigger role in campaigning, it may lose some of the distinctive characteristics that encouraged those who hoped it would reduce the power of money in elections. As the Internet is increasingly merged with video and audio output, the possibility for media companies to produce sophisticated campaign material, but this time tailored much more precisely to the concerns of individual voters that have been identified by prior surveys, will reopen the opportunity for those with deep pockets to impress. Even a cursory glance at the web pages for the Democratic and Republican parties in the US suggests that these organizations are bringing the more professional techniques that they learnt in the television age of campaigning to the Internet. Bieber, too, has shown how the main political parties in Germany have been actively embracing the new technologies to revive citizen interest in politics, although he is more doubtful about their likely success and the depth of their commitment to make the most of what the technologies can offer.

Also, Lekhi has reminded us that the new opportunities for access through the Internet have not always proved as liberating as the more enthusiastic advocates would have predicted. This is particularly the case for disadvantaged groups and minorities. Obviously one problem is that minorities cannot afford to get on to the Internet. Figures from a report prepared for the Rand Corporation in 1999 show that the inequality of access to the Internet between African-American and Hispanic citizens on the one hand, and white Americans on the other has widened as general access has surged.[2] But in addition, even when members of minorities get on to the Internet, they may not take part in the full range of services that are available. African Americans, for instance, are more inclined to use only their own sites. The Internet has not had the liberating effect that might have been expected. African American users of the net have not become more cosmopolitan because they use the net, which is in principle open to everyone equally. The racial and social divide in American society has been replicated on the net, at least for the time being.

As for parliaments, even a brief survey of their web sites in the US and in Europe shows that a lot of progress has been made in recent years in making them more accessible to outsiders. Yet at the same time, most of these efforts have replicated the fairly hierarchical relationship that existed between them and the rest of society. This relied upon individuals and groups communicating their views on policy to legislators, who then decided what to do and communicated the outcome back to society. Most of these web sites have not set out to stimulate public debate in general with the aim of raising the level of understanding of issues among citizens. The only ones that have even begun to do this systematically are the German and Scottish parliaments and, here too, it is too early to judge the long-term effect.

In any case it would be premature to expect a transformative effect on politics for three other major reasons. The first is the cost of Internet access in most countries. The simple fact of having to pay telephone charges for all of the time that people are on-line in most countries is an obvious disincentive against extended logging-on, as compared with the US where local telephone calls are free. As long as this persists, it is bound to slow down the rate of take-up.

The second reason is the scale of transformation that will be needed for current post-industrial societies to become genuinely 'information societies', where all, or almost all, citizens are roughly equal in their access to all new channels of information, as well as all the old ones, and where they also have the sophistication to make the best use of them. When even the US still suffers from widespread, inadequate levels of education and even shortcomings in literacy, all the other societies are bound to find the task even more daunting. Achieving that will take decades. As it is at present, despite the very rapid expansion of Internet usage, a 1999 study from the Rand Corporation showed that inequalities in usage of the Internet between different social categories had either widened or, at best, remained the same.[3] The same picture will be even more true for other countries.

The third reason is still more fundamental. That is the information overload that the new technology can impose upon decision-makers and representative politicians. The more that they are contacted by individual citizens, the more difficult they will it find to respond in a reflective way that responds to the particular concerns of each citizen. Stromer-Galley mentions the difficulty already of receiving responses from candidates to basic Internet queries during election campaigns. This problem will become more acute and it will put increasing pressure on both candidates and representatives to appoint more and more spokespersons who can handle relations with outsiders. But that means either sharing power and responsibility – which could challenge the power of those elected or seeking election, or it means retreating even more from direct contact with voters, thereby exacerbating the general problem of perceived inaccessibility..

The same sort of problem has apparently arisen for public administration in the US with the advent of new technology. Coupled with the individual's right to know about information held on file, this has enormously increased the workload of the agencies responsible for making that information available.[4] Simply coping with the increased demand for information and responses that can be accessed on-line will be an enormous administrative, as well as political problem.

Possibly the impact of the Internet has been greater in authoritarian or semi-authoritarian regimes. The example here is Indonesia. Hill and Sen have emphasized the very important role that the Internet played as a catalyst for political change there. The authoritarian government deliberately encouraged the spread of home computers and the Internet because it offered the prospect of greater international competitiveness for Indonesian business and also because it became a symbol of modernity. Even though the ownership of personal computers was still tiny as a proportion of the total Indonesian population, elites did take to it with a will, and not just for business purposes. Muslim intellectuals associated with

ex-President Habibie, for instance, launched an extensive web-site to discuss issues of Islamic doctrine.[5] But the habit of relatively unfettered discussion on the Net then turned to political issues when the economic crisis hit the country in 1997. Indonesians both at home and abroad began to bombard each other with messages of concern, rising to anger, over perceived government incompetence and corruption. They were able to link up and derive collective self-confidence from this fact. At the same time, the government had devoted little attention of ways of checking on net users, let alone controlling them. So the freedom of speech on the net then fed into political action within the country. As the crisis deepened, the net became a source of information on protests and official responses that was universally and immediately available, with the result that it could be fed into the events as they unfolded. Protesters were both emboldened and better informed about the general impact of their actions. Surprisingly quickly the tide of protest swept President Suharto away.

Despite this the achievements of the Internet in changing authoritarian regimes seem more modest than might have been expected. Leaving aside societies such as Singapore's, where the government has deliberately set out to tame the political impact of the Internet,[6] none of the other cases that we have considered show conclusively that the Internet can transform politics.

In the case of Indonesia Hill and Sen noted that once the Suharto regime had fallen and more 'normal' democratic political activity was allowed, the significance of the Internet declined. Public meetings and open electoral campaigns aimed at large numbers of voters became the norm. The Internet did not play nearly as important a role in the general elections of 1999. Under those circumstances the still limited penetration of Indonesian society as a whole by the Internet became much more crucial.

A more recent analysis of the Chiapas uprising also suggests a more sober conclusion about the long-term impact of the Internet than was common in 1996. The authors there suggest that it was not just the Internet in itself that was crucial. It was also the involvement in the events by international non-governmental organizations. Without their role in broadcasting the events to a wider international public, the *Zapatistas* would have been much more easily suppressed.[7] And although in 1996, for instance, when Castells was writing,[8] it was possible to be sceptical about the chances of the ruling Institutional Revolutionary Party hanging on to power into the twenty-first century, the introduction of an open party-wide vote on the candidate for the year 2000 presidential elections seems to have revived the party's fortunes and given it a much greater chance of retaining control.

The Serbian experience is similar too. There was no doubt that the ability of the Serbian Democratic Party to use mirror servers abroad for its web site to maintain its profile within the country was extremely important in frustrating government attempts to ban it. As was mentioned earlier, the party also for a while linked its web-site to that of an independent news agency within the country, so that it could better inform Serbs about what was really being done by the government in Kosovo and elsewhere. So it was a pluralizing voice presenting alternative, objective information to Serbian public opinion. And the independent radio station B92 also used the Internet to gather information and disseminate reports. Yet the NATO (North Atlantic Treaty Organisation) attacks over Kosovo made life much more difficult for independent voices inside Serbia, especially since the regime alleged that these voices were being in part subsidised by NATO countries. So President Milosevic is still in power and the opposition groups, whilst not silenced, are still divided and on the defensive.

Lastly, in Malaysia, there is no doubt that the emergence of Internet-based groups supporting former Deputy Prime Minister Anwar Ibrahim was both a shock and a challenge to Prime Minister Mahathir. It showed that his control over the Malay community was becoming more fragile. Yet when in the end he called a general election in November 1999, he won yet again with a two-thirds majority. Admittedly the result was less reassuring to him than previously, because his support among the Malay community had dwindled. There opposition to him had turned to the Islamic opposition party PAS (Pan-Malaysian Islamic Party) more than ever before – something that he had always tried to prevent during his tenure in office. Yet he expressed understandable satisfaction with the result since he had, after all, won handsomely again. The election outcome was no victory for the power of the Internet.

If we turn to the attempts to use the Internet internationally to encourage democracy, here too the picture is only modestly encouraging. Bray shows how on occasions the pro-Tibet protesters have been able to embarrass the Chinese authorities because of protests that they have orchestrated through the web in a way that would not have been possible before. The World Bank has been pressured into much greater caution in granting loans to China that might affect Tibet or the Tibetans. Yet it would be difficult to suggest that, at least at the moment, Beijing's rule in Tibet had been shaken.

And as for using the Internet to encourage democracy in Africa, Ott and Rosser rightly emphasise the potential that exists for using this as a tool of western aid policies. Yet they also caution against expecting any immediate breakthrough, since Internet penetration on the continent remains very low.

It may be that the impact of the Internet will be greater on the media than on politics. There is a striking consensus, even among those who are sceptical about the extent of the impact of the Internet upon politics, that it will certainly not leave the media unaffected as far as its coverage of politics is concerned. As an official in the Pentagon, Charles Swett predicts (possibly hopes):

> The monopoly of the traditional mass media will erode. No longer will the news editors and anchorpersons of television networks and newspapers solely determine what the mass audience learns and thinks about current events. Raw news reports from local, national and international news wires and alternative news sources, and from unaffiliated individual observers on the scene of events acting alone, will be accessible by all Internet users. The filtering and slanting of the news currently performed by traditional media will give way to some extent to direct consumption of un-analyzed information by the mass audience, diminishing the influence now enjoyed by those media. An increasingly skeptical audience will be able to compare raw news reports with the pre-digested, incomplete, out-of-context and sometimes biased renditions offered by televisions and newspapers.[9]

In fact part of the challenge may come from the political parties themselves. Bieber showed how the main parties in Germany have developed web-sites which combine party news with interpretations of current events. They are not just limited to press releases of speeches by party representatives, as tends to be the case for the web-sites of British parties. They also include extracts from newspaper articles that comment on particular events in a way favourable to the given party. This is similar to the main web pages of the Democratic and Republican parties in the US. They too include extensive extracts from media comment in a sophisticated way. And in Yugoslavia the Democratic Party of Serbia for a while combined its web-site with that of a news agency so as to counter official propaganda. One consequence of the Internet revolution, therefore, may be that parties become, or at least try to appear, more 'objective' in their assessment of what needs to be done, as a way of winning support.

Certainly one of the chief impacts of the Internet so far has been to accentuate the impact of political crises. It can bring together direct participants as well as commentaries or views from all over the world. Hill and Sen mentioned an occasion in 1998, when the crisis of the Suharto regime was reaching its peak, that information about protests in Jakarta was relayed through the Internet directly from the parliament building to Washington. In these sorts of circumstances, when the authorities are already in turmoil and cannot speak with one voice, the ability to counter Internet-based information so as to 'calm' public opinion is much more restricted. It is precisely at these times that governments find it most difficult to 'manage' the news. The problem is further exacerbated if they are the targets of the crisis. So it is fair to assume that however much authoritarian regimes may attempt to control political use of the Internet, they will still find it extremely difficult in these moments of crisis. In that sense the Internet will always heighten challenges in a crisis.

Because of this the term coined by Bimber of 'accelerated pluralism' to describe the effect of the Internet upon politics seems persuasive. Because the Internet will lower the obstacles to grass-roots collective political organization, it will speed up the process of 'intensification of group-centered, pluralistic politics'. The result may be 'a political system in which issues develop and move more quickly because of the quicker cycle of mobilization and response, and in which government officials increasingly hear from and respond to new kinds of groups – those without large, stable memberships or affiliations with established institutions'.[10]

So far the assessment of the Internet effect upon politics has been cautious. But over a longer period of time it still seems reasonable to assume that the Internet *will* transform politics, both domestically and internationally. This is because it will be reinforced by another major factor – generational change. Some of the more enthusiastic prophets of dramatic change caused by the Internet have begun to focus upon the attitudes of the younger generations who have developed an ease and a familiarity with computers as they have grown up. From this they extrapolate into the future. Surveys have suggested that the newcomers' expectations of politics will be heavily influenced by the new technologies.

> The biggest storm warning is the N-Gen [i.e. Net generation] attitude that young people need to control their own destiny. We can expect that this will evolve to embrace political control. This is a generation that will not be happy just watching politicians from the vast selection of 2 parties doing 30-second ads in election campaigns and then watching them doing 20-second clips on the evening news for the next 4 years.
>
> Just as the new media and the N-Gen spell trouble for broadcast learning and the schools, they also spell trouble for broadcast democracy and current forms of governance: demographic,

> technological, and economic shifts typically bring far-reaching changes in the political infrastructure. Democracy as TV show is in deep trouble … .
>
> Older generations of lawmakers and citizens can't even think about changing the paradigm of democracy. But the Net Generation can and will … The Net Generation will want to use their media to shape the body politic.[11]

Admittedly, some of these kinds of predictions about the attitudes of this generation bear striking resemblances to earlier very optimistic descriptions of the 1960s generation and how they were going to transform politics.

> They are accustomed to empowerment, open discussion, and immediacy – all antithetical to the disempowerment, myopic discussion and bureaucratic governance processes of today. They want to interact and get to the bottom of things, to sift information and decide. They care deeply about social problems and cannot understand why governments seem so ineffectual. Their orientation is their neighbourhood and their virtual global communities, not the nation-state. They are used to being actors, not spectators … When the N-Gen comes of age, … one thing is for sure: democracy as we know it will be finished.[12]

In the event the impact of the 1960s generation upon politics has not been so revolutionary. Nevertheless, it has not been negligible either.

Teenagers in various countries already engage in international e-mail debates about great moral and political issues. Politically concerned, Internet-literate citizens will probably not pay a great deal of attention to geography in the causes that they take up. And they will do so without necessarily deferring to governments or politicians. There is for example a thriving e-mail debate between activists on both sides of the Taiwan Straits about Taiwan's relations with mainland China that is only loosely linked to what governments say and do.

And when large numbers of citizens have become used to ordering goods on the net and receiving them within days, once they have got used to what Negroponte calls 'Anything, Anytime, Anywhere Television',[13] where the Internet can be programmed to provide services at the time that they wish, they may well become much more impatient of a political system that will only talk to them at predetermined intervals, and then only briefly. But whether the Internet will indeed bring about a revolution in political institutions, as opposed to political behaviour, remains more difficult to predict. It seems, in the words of Zhou Enlai about the significance of the French Revolution, 'still too early to tell'. But if it does have anything like the effect that its most enthusiastic advocates predict, we will not have to wait two centuries to find out. According to Mulgan, one of the architects of the British Labour Party's 'third way', the history of the diffusion of major new technologies shows that they take 50–60 years to work through the whole of society.[14] Whether one takes the launch of the Internet as taking place in the 1960s, or in the 1990s when it suddenly became popularly available outside the defence sector, this would give it 30–50 years. So in one to two generations we will be much clearer about its effect.

## NOTES

1. Bruce Bimber, 'The Internet and Political Transformation: Populism, Community and Accelerated Pluralism', *Polity*, Vol.XXXI, No.1 (1998), p.159.
2. C. Richard Neu, Robert H. Anderson and Tora K. Bikson, *Sending Your Government a Message: Email Communication Between Citizens and Government* (Santa Monica, CA: Rand, 1999), pp.185–6.
3. Neu *et al.*, *Sending Your Government a Message*, Appendix A, pp.177–87.
4. Peter J. McGeoch and Jeffrey B. Ritter, 'Operating Government in an On-line World: Balancing Access with the Needs to Govern Effectively' at the G8 Democracy and Government Online web site, www.statskontoret.se/gol-democracy
5. See www. isnet.org/archive-milis/
6. Garry Rodan, 'The Internet and Political Control in Singapore', *Political Science Quarterly*, Vol.113, No.1 (1998), pp.63–89.
7. David Ronfeldt *et al.*, *The Zapatista 'Social Netwar' in Mexico* (Santa Monica, CA: Rand Corporation, 1999), p.103.
8. Manuel Castells, *The Power of Identity. The Information Age: Economy, Society and Culture*, Vol.2 (Oxford and Malden, MA: Blackwell, 1997), p.286.
9. Charles Swett, *Strategic Assessment: The Internet (www.fas.org/cp/swett.html)*; cf. 'We are likely witnessing the last days where the big media control the national agenda' (Selnow, *Electronic Whistle-Stops*, p.187); 'At the very least, the Net appears likely to decrease the influence of established media organizations over formation of the political agenda' (Bimber, 'The Internet and Political Transformation', p.159).
10. Bimber, 'The Internet and Political Transformation', pp.156, 158.
11. Don Tapscott, *Growing Up Digital: the Rise of the Net Generation* (NY: McGraw-Hill, 1998), pp.301, 303.
12. Ibid., p.304.
13. Nicholas Negroponte, *Being Digital* (London: Coronet Books/Hodder & Stoughton, 1995), p.174.
14. Geoff Mulgan, *Connexity* (London: Chatto & Windus, 1997), p.29.

# Abstracts

*The Internet, Democracy and Democratization*
PETER FERDINAND

The impact of the Internet upon business, upon government organization and efficiency, and then upon democracies and processes of democratization are investigated in a manner that sets the context for the contributions that come later. What is the nature of the challenge to individual political systems? Does it come from within individual states or from international pressures? For established democracies, the study looks at political campaigning, parliaments, minority activism and local democracy. For authoritarian regimes, it looks at the impact of the Internet upon recent developments in Mexico, Serbia and Malaysia. Lastly, it raises the question of the possible use of the Internet to strengthen international civil society.

*Paradoxical Partners: Electronic Communication and Electronic Democracy*
BETH SIMONE NOVECK

Although we are living in a communications revolution, the explosion of electronic speech has not significantly improved democracy. The Internet poses a series of paradoxical challenges to the development of a culture of democracy on-line. It makes information easier to obtain and knowledge more difficult. It facilitates both privacy and surveillance. It makes communication more freely available, but it does not result in public discussion of policy choices. It may encourage a sense of community or anomie. The inquiry concludes by arguing for the need to create spaces on the Internet for public deliberation so as to enhance democracy, not just e-commerce. Otherwise our virtual world will be one of information, not knowledge, privacy without intimacy and networks without community.

*Democratizing Democracy: Strong Democracy, US Political Campaigns and the Internet*
JENNIFER STROMER-GALLEY

The Internet's achievements in facilitating Benjamin Barber's notion of 'strong democracy' are assessed by way of analyzing its impact upon selected American political campaigns since 1996. The study focuses upon six features that might affect its application. Campaigning on the Internet is cheaper than using other forms of media. It shrinks distance. It can store and apply much greater volumes of information on individual voters and groups of them, allowing much more targeting of political messages. It can amalgamate messages from various types of media. It can provide greater interaction between candidates and voters, and at much greater speed. The study concludes that candidates have only just begun to tap these features. Citizens must pressure candidates to utilize the Internet for strong democratic ends.

*Revitalizing the Party System or* Zeitgeist*-on-Line? Virtual Party Headquarters and Virtual Party Branches in Germany*
CHRISTOPH BIEBER

This study examines the use of the Internet by the main party organizations in Germany. It argues that there has been a gradual evolution in the direction of more complex applications and away from simple recruitment of members, although all the parties in Germany are confronted by declining and ageing memberships. Party headquarters now attempt to present a more co-ordinated picture of news as it affects them so as to turn it to their advantage. They are also beginning to use the Internet for intra-net discussions of topical issues, to which non-party members may get access. The future might take the form of increasing synthesis of media forms and party information, and possibly 'virtual' local party organizations. So far, however, proposals along these lines have been resisted by the leaderships.

*The Politics of African America On-Line*
ROHIT LEKHI

This examination of the use of the Internet in African American politics begins with an investigation of how access to and wider structural forces in United States society and economy shape usage of the Internet within African America. The second part examines the qualitative experiences of African Americans on-line. It looks at a variety of resources available across the Internet and assesses the extent to which these have facilitated, or are likely to facilitate, opportunities for deeper political engagement by African Americans. However, the third and concluding part of the paper asks whether the effectiveness of the Internet as a medium for political communication and interaction for African Americans can be assessed adequately through a focus on the impact of the Internet on 'traditional' forms of political activity. Here, it suggests an alternative way of understanding African American on-line activity. It argues that the true significance of the Internet for African Americans may lie less in its ability to increase levels of political activity within existing institutions than in its ability to facilitate new forms of activity that either bypass those institutions or directly compete with them.

*Neo-Nazis and Taliban On-Line: Anti-Modern Political Movements and Modern Media*
PETER CHROUST

One of the challenges to democracies and democratization posed by the Internet is its use by anti-democratic groups to mobilize support. Two examples are the Taliban in Afghanistan together with their supporters elsewhere in the world, and right-wing neo-Nazi groups in Germany and elsewhere. This study examines their use of the Internet to try to achieve ideological hegemony within their societies and it sets their ideas in the context of theories of modernization. Even though they may appear backward-looking movements, this does not prevent them making use of the most advanced forms of communication to create new networks of their own, even sometimes to provoke violence. At the same time, their use of the Net can reveal at least some of their activities to opponents.

*The Internet in Indonesia's New Democracy*
DAVID T. HILL and KRISHNA SEN

The Internet has not yet achieved very deep penetration of Indonesian society, but it played an important part in the downfall of President Suharto. This study begins with an outline of its introduction into the country. Modernizers within the New Order regime welcomed it because of the opportunities that it offered for increasing the efficiency of business. The sudden financial crisis in 1997 provided an opportunity for critics at home and abroad to associate, network and condemn the regime with a vehemence that would have been repressed if they had taken to the streets. Once the New Order regime had collapsed, politics did go on to the streets, but the Internet continues to provide up-to-date, alternative information on political events. At the very least it provides an insurance against a reversion to authoritarian rule and control of the media. It remains to be seen what more positive political uses the Indonesians find for the Internet.

*The Electronic Republic? The Role of the Internet in Promoting Democracy in Africa*
DANA OTT AND MELISSA ROSSER

With the dramatic expansion of various forms of electronic interchange, including electronic mail and the Internet around the world, opportunities for communication across national boundaries, and cross-fertilization of ideas are greater than ever before. Access to these electronic communication tools can have a positive impact in promoting democracy in Africa. It can give civil society greater leverage *vis-à-vis* the state and political elites; increase the free flow of information and Networking opportunities; and decrease barriers to political participation, such as cost, through improved communications technologies and greater access to information. However, without parallel efforts to ensure that access to the Internet is not restricted to urban and elite populations, governance will not improve and political instability may result. The study is organized in four sections. Section I makes the theoretical case for the role of increased access to information and communication in the promotion of democratic political regimes. Section II presents an overview of the state of electronic access in Africa, including international donor supported initiatives to promote African connectivity. Section III presents an empirical analysis of the relationship between access to the Internet and indicators of economic and political freedom in Africa. Section IV offers conclusions and recommendations.

*Tibet, Democracy and the Internet Bazaar*
JOHN BRAY

This study examines the use of the Internet made by the Chinese authorities to explain their rule in Tibet and by their opponents. Most of the latter are found in India and the West. It argues that Internet pressure led the World Bank to re-examine a project for resettling non-Tibetan farmers from other parts of China in Qinghai province. For the moment, the chief roles of the Internet are two-fold: disseminating information on recent developments in Tibet among sympathizers abroad more rapidly than was previously possible, and facilitating the co-ordination of campaigns. It will take much wider use of the Internet inside China for it to have a transformative effect there.

*Fair Play at Voting Precincts: A Comparison of Mexican and Chilean Elections*
PATRICIO NAVIA

This article investigates electoral data from voting precincts in Mexico 1994 and Chile 1993. It finds that electoral results in Chile are more homogeneous across precincts than in Mexico. In Chile almost all the precincts returned results that resemble the aggregate national results. In Mexico, there are significant differences across precincts and across regions. It argues that perhaps the heterogeneity of the results across regions in Mexico helps explain the lack of credibility in the electoral process that persisted there in 1994 despite the reforms and measures adopted to make the process more fair. Also, there were significant regional differences in the level of support for all candidates in Mexico but not in Chile. There were instances of apparent electoral tampering in Mexico, but no evidence that possible electoral fraud significantly altered the electoral results. Finally, because support for different presidential candidates varied significantly across regions in Mexico, the inconsistencies between national aggregate results and precincts results aided by a history of electoral tampering might also help explain the credibility problem of elections in Mexico.

# Notes on Contributors

**Christoph Bieber**, Ph.D., is Associate Professor at the Institute for Political Science at the Justus-Liebig University in Giessen, Germany.

**John Bray** is an Asia specialist at Control Risks Ltd. in London.

**Peter Chroust**, political scientist, is a staff member of the Hessisches Landesinstitut für Pädagogik, and lecturer at the University of Kassel, Germany.

**Peter Ferdinand** is Director of the Centre for Studies in Democratisation at the University of Warwick.

**David Hill** is a Professor of South East Asian Studies at Murdoch University, Australia.

**Rohit Lekhi** is a Lecturer in the Department of Politics and International Studies at the University of Warwick.

**Beth Simone Noveck** is Director of International Programs at the Yale Law School Information Society Project and practices Internet and telecom law in New York City.

**Dana Ott** is a democracy analyst in the Africa Bureau at the United States Agency for International Development, Washington, DC, specializing in democracy promotion programming.

**Melissa Rosser** is a civil society analyst in the Africa Bureau at the United States Agency for International Development, Washington, DC, specializing in democracy promotion programming.

**Krishna Sen** is Associate Professor in Media Studies at Curtin University, Australia, and is an editor of *Inside Indonesia* quarterly.

**Jennifer Stromer-Galley** is a doctoral student in the Annenberg School for Communication at the University of Pennsylvania.

# Index